The United States and China

The United States and China

Into the Twenty-First Century

MICHAEL SCHALLER
University of Arizona

FOURTH EDITION

New York   Oxford
OXFORD UNIVERSITY PRESS

Oxford University Press is a department of the University of Oxford.
It furthers the University's objective of excellence in research,
scholarship, and education by publishing worldwide.

Oxford   New York
Auckland   Cape Town   Dar es Salaam   Hong Kong   Karachi
Kuala Lumpur   Madrid   Melbourne   Mexico City   Nairobi
New Delhi   Shanghai   Taipei   Toronto

With offices in
Argentina   Austria   Brazil   Chile   Czech Republic   France   Greece
Guatemala   Hungary   Italy   Japan   Poland   Portugal   Singapore
South Korea   Switzerland   Thailand   Turkey   Ukraine   Vietnam

For titles covered by Section 112 of the US Higher Education
Opportunity Act, please visit www.oup.com/us/he for the
latest information about pricing and alternate formats.

Published by Oxford University Press
198 Madison Avenue, New York, New York 10016
http://www.oup.com

Library of Congress Cataloging-in-Publication Data
Schaller, Michael, 1947-
    The United States and China : into the twenty-first century / Michael Schaller, University
of Arizona. -- Fourth edition.
        pages cm
    Includes index.
    ISBN 978-0-19-020006-0 (pbk.)
    1. United States--Foreign relations--China. 2. China--Foreign relations--United States.
3. United States--Foreign relations--20th century. 4. United States--Foreign relations--21st
century. I. Title.
    E183.8.C5S323   2015
    327.73051--dc23

                                                                        2015003006

Printing number: 9 8 7 6 5 4 3 2 1

Printed in the United States of America
on acid-free paper

To Gail, for her kindness and wisdom

CONTENTS

ACKNOWLEDGMENTS

This work builds on the scholarship of many researchers, as well as my own. I have included at the end of each chapter suggestions for further reading that acknowledge the key contributions of these many authors.

Thank you to the reviewers of the fourth edition, Judy Barrett Litoff, Harold J. Goldberg, Arlene Lazarowitz, Joseph C. Morreale, Shuo Wang, and those who wish to remain anonymous.

A note on transliteration: well-known, historic Chinese personal and place names are generally rendered in traditional form, followed initially by pinyin transliteration in brackets. For example, Chiang Kai-shek (Jiang Jieshi), Yenan (Yan'an), and Chungking (Chongqing). Less well known or recently prominent personal and place names are rendered in pinyin. For example, Xi'an (Sian), Xi Jinping.

PREFACE

I initially intended to simply add a new chapter for the fourth edition, covering developments between the United States and China since 2001. I did add a chapter, Chapter 13, "China Ascending," covering this time period. But as I engaged in the writing, I realized that so much new scholarship by both Western and Chinese authors had appeared in the past 15 years, along with much government documentation, that the entire book deserved a rewrite. The suggested readings listed at the end of each chapter reflect this new scholarship.

I began, quite literally, at the beginning, discussing the clash of cultures, power, and economics that categorized the U.S. encounter with China in the first half of the nineteenth century. This edition also examines in greater depth the cultural interaction and clash between China and the United States during the late nineteenth and early twentieth centuries. The second and third chapters describe the impact of "yellow peril" literature on American views of China and the countervailing image of "heroic" China popularized by writers such as Pearl Buck and Edgar Snow in the 1930s.

The chapters on the World War II era reflect recent scholarship on the sources of both conflict and cooperation among the United States, the Nationalist Chinese, and the Chinese Communists between 1936 and 1945.

Chapter 6, on the emerging Cold War, examines how China became a political flashpoint in U.S. politics and how the United States became defined as China's main enemy.

Chapters 8 through 12, covering the 1950s through the 1990s, have been completely rewritten. Again, new scholarship and documentation has led to re-examining how the Eisenhower, Kennedy, and Johnson administrations responded to the "Communist menace" and the breakup of the Sino–Soviet alliance. The Kennedy administration's fear of China and China's role in the Vietnam War are also explored in greater depth.

The long Chapter 10 on the Nixon administration's opening to China incorporates substantial new scholarship. Earlier discussions of the opening relied largely on the memoirs of Henry Kissinger. That information has been supplemented by the opening of many U.S. and Chinese primary sources and by a lively scholarly debate on the question.

Chapters 11 and 12 examine how the process of normalization of relations created new cleavages within the U.S. government and how the status of Taiwan reemerged as a political and diplomatic flashpoint. These chapters also examine the influence of China—real and imagined—on the U.S. political process. These two chapters, as well as the concluding chapter, chronicle the rise of the new U.S.–China trade relationship (the creation of what has been called "Chimerica") and geostrategic rivalries as China asserts its regional power. Chapter 13 also examines "soft power," the ways in which the two nations interact culturally, through trade and tourism.

NEW TO THIS EDITION

- Completely new coverage of post-2001 events, focusing on the rise of China.
- New emphasis on cultural interaction and clashes in early chapters.
- Completely rewritten chapters on the 1950s to the 1990s (Chapters 8–12) based on new documentation and scholarship examining the roots of the Cold War conflict between the United States and China and how and why the Nixon administration broke the logjam.
- New discussion of charges raised in the 1990s and beyond that China has tried to influence U.S. politics and steal secrets.
- Expanded discussion of the role of Taiwan in U.S.–China relations since Nixon.

INTRODUCTION

Before 1991, Soviet academics joked that under Communism historians were tasked with "predicting the past." Living under a regime that routinely "air brushed" out of photos disgraced leaders, historians had to carefully parse the version of events they told. In freer societies historians faced different complications. They, too, revise and reinterpret stories about the past based on the appearance of new materials and methods of interpretation. Since the third edition of this book appeared in 2001, the relationship between the United States and China has evolved in ways no one could have predicted. Abundant new scholarship, based on both Chinese and American source materials, has enriched and sometimes overturned past certainties.

Writing in 2001, it seemed almost a thing of wonder that a Starbucks coffee franchise had opened inside the Forbidden City. But who would have imagined that just 12 years later Chinese officials, managing what had become the world's second largest economy, would criticize the U.S. Congress for being "irresponsible" capitalists mismanaging the domestic and world economies? Holding more than a trillion dollars in U.S. government bonds, Chinese economists wondered whether the time had come to replace the dollar as the global standard of exchange.

Other recent headlines seemed to defy the logic of the previous half century. For example, as millions of newly well-off Chinese tourists flocked to foreign destinations in Europe, many locals complained that they had become the new "ugly Americans," originally a French phrase to denigrate crass American tourists in the 1950s. Growing numbers of wealthy Chinese families sent their teenage children to private schools in the United States as preparation for admission to American universities. Perhaps most astonishing, in vitro fertility clinics in California reported that by 2014 thousands of childless Chinese couples routinely sought American women—preferably "tall, blonde, and blue-eyed"—to serve as surrogate mothers and deliver their children as U.S. citizens.

But the past, like the present, holds many surprises. Only a decade ago, no one took notice that China's first modern revolutionary, Sun Yat-sen, attended the same missionary school in Hawaii, Punahou, as did future American president Barack Obama nearly a century later. Recent scholarship has enriched our understanding of how events as varied as the Opium Wars, unequal treaties, global trade, and decolonization impacted the Chinese–American relationship. China's role as an American ally during World War II, long relegated to the shadows, is now understood as far more consequential. Our understanding of the period from 1949 to 1971, two decades of seemingly unremitting hostility between the United States and the People's Republic of China, is now seen as more varied and full of missed opportunities. During the past 15 years, scholars have revealed in great detail how the failures of Maoism within China, the Sino–Soviet split, and the crisis faced by the United States during the Vietnam War created the conditions for reconciliation in the early 1970s. As China progressed economically during the 1980s and beyond, it emerged not only as one of America's top trading partners, but also as an economic engine that lifted more people out of poverty more rapidly than any regime in history. At the same time, China's efforts to project power in Southeast Asia and in nearby maritime regions have rekindled fears in the West of the perils of Chinese expansion dormant since the end of the Cold War. This edition integrates the new scholarship that enriches our understanding of past Sino–American relations and, I hope, encourages readers to understand unfolding events in their complex historical dimension.

TUCSON, ARIZONA, March 2015

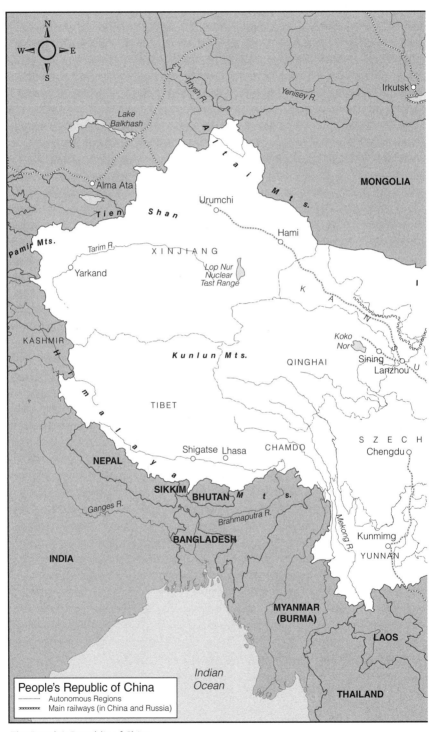

The People's Republic of China

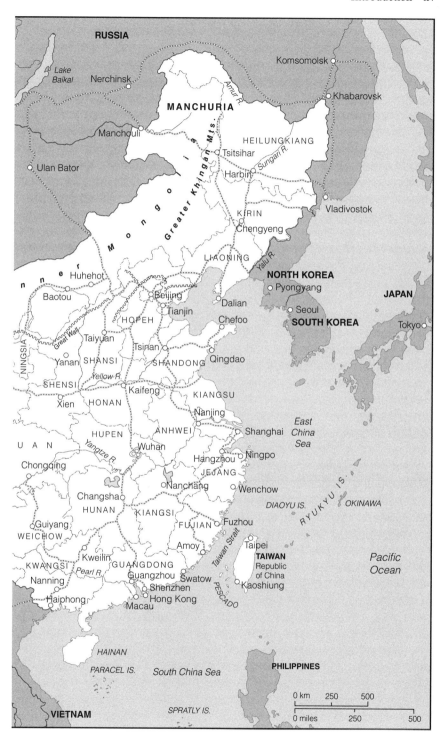

CHAPTER 1

The American Discovery of China

For more than a century, Americans perceived the massive Gate of Heavenly Peace (Tiananmen), the portal separating the Forbidden City of China's imperial past from Beijing, as a backdrop for the drama of modern China. Standing on the platform atop the gate on October 1, 1949, Mao Zedong proclaimed creation of the new People's Republic of China (PRC). Mao had already declared that China would "no longer be a nation subject to insult and humiliation" as it had been for the past century. The Chinese people had "stood up" and swept away the remnants of Chiang Kai-shek's (Jiang Jieshi) army. Most Westerners and their privileged institutions were also on the way out. In the global contest between the Soviet Union and the "imperialist" United States, Mao asserted China would "lean" toward the socialist camp.

In the United States, government officials and opinion leaders condemned what they called "Red China." Hoping to shame Mao and his followers, in August 1949 the State Department had issued a long report, called the China White Paper. After laying out the case that the United States had done all it could to help Chiang's doomed regime, it blasted the PRC as a Soviet puppet, unable to "pass the first test of legitimacy . . . it is not Chinese."[1] *The New York Times*, America's most respected newspaper, ridiculed Chinese Communism as a "nauseous force" dominated by "Moscow's nominees." *Time–Life* publisher Henry Luce, born to American missionaries in China and a fervid supporter of Chiang, added that Mao's anti-Americanism "shattered the illusion cherished by many . . . the illusion that China's Communists are different." More ominously, the publisher's wife and Republican activist, Clare Boothe Luce, charged that not only mistakes but also "traitors in the State Department" had conspired to bring about a Communist victory. Even before the fall of 1950, as Chinese "volunteers" fought

---

[1]The full report blamed the Nationalist regime for its own collapse. Unfortunately, the lengthy document's cover letter ignored much of the actual contents and heavily criticized the Chinese Communists and Soviet Union for the Chinese civil war and its outcome.

U.S. soldiers and Marines on the Korean peninsula, Republicans in Congress, led by Wisconsin Senator Joseph McCarthy, accused treasonous diplomats and President Harry S. Truman's closest advisers of "losing China."

After 20 years of near complete estrangement between the United States and China, Tiananmen again became a backdrop to diplomatic maneuvers. On October 1, 1970, the Communist Party chairman Mao Zedong had the United States on his mind as he reviewed the National Day parade from atop the famous gate. An old friend, the American journalist Edgar Snow, who had introduced the Chinese Communists to the Western world in his 1937 book, *Red Star over China*, stood beside the aging chairman. Snow's place of honor, along with an interview Mao gave Snow in which he suggested that President Richard M. Nixon visit China, signaled renewed interest in opening a dialogue with Washington. During the next three years of secret dialogues and then open visits, the relationship between China and the United States underwent a dramatic transformation. By 1973, Nixon's close aide, Henry Kissinger, confided to the president that "with the possible exception of the United Kingdom, the PRC might well be closest to us in its global perceptions." Remarkably, the United States and China, Kissinger explained, had become "tacit allies."

That nascent alliance nearly broke in June 1989 when tens of thousands of students and their supporters demonstrated in the square before Tiananmen. The political activists demanded democratic reforms and challenged the political monopoly of the Communist Party. Playing to Western sensibilities, the demonstrators unveiled a giant papier mâché model resembling the Statue of Liberty and dubbed the Goddess of Democracy, which faced off against the grim portrait of the now deceased Mao that still hung on Tiananmen. On June 4 the de facto leader of the PRC, Deng Xiaoping, ordered troops to disperse the protestors. Hundreds were killed that night and thousands arrested after the students fled into surrounding streets. A day later, television viewers around the world witnessed via satellite the defiance of a lone protestor who attempted to block a column of tanks in Beijing by standing in the street.

What soon became known as the "Tiananmen massacre" revived memories of past confrontations and stoked fears among many Americans that China's government remained a ruthless threat to civilized norms. In Washington, President George H. W. Bush condemned Chinese actions and suspended some trade and security exchanges. In response, the PRC accused Washington of meddling in its internal affairs. But after a few months of private talks, most commercial and diplomatic contact resumed.

A decade later, after U.S. warplanes accidentally bombed the Chinese embassy in Belgrade during the 1999 Balkan War, angry mobs in Beijing partially sacked the U.S. embassy, located near Tiananmen. Congressional Republicans, sensing that Chinese behavior had become a hot-button issue, stepped up their investigation of alleged illegal Chinese donations to President Bill Clinton's 1996 campaign. Some Republicans even charged that Chinese émigrés and Chinese Americans were widely recruited to steal U.S. nuclear secrets. Thinly veiled racial epithets voiced by some members of Congress echoed "yellow peril" language from the late nineteenth century warning of a Chinese plot to take over the United States. Although by the start of the twenty-first century China had become the fourth largest U.S. trading partner (after Canada, Mexico, and Japan), the new administration of President George W. Bush in 2001 described China as a "strategic competitor."

By the second decade of the twenty-first century, the U.S. and Chinese economies had become so enmeshed that one commentator coined the term "Chimerica" to describe the relationship. Each year, hundreds of thousands of tourists, students, and business representatives moved between the two nations. At the same time, China's increasingly assertive foreign policy, such as its claims to sovereignty over various uninhabited but strategically located islands in the South and East China Seas, alarmed China's neighbors, several of whom had security treaties with the United States dating back to the 1950s.

The turbulence in U.S.–China relations over the past 150 years had roots in two cultures that barely understood each other. China, one specialist remarked, has long served as a kind of "national Rorschach test [a psychological evaluation in which subjects are asked to describe what they see in a series of irregularly shaped ink blots] for the United States onto which we project our hopes and fears" of the moment. Since their initial contacts in the 1780s, Americans perceived China—sometimes simultaneously—as an advanced civilization, a barbaric anachronism, a vast export market, a threat to the nation's economy, a military ally, a warlike rival, an emerging democracy, a repressive dictatorship, a culture hostile to foreign ideas, and a society eager to embrace Western models. At different times and to different degrees, all these perceptions contained a grain of truth.

When seen in the perspective of the past two centuries, the many reversals since 1949 appear less startling. From their initial contact in the 1780s, both ordinary and influential Americans and Chinese misunderstood one another more often than not.[2] Compared to the influx of millions of Europeans, only a handful of Chinese came to the United States while the immigration window remained opened to them between the 1860s and 1882. Then, until 1965, nearly all Chinese were excluded from migrating to the United States. Between 1949 and 1971, even travel between the two countries was virtually impossible. For most Americans, a trip to an exotic shop or restaurant in "Chinatown" in New York or San Francisco was about the only routine contact with ethnic Chinese, their culture, or their language.

Colonial America and, after 1783, the United States had some commercial contacts with China, but limited social interaction. Overwhelmingly Christian and dominated by European Americans, the United States saw itself as a bold

---

[2]A pathbreaking documentary produced by Irv Drasnin in 1972 bore the evocative title *Misunderstanding China*. It explored how for a century popular culture in the United States—including films, comics, slang, and religious publications—routinely distorted the image of China.

experiment in representative government, at least for white males. Even before independence, American colonials had grown fond of imported Chinese tea and the upper classes often displayed Chinese porcelains and silks in their parlors.

A dispute over Chinese tea became one of the founding legends of American independence. British law gave the East India Company monopoly rights to import Chinese tea to the colonies. American smugglers, however, illegally imported substantial amounts of tea, often undercutting the monopoly price. In 1773, in a bid to bail out the financially troubled East India Company, Parliament passed the Tea Act, which combined a modest tea tax to be paid by colonial consumers with enhanced antismuggling efforts. This effectively reduced the price of legally imported tea below that of the smuggled product, threatening to ruin the black market. In Boston, political activists who objected to all parliamentary taxes joined with irate smugglers to attack several British merchant ships. Disguised as Indians, they dumped hundreds of tea chests into the harbor. In ways none of the participants could foresee, their act foreshadowed by some 60 years the Chinese seizure and destruction of British and American chests of illegally imported opium in Guangzhou (Canton).

A decade after the Tea Party, following America's successful war for independence, the president of Yale University, Reverend Ezra Stiles, delivered a widely reprinted sermon on the nation's future prospects. Stiles predicted that with independence and the lifting of British commercial restrictions, the nation's trade would become truly global. Ships carrying the American flag would sail to "Bengal and Canton, on the Indus and Ganges, on the Whang Ho [China's Yellow River]," and along with commerce they would "import the wisdom and literature of the East." In this early vision of globalization, there would be "universal traveling to and fro."

In February 1784, a few months after Stiles spoke, the U.S.-flagged *Empress of China* sailed from New York to south China, carrying a cargo of sea otter and beaver pelts, woolen cloth, lead, 30 tons of ginseng, and about $20,000 in Spanish silver coins. By the 1790s around 90 American vessels, second only to Great Britain, engaged in China trade. Through the 1820s, American ships bound for China carried animal pelts (until overhunting nearly exterminated Pacific seals and sea otters), Hawaiian sandalwood, and ginseng, desired as an aphrodisiac.

Because the value of goods purchased in China—mostly tea, porcelain, and silk—exceeded that of Western imports, British and American merchants had to carry large amounts of silver, China's metallic currency, to make up the difference. After the 1820s, "bills on London," a sort of international paper credit system, gradually replaced silver as a medium of exchange.

Many American opinion leaders in the late eighteenth century were impressed by what they knew—or thought they knew—about China. For example, Benjamin Franklin, Thomas Paine, and Thomas Jefferson all praised China as an advanced civilization and the imperial examination system as a form of meritocracy. Paine and Jefferson even compared the Chinese philosopher, Confucius, to Jesus. Although some dissenters, such as Ralph Waldo Emerson, dismissed China as a "booby nation," most Americans who interacted at all with the so-called Middle Kingdom through the 1820s praised it. One typical booster was trader Amasa Delano, who published a book in 1817 that celebrated China as "foremost in the arts and sciences and agriculture" and "one of the best regulated governments in the world."

Before the mid-nineteenth century, Chinese officials had little regard for or understanding of the United States. As late as 1844, when China concluded its first trade and diplomatic pact with the United States, the Chinese negotiator informed the emperor that the United States was "the most uncivilized and remote of all countries . . . in an isolated place, outside the pale, solitary and ignorant."

China's disdain for the United States, along with most of the outside world, had roots in culture, geography, and economics. For nearly 1,000 years China was by most measures the most productive economy in the world. Under the Qing Dynasty (1644–1912) the country roughly doubled in size between 1700 and 1800, absorbing Mongolia, Xinjiang, and Tibet. With the introduction of new world crops such as potatoes and peanuts, agriculture expanded and the population grew from about 150 to 400 million. Most of China's smaller neighbors, such as Korea, Burma, and Vietnam, were generally allowed to go their own way so long as they acknowledged China's centrality and engaged in a form of ritualized trade and diplomacy known as the tribute system. Before the mid-nineteenth century, with the exception of Czarist Russia, China had limited contact with non-Asian governments. In the late seventeenth and early eighteenth centuries the Qing Dynasty signed several treaties with Czarist Russia delineating their inner-Asian border and permitting some overland trade.

Western ships, led by the Portuguese and Spanish, appeared off the south China coast in the mid-sixteenth century and Portugal secured a lease to Macao in 1557. But for most of the next 200 years, China officially ignored the growing number of European trading vessels that came to its southern shores. Then, in 1757, the dynasty established a system to regulate and limit foreign trade. The so-called Canton system (named for the city of Guangzhou, or Canton, along south China's Pearl River) stipulated that foreign ships must register at a customs house some distance from Guangzhou and take on a Chinese pilot to head up the Pearl River. Once the ships reached Whampoa, about 12 miles south of Guangzhou, the vessel and its cargo were placed under the supervision of one of 12 or 13 authorized Chinese merchant guilds, or *hongs*. Under *hong* supervision goods were taken from Whampoa to Guangzhou for sale. For about half a year, a limited number of foreign merchants were allowed to reside in a walled compound in Guangzhou known as the foreign factories where they could indirectly participate in commerce. The system was cumbersome and involved payment of bribes to an array of Chinese officials. Western merchants, technically forbidden to learn Chinese, communicated using a language called "*pidgin*," an amalgam of English, Portuguese, Chinese, and assorted local idioms.

The Canton system kept foreigners at arm's length while allowing wealthy Chinese to buy Western luxury goods. The arrangement also affirmed China's

An artist's depiction from the 1820s of the European and American warehouses near Canton from which opium and other goods were traded. (Private Collection Roy Miles Fine Paintings/Bridgeman Images)

mindset that it was aloof from and superior to the outside world. The Chinese word for their own country, *Zhong guo* (middle or central kingdom), embodied this ideal. Chinese considered outsiders "barbarians" or, less charitably, "foreign devils." Foreigners entering China were expected to *ke tou* (kowtow, in English), ritualized bowing and "knocking of the head on the floor," in front of Chinese officials.

Chinese concepts of political order, often called Confucianism, after the philosopher who described the system, rested on notions of ritual and formal hierarchy in which power radiated down from the emperor, or "son of heaven," through appointed officials to local elites. Those at the bottom of the hierarchy, the vast majority of Chinese, were like children in a well-ordered family. Confucian ideology relied on norms of an imagined natural hierarchy of men over women, age over youth, mental over physical labor, and educated and landed elites over peasants. The Son of Heaven presided over this human family and commanded obedience like a father over his wife and children.

The emperor ruled through an imperial bureaucracy, mostly selected through a competitive examination. In theory, anyone could qualify to take the exam and, if successful, enjoy the door to wealth and power it opened. In reality, passing the exams required years of arduous study of Chinese classics. Only those with wealth had the opportunity to master written Chinese and the formal structures of the language. High culture served the privileged class and was more of an impediment than a ladder of mobility. The vast majority, and nearly all women, remained illiterate peasants, working either small family plots or rented land. Before the twentieth century, Chinese typically identified themselves as members of extended families and clans, not as citizens of a nation-state.

Most of those passing the imperial examination and entering government service were the sons of well-off landowners, the so-called gentry. This created strong bonds between provincial officials and large property owners. The gentry often assumed responsibility for local security, tax collection, and maintenance of roads and irrigation systems. In return, the government recognized the gentry's unofficial domination of rural life.

Dynasties had risen and fallen for more than 2,000 years before the Qing, conquerors from the northeast, seized power in 1644. But imperial reshuffling had only limited impact on the underlying order or living conditions for most Chinese. Qing power and efficiency peaked around 1800, with the rule of the Qianlong emperor. His successors proved less able to administer the huge empire acquired over the past century or to manage domestic and foreign challenges. At the same time as China's political system and economy stagnated, the Western world, epitomized by England, experienced a revolution in both industrial and military technology.

THE WESTERN IMPACT

Until about 1800, China had limited trade or cultural contact with non-Asians. Since Roman times, some caravans crossed inner Asia along the so-called Silk Road, carrying small amounts of luxury items. The thirteenth-century adventurer, Marco Polo, allegedly followed this route, although scholars are unsure whether his famous chronicle is based on his own travels or tales told to him by others. In the fifteenth century a daring Chinese admiral led naval expeditions to Africa and Southeast Asia, bringing back exotic animals and products, including a hapless giraffe, before the Ming Dynasty lost interest and canceled future voyages. The most sustained Western contact began in the early 1600s when a small number of Jesuit missionaries took up residence in Beijing. They assisted astronomers and mathematicians in the Ming court in improving methods for calculating time and the calendar and demonstrated techniques for casting better cannon. Many of the elaborate bronze models they produced are still on display in China. The Jesuits avoided challenging the sacred position of the "Son of Heaven" and soft-pedaled their efforts to convert Chinese to Catholicism.

Rival religious orders in Rome, such as the Franciscans, criticized the Jesuits' approach and soon turned the Pope against them. By the time the Qing assumed power in 1644, the Jesuits and other Catholic missionaries were looked upon with suspicion because of their collaboration with the deposed Ming and within a few decades most left China. Nearly a century elapsed between the departure of the Jesuits and the large-scale return of Westerners. In the interim, revolutionary advances in industrial and military technology had transformed Western Europe and then the United States into centers of global power.

Chafing under the Canton trading system, British merchants and their government took the lead in pressing China to "normalize" commerce. This meant signing treaties to regulate trade, protect merchants, establish regular tariffs, and allow foreigners more direct contact with Chinese consumers.

In 1793 King George III, the villain of the American Revolution, sent an envoy, Lord McCartney, to China in hopes of convincing the emperor to sign agreements expanding commercial and diplomatic ties. The Qing court balked. McCartney was permitted to visit Beijing as a tribute bearer, not a royal representative. But when he refused to perform the kowtow, court officials denied him an audience with the emperor. Instead, McCartney was handed a letter addressed to the British king. In condescending prose, it expressed sympathy for Britain's desire to acquire the "rudiments of our civilization" but declined to make any deals with the British. China, the letter explained, "possesses all things . . . and has no use for your country's manufactures." McCartney was sent home empty handed.

Despite this formal rejection, Qing officials permitted some expansion of the limited commerce in Guangzhou. Several times over the next 40 years, the British and then the American government requested that China enter into modern trade agreements, but the Qing rebuffed these initiatives. Soon, however, the economic engine of the global narcotics trade overwhelmed China's effort to remain aloof.

THE OPIUM WARS AND THE UNEQUAL TREATY SYSTEM

Opium had been known in China for 1,000 years before the crisis of the 1830s. Traditionally, it had been used as a liquid medicine to kill pain and alleviate intestinal ailments. After 1600, with the introduction of tobacco in China, it was often smoked in a mixture with tobacco or on its own. Imperial edicts had outlawed opium consumption in 1729 but the law was widely flouted. In 1793, the British East India Company, which effectively ruled the colony, asserted a monopoly over most opium production in India and promoted its export. (The East India Company lost its monopoly in 1833.) By 1839, somewhere between 2 million and 10 million Chinese smokers consumed 40,000 imported chests of opium per year, each weighing 133 pounds. American merchants, carrying mostly Turkish opium, controlled about 10 percent of the market. Although opium poppies grew in China, consumers preferred imported product.

The British government and East India Company denied formal involvement in the drug trade. The Company made money by licensing the cultivation of opium, refining the sap, and auctioning off the finished product in Bombay to private merchants who transported the drug to China on their own ships. The Company and the British government earned profits from licensing cultivation, selling the refined drug, and charging a tax on the chests carried off to China. But technically the opium was out of their control after leaving India.

Despite periodic decrees against opium, Chinese imports grew to 8,000 chests in 1823, 24,000 in 1833, and 30,000 in 1835. Chinese smugglers along with corrupt officials facilitated the trade. The Chinese paid for imported opium in silver, reversing the balance of payments that had previously benefitted China. By the 1840s, opium, along with the closely connected slave, cotton, and sugar trade, was one of the most lucrative commodities in world markets.

British and American opium merchants often relied on Christian missionaries as interpreters and go-betweens as they plied their wares along the south China coast. Both the merchants and the missionaries considered themselves moral actors, fulfilling, not creating, demand. In any case, opium was a legitimate product in both the United States and Great Britain, widely used in over-the-counter medicines. As one merchant wrote in his diary in 1832, "employed delivering briskly . . . no time to read my Bible." Warren Delano II, an official of the American firm Russell & Company and grandfather of the president Franklin Delano Roosevelt, insisted he engaged in a "fair, honorable, and legitimate trade," no worse than the sale of liquor.

Stunned by the economic and social consequences of this trade, Chinese authorities in Canton beginning in 1838 made more serious suppression efforts, including the public execution of several Chinese opium dealers in Macao and in front of the foreign factories in Guangzhou. In Beijing, the Daoguang emperor endorsed the crackdown and appointed Lin Zexu as special commissioner to suppress the opium trade. By the time Lin arrived in Guangzhou in the spring of 1839, he had devised detailed plans to destroy drug paraphernalia, punish Chinese users, and confiscate opium stockpiles. He apparently had not given much thought to how the British might react. Lin ordered the *hongs* to cease dealing in imported opium and demanded that British merchants turn over their inventory for destruction. After refusing a British offer of 1,000 chests, Lin embargoed all foreign trade in Guangzhou and put the foreign factories under siege.

Captain Charles Elliott arrived in Guangzhou in March 1839 as a superintendent of trade appointed by Parliament. Despite his own misgivings about the opium trade, he resented Lin's pressure tactics. To get Lin to lift the siege, Elliott arranged for British and American merchants to turn over to him the 20,000 chests of opium they controlled, about 1,500 of which were owned by Americans. He then surrendered what was now technically British government property to Lin, who publicly burned the opium. British merchants were then allowed to retreat to Macau and other locations off the coast. What began as a nominally private trade dispute had become a conflict between the Chinese and British governments.

British commercial interests in London argued that the issue in China really had nothing to do with opium. The root of the conflict, they insisted, was China's assault on British lives, property, and honor. The British press and exporters invoked international law and the spirit of progress to justify retaliation. Britain's promotion of free trade was depicted as a spearhead of progress against a decrepit society. Britain was honor-bound to both avenge the wrong done to its citizens (who lost their property) and uplift and civilize China. In short, British merchants wanted to sell products, including opium, legally all over China. The Chinese government wanted to bar opium altogether and confine the remaining trade to the area around Guangzhou. The British wanted their nationals to be exempt from most Chinese laws, whereas the Qing insisted that foreigners in China remain under Qing jurisdiction.

In February 1840, British foreign minister Lord Palmerston composed a message to the Chinese emperor stating that since China had failed to effectively enforce its own laws against opium use, it had no right to impose restrictions on British merchants. China must now return or pay for the confiscated opium, agree to deal with British officials "in a manner consistent with the usages of civilized Nations," turn over one or more islands along the coast as a "place of residence and commerce for British" nationals, and allow British merchants to trade with whomever they wanted in numerous Chinese ports. In addition, China must place "fair duties" (meaning low) on imported goods and agree that British subjects who committed crimes in China be tried under British, not Chinese, law, a legal concept known as extraterritoriality. Palmerston sent his letter via a flotilla of 16 warships, 4 armed steamers, 27 transports, and 4,000 troops, all sent from India. The commander was empowered to blockade Chinese ports, sink ships, and seize territory until the emperor acceded to these demands. Once hostilities ended, China would be assessed costs of the entire operation.

After surrender of the opium, American merchants signed a pledge to temporarily stop dealing in the drug. This allowed them to continue to trade in Guangzhou while the British fought. Although some Americans at home criticized British motives, many opinion leaders took England's side. For example, former president John Quincy Adams, a congressman in 1841, considered the war a righteous crusade. Opium, he argued, was no more a cause of war than was "throwing overboard the tea in Boston harbor . . . a cause of the North American Revolution." Adam's attributed the war to the kowtow, a symbol, he argued, of China's "arrogant and insupportable pretension" that she could do business with Western nations "not upon terms of equal reciprocity, but upon the insulting and degrading forms of the relations between lord and vassal." Several outspoken American missionaries criticized the opium trade but also predicted, in the words of one, that a British victory "may break down the barriers which prevent the Gospel of Christ from entering China."

In the summer of 1840 British naval forces attacked the east China coast, far north of Guangzhou. They intended to force the Qing government to come to terms by cutting off grain shipments from south and central China to Beijing. British artillery and soldiers armed with rifles easily routed Qing warriors brandishing bows and arrows and spears. Steam-powered, iron-clad warships destroyed Qing vessels and pulverized coastal fortifications. Malaria and dysentery posed more of a danger to British forces than did the poorly armed and motivated Qing soldiers.

In August 1840, the emperor finally received Palmerston's letter. He and his advisers mistakenly concluded that simply sacking Lin Zexu would appease the

British. Instead, the British expanded their offensive and captured Guangzhou in May 1841. By 1842 British forces controlled most key Chinese ports and began moving up the Yangtze River, putting the city of Nanjing under siege. The emperor and his advisers decided to accede to British demands rather than continue a war that was unsettling central China and exposing the dynasty's weakness. The terms of the Treaty of Nanjing, signed in August 1842, compelled China to pay for the destroyed opium, turn Hong Kong Island over to Britain, pay a large indemnity for the cost of the war, open five ports for trade, and give British citizens the right to reside in these so-called treaty ports. A supplementary agreement in 1843 gave British residents extraterritorial legal protection. Aside from the indemnity, the treaty did not even mention the opium trade. These so-called unequal treaties initiated China's "century of dishonor."

Following closely on England's victory, President John Tyler sent the former Massachusetts congressman Caleb Cushing to head a diplomatic mission to China. Although he claimed he traveled to China "on behalf of civilization," Cushing hoped to win the same terms as the British had, but without war. He described his mission as "open[ing] the doors of the hundreds of millions of Chinese to America." The use of the term "open door" would come to define American goals in China—and beyond—for the next century. By the time Cushing reached China in February 1844, the Qing court had issued a decree granting American merchants essentially the same rights as their British counterparts and the court saw no need to confer with Cushing. But the American pressed his case, ably assisted by his interpreter, the missionary Peter Parker, and in July 1844 signed the Treaty of Wangxia (a village near Macao) with Chinese officials. The treaty gave the United States nearly identical privileges to those granted Britain, except without territory like Hong Kong. Some of the privileges exceeded those given the British. In treaty ports, Americans could build not only houses but also hospitals, churches, and cemeteries. In return, Cushing agreed to a clause committing Americans to "take measures" to see that U.S. ships and merchants did not import opium in violation of Chinese law. Despite Cushing's accomplishment, Washington more or less ignored China till the late 1850s, often neglecting to appoint any U.S. representatives in the treaty ports.

The treaties negotiated by the United States, Great Britain, and other foreign governments in the wake of the Opium War typically included a "most favored nation clause." This assured that whenever China granted commercial or other rights to one foreign power, the benefits passed automatically to all. Americans often complemented themselves on not using direct force to extract privileges from China. But Chinese critics saw things differently, disparaging the American strategy as "jackal diplomacy."

Eventually, the Western powers and Japan controlled dozens of treaty ports along China's coasts and major rivers. In addition, some Western countries such as France and Germany seized whole cities or, in Germany's case, all of Shandong Province, as "special concessions." Ultimately, only a few of these treaty ports and concessions were economically and culturally significant. Before 1949, China's lack of transportation infrastructure and rural poverty limited the value of these foreign enclaves. The exceptions, partly because of their strategic locations, included Guangzhou, Tianjin, Harbin, and, especially, Shanghai. As the "foreigners' capital of China," Shanghai attracted nearly half of all foreign investments that flowed to China in the century after the Opium War and was home to the largest number of foreign residents. Most of the treaty ports resembled small European-style cities, generally walled and surrounded by larger Chinese settlements. These special zones contained warehouses, shops, restaurants, churches, homes, clubs, parks, and banks. Social segregation limited the rights of Chinese within the special zones and most were only allowed in to do physical labor.

According to legend, a sign in a Shanghai park warned strollers: "No dogs or Chinese allowed." Whether or not the sign actually existed, it certainly reflected a system of unequal relations that gave foreigners a privileged position within China and exempted them from local laws and traditions. When Mao Zedong spoke in 1949 of suffering a "century of dishonor," he tapped into raw feelings shared by millions of Chinese.

From the mid-1840s through 1880, overall Western trade with China grew modestly. American exports fluctuated in the range of $15 to $22 million, with opium accounting for roughly 10 percent. Although some American trading companies did well, the China trade comprised a tiny portion of U.S. commerce between the 1840s and the early twentieth century, typically between 1 and 2 percent of U.S. exports.

American naval architects improved ship construction in the 1840s, designing the classic "China Clipper" such as the fabled *Sea Witch*, able to make a round-trip voyage from New York to China in less than six months. Despite hopes that speedier transport would yield bigger profits, the volume of trade never matched expectations and by the late 1840s and 1850s, the clippers were repurposed to transport miners and supplies to California in the wake of the gold rush. Politicians and pundits spoke periodically of a vast "China market" but rhetoric never matched reality until before the late twentieth century.

For a decade after the British victory in China, disputes continued over the rights of foreign citizens to reside permanently in the treaty ports and to send diplomatic representatives to Beijing. Frustrated by what they considered Chinese harassment, late in 1857 British and French naval forces bombarded coastal cities and followed up by occupying the city of Tianjin in the spring of 1858. The Qing government agreed to foreign demands for greater access to Beijing, but then reneged. In the spring of 1860, Anglo-French troops fought their way from Tianjin to Beijing, destroying nearly everything in their path. Outside Beijing, the troops looted and burned the imperial summer palace (Yuanmingyuan) in supposed retaliation for the torture of several dozen British soldiers. One British officer wrote of the event that he could "scarcely imagine the beauty and magnificence of the palaces we burn . . . in fact, these palaces were so large, and we were so pressed for time, that we could not plunder them carefully . . . everybody was wild for plunder."

(Belatedly, the Qing agreed to a new treaty in 1860 that required their payment of huge indemnities to the invaders, affirmed the right of foreign powers to establish embassies in the Chinese capital, expanded the rights of foreign merchants and missionaries to live and work beyond the treaty ports, set low import tariffs on imported goods, and, unlike the earlier treaties, formally legalized opium imports.) Around the time the British and French fought their way into Beijing, the Buchanan administration in Washington appointed its first minister, or ambassador, to China and prepared to enjoy the newly won privileges.

Emboldened by China's weakness, during the 1850s and 1860s Czarist Russia forced China to concede control over large parts of Mongolia and Manchuria. In the 1870s and 1880s, France fought local skirmishes with Qing forces and seized most of Vietnam and some enclaves in south China. Newly industrializing Japan seized Taiwan and Korea after defeating China in 1895. (Although the United States did not fire a shot, through the most favored nation clause in its own treaty with China it automatically received most of the legal and commercial privileges extracted by other powers.)

Following the second Opium War, opium imports rose steeply, peaking at about 90,000 chests per year in the early 1880s. At the same time, however, the anti-opium movement, spurred by religious and health reformers in Britain and the United States, gathered strength. Missionaries, who earlier collaborated with opium sellers, now argued that opium was destroying the bodies and souls of the same Chinese they hoped to save. As one put it, "the opium traffic is doing more evil in China in a week than Missions are doing good in a year." Also, by the 1880s, an increase in China's domestic opium production undermined imports. Most American traders left the drug business by the 1880s and it declined as a portion of British trade as well.

Opium, missionaries decline.

Beyond the sphere of Qing officials, the foreign presence impacted the lives of ordinary Chinese. Western military incursions, Christian proselytizing, Qing mismanagement, and population pressure in south and central China set off a series of rebellions during the 1850s and 1860s that nearly toppled the dynasty. For example, the massive Taiping Rebellion that raged in south China from 1850 to 1864 led to between 20 and 30 million deaths. Its leader, Hong Xiuquan, had absorbed Christian ideas from a missionary in Guangzhou and held himself to be a younger brother of Jesus destined to establish an egalitarian kingdom on earth. The Qing barely managed to suppress the rebellion, with some help from British and American mercenaries.

Stunned by the Taiping's challenge, during the 1860s and 1870s some Qing officials concluded they must "understand the Barbarians in order to control them." In a series of reforms, dubbed the Self-Strengthening Movement, the dynasty created an agency to deal with foreign powers, promoted the study of Western science, and even sent study delegations abroad. The aim, an imperial adviser explained, was the hope that by gaining the knowledge possessed by Westerners, the Qing could "control them and make them exploitable by us." In 1872, two leading reformers, Zeng Guofan and Li Hongzhang, sponsored an educational mission to the United States by 120 Chinese students. However, by the 1880s, anti-Chinese sentiment in the United States closed the door to most Chinese, whereas within China conservatives who feared losing power to Westernized rivals hobbled reform efforts.

Despite China's enfeeblement and land grabs by outside powers, the foreign beneficiaries of China's weakness neither wanted to colonize China nor destroy the dynasty. As described by the historian Joseph Levenson, the situation between the 1860s and the early twentieth century resembled that in ancient Rome. The Roman power broker Crassus, Levenson noted, "had both a private fire department and a private arson squad, and . . . he made many talents out of using the two in judicious combination." The Western powers, he explained, played the part of Crassus in late-imperial China. Their interests were best served when the "Chinese government had a fire lit under it, the fire of at least partly western inspired" domestic rebellion. The threat posed by rebellion forced the Qing to make concessions to foreigners "to qualify for the foreign aid which alone could save them at home." There were, however, limits to this protection scheme. "The Chinese government should not become so helpless before its domestic foes that effective foreign aid [would] overtax the foreigner or over-encumber the Chinese client; the former will not dispense more [aid] than his stake is worth, the latter will not repay more than he stands to lose."

CHINA COMES TO AMERICA

Upheavals in south and central China in the mid-nineteenth century, along with a growing demand for cheap plantation, mining, and construction workers around the globe, spurred a huge diaspora. Between the 1840s and 1880s, more than 1 million Chinese, mostly from the Pearl River delta, emigrated to Southeast Asia, Latin America, and the United States. (After 1900, millions more moved abroad, nearly all to Malaya, Thailand, French Indochina, the Dutch East Indies, and the Philippines.) In the mid-nineteenth century, the demand for cheap labor increased with the end of the Atlantic slave trade and after Britain, the United States, and Brazil gradually abolished slavery.

Few Chinese visited or immigrated to the United States before the Civil War. Some Chinese sailors "jumped ship" during the 1820s and 1830s and settled in American cities. The best-known Chinese were two conjoined twins, named Chang and Eng, ethnic Chinese from Thailand. Joined at the abdomen, they were brought to Boston in 1829 as indentured servants and put on display as "freaks of nature." In 1832, they struck off on their own, touring the United States and Europe as the "eighth wonder of the world." The entrepreneurial brothers settled in North Carolina in 1839 where they married two sisters, became slave owners on a plantation, and died within hours of each other in 1874.

The so-called *coolie trade* (a word probably derived from the Chinese term for bitter labor) began in the 1840s and continued into the 1880s. The British, as usual, took the lead, recruiting Indians as plantation workers, and the practice soon expanded to south China. Technically, coolies were free, contracted laborers who signed up for eight-year terms as indentured workers. Chinese recruiters received a fee from ships' captains for delivering men for transport. In reality, many coolies were little more than slaves. Many of the American and British ships that transported some 250,000 Chinese to plantations and mines in Peru and Cuba had previously carried enslaved Africans across the Atlantic. Shipboard mortality rates reached 12 percent, and by some estimates half the laborers died before completing their eight-year contract. U.S. abolitionists succeeded in getting President Abraham Lincoln to sign a bill in 1862 prohibiting American-owned ships from engaging in the trade.

Although slang often referred to nineteenth-century Chinese laborers in the United States as coolies, most of the 300,000 who arrived after 1850 came voluntarily, either paying their own way or buying tickets on credit from merchants. A small number of Chinese women were also brought along, many coerced into the sex trade.

The first large influx of Chinese came in the wake of the California gold rush that began in 1849. About 100,000 Chinese sailed from Guangzhou to "Old Gold Mountain" (San Francisco), where they typically worked as miners, launderers, cooks, and shopkeepers. A relaxed immigration law along with the chronic labor shortage in the West initially eased their acceptance.

During the Civil War, Secretary of State William Seward sent Anson Burlingame as Washington's chief diplomat in China with instructions to promote trade and immigration. After the Civil War, Burlingame resigned his post and was hired by the Chinese to represent their interests in the United States and Europe. Secretary of State Seward, who also promoted the purchase of Alaska as a gateway to transpacific shipping, negotiated a treaty with Burlingame, acting on China's behalf, in 1868. Seward, like many Americans, thought that Chinese laborers were ideally suited to construct the western leg of the transcontinental railroad because, as one medical text of the time explained, their "primitive" nervous systems made them immune to ordinary pain. The treaty promised that Chinese immigrants would receive fair treatment and government protection.

In the decade after 1868, about 200,000 Chinese flocked to the western United States. About 25,000 worked on construction crews for the Central Pacific Railroad, laying track, blasting tunnels, and building bridges across the rugged Sierra Nevada mountains. Construction bosses acknowledged they could never have completed the western link of the transcontinental railroad without Chinese labor.

Although many other immigrant groups suffered initial discrimination and abuse in their adopted country, hostility toward the Chinese increased over time. Stark differences in language and culture separated the Chinese from both Anglo-Saxon Protestants and other newcomers such as the Irish, Slavs, Italians, and Jews who came to America around the same time. The fact that many Chinese considered themselves "sojourners," temporary residents who hoped to earn some money and return to their ancestral home, further separated them from "old-stock" Americans and other recent arrivals. Sometimes by choice but often because of hostility, Chinese lived apart from other ethnic groups and some found solace in gambling, opium, and prostitution. At one point, nearly half the Chinese females in America worked as prostitutes, largely servicing Chinese men. These circumstances, along with the willingness of many Chinese to accept low pay for unskilled jobs, aroused the anger of white working-class males, who saw them as a threat.

Despite wording in the 1868 treaty promising full protection to Chinese immigrants, waves of anti-Chinese violence swept western states during the 1870s and 1880s. Attacking the "heathen Chinee" became a popular sport in many California cities and Rocky Mountain mining towns. Even when 28 Chinese were brutally murdered by a mob in Rock Springs, Wyoming, in 1885, the perpetrators went unpunished. The American satirist Bret Harte captured the plight of these victims in a mock obituary he wrote for "Wan Lee: Dead my reverend friend, dead. Stoned to death in the streets of San Francisco in the year of grace 1869 by a mob of half-grown boys and Christian school children." America's most famous political cartoonist, Thomas Nast, summed up America's handling of the "Chinese problem" in a sketch from 1880. Nast depicted a terrified Chinese man cowering before a crazed lynch mob. Pinned to the "coolie's" shirt were labels bearing words such as "slave, pauper and rat eater." The violence chronicled by Harte and Nast added a vivid phrase to the language: "Not a Chinaman's Chance."

For decades, Western powers had justified armed intervention and punitive military strikes in China as a response to antiforeign violence. Yet neither state nor federal authorities displayed much interest in protecting the Chinese from mob attacks. China's few diplomatic representatives in the United States (the first Chinese ambassador in Washington arrived in 1878) protested mob violence, but their voice carried little weight.

Anti-Chinese violence and laws were most prevalent in California and the Rocky Mountain states, home to nearly all Chinese immigrants. In the words of California Senator Aaron A. Sargent, the nation faced a "great and growing evil" from "Mongolian immigration" that threatened both "republican institutions" and "Christian civilization." Although most large employers lobbied Congress against halting Chinese immigration during the 1870s, western states connived to discourage new arrivals and drive out those already settled. State and local governments imposed special taxes on foreign miners and laundries that singled out Chinese. Authorities ignored vigilante attacks, such as when mobs cut off the queues (pigtails) worn by many Chinese men. Federal laws imposed new impediments to Chinese becoming citizens, although they did not bar it. To hinder family formation, the Page Act of 1870 banned most immigration by Chinese women, whereas state antimiscegenation laws forbade marriage between whites and most Asians.

In 1879 Congress enacted a law limiting to 15 the number of Chinese laborers permitted to enter the country on any one ship. President Rutherford B. Hayes

[February 18, 1871.]   HARPER'S WEEKLY.   149

"Columbia protecting John Chinaman from a lynch mob." In this 1871 cartoon, Thomas Nast turned his attention from his usual target, urban political corruption, to depict the plight of Chinese immigrants in the American West. After torching a "colored orphan asylum," a mob sets out after "John Chinaman." (Courtesy of the Library of Congress, LC-USZ62-53346) vetoed the law, but Congress took further action. In 1880, the platforms of both the Democratic and the Republican parties endorsed strict curbs on Chinese immigration. In 1881, the Senate ratified a treaty forced on China by the State Department that permitted the United States to "suspend" the coolie trade. Congress then enacted the Chinese Exclusion Act of 1882, suspending for 10 years *all*, not just unskilled, Chinese immigration. Periodically renewed after its first iteration, the law classified Chinese along with imbeciles, paupers, and prostitutes as barred from immigration. Over the next half century, Congress and state legislatures imposed increasingly harsh versions of these restrictions. Faced by violence and insult, about two-thirds of the 300,000 Chinese who came to the United States after 1850 returned home by the 1880s.

Between the 1890s and 1920s, state and federal laws, backed by court decisions, stripped most resident Chinese (and many other Asians) of their legal and property rights. In 1913, California barred persons "ineligible for citizenship" (in effect, Asians) from owning land. The National Origins Act passed in 1924 barred all new Asian immigration. The Supreme Court affirmed that Asians already resident in the United States but not born here could be refused the right of naturalization.

These restrictions remained virtually intact until the middle of World War II. Then, with China a U.S. ally fighting against avowedly racist Germany and Japan, Congress approved a token quota of 105 Chinese immigrants per year. After World War II, some of the most egregious wording in treaties between the United States and China was modified. But when Congress enacted the McCarran–Walter immigration act in 1952, it imposed strict immigration limits on Asians, limiting each country to about 100 persons per year. These restrictions continued until passage of the landmark Immigration and Nationality Act of 1965.

AMERICANS IN CHINA

From the time Cushing negotiated the first treaty with China in 1844 through the end of the century, the U.S. government minimized its direct role in China. The United States stationed no troops in the region, fought no wars (aside from some indirect assistance to British naval vessels in various bombardments of Chinese fortifications), and was content to enjoy the various privileges extracted from China by others. With the decline of American participation in the opium trade after 1880, the nation's merchants had few things to sell. Christian evangelism emerged as the only "growth product" in the Chinese–American relationship. From the mid-nineteenth century through World War II, missionaries served as the key interface between China and the American public. These Americans lived in China, learned the language, established institutions, and reported to the public at home through church newsletters, magazines, and, eventually, films. More than any other group they created the notion of tight and growing bonds between the United States and China.

Although China had banned Christianity in the eighteenth century and limited missionary efforts before 1860, American Christians saw China as a vast market of souls. Evangelical Protestants believed that Christ's Second Coming awaited the conversion of heathens and nowhere on earth had more heathens than China. Some early missionaries and the church boards that sponsored them exuded intolerance. S. Wells Williams remarked in 1843 that "God's plan of mercy" for Chinese included "harsh measures to bring them out of their ignorance, conceit and idolatry." Williams, like many of his contemporaries, tacitly approved Britain's war in China, even if they opposed opium, as clearing the path for Christian uplift. At least some missionaries seemed to peddle the "imperialism of righteousness."

In reality, most missionaries were neither intolerant Bible thumpers nor naive do-gooders. Typically, they were idealists motivated by dual desires to spread the Gospel of Jesus along with what they considered the superior American way of life. Like Western merchants who hoped to end China's isolation and create new material wants, they envisioned themselves selling salvation and progress. The missionaries bore a resemblance to America's secular "nation builders." A century later, similar idealism motivated many of the young men and women who flocked to the Peace Corps. In 1895, Charles Denby, the chief American diplomat in China, made this point in a message to the State Department. Missionaries, he explained, were "pioneers of trade and commerce. Civilization, learning, instruction breed new wants which commerce supplies." Like their military and commercial counterparts, missionaries often described their challenge in martial terms. For example, a report issued in 1895 by the Young Men's Christian Association on the effort to spread Christianity bore the title "Strategic Points in World Conquest."

Until 1860, missionaries were confined to a handful of treaty ports. Thereafter, most of China was thrown open to proselytizing. The Protestant and Catholic missionaries who ventured to China were part of a larger cohort that set out to do God's work in Latin America, Africa, the Near East, and Hawaii. They targeted not only pagan worship but also the disease and ignorance they saw everywhere in China. Funds for the work came from donations raised at Sunday services in thousands of churches across America.

Aside from opposition by Qing authorities and local elites who feared that the egalitarian aspects of Christianity would undermine their authority, missionaries faced cultural resistance. Most Chinese who concerned themselves with religion were reluctant to embrace one faith exclusively. Chinese often blended their devotions, combining aspects of Buddhism, Taoism, ancestor worship, and prayer to local spirits. This held true for the Taiping leadership. Hong Xiuquan and his followers, to the great disappointment of the missionary community, combined vague Christian notions with various folk beliefs that bore little resemblance to traditional Christianity.

The number of missionaries in China increased gradually after 1860. By the 1920s, some 6,000 Protestant missionaries, in addition to Catholic priests, worked in China. About 3,000 of the missionaries were American and, of these, half were women. Many more Christian lay workers assisted in the hospitals, schools, orphanages, and other charitable institutions established under church auspices. The number of Chinese converts remained small: perhaps 100,000 by 1900 and between 2 and 3 million by the 1930s. Christians were more heavily represented in the ranks of graduates from the many high schools and colleges founded by missionaries. Given a population of around 400 million in the late nineteenth and early twentieth centuries, the achievement was a modest one.

Numbers aside, the efforts by missionaries and lay workers found a receptive audience among American Protestant and Catholic churchgoers. Sermons, newsletters, magazines, and testimonials were supplemented by church films beginning in the 1920s. With titles such as *The Cross and the Dragon*, *The Conquest of Cathay*, and the *Missioner's Cross*, these films showed dedicated missionaries amid throngs of eager converts.[3]

Almost from its origins, however, missionary activity in China provoked a reaction. Isolated acts of violence against church property, missionaries, and Chinese Christians were common. Occasionally, the violence escalated into major riots. The most dramatic outbreak occurred in 1900 during the so-called Boxer Rebellion, discussed later. Attacking a defenseless missionary or Chinese Christian, after all, was about the only way an ordinary Chinese could strike out against foreign domination. Few Americans paid attention to more nuanced criticism of merchant, missionary, or military activity in China. For example, stunned silence followed a speech in Philadelphia in 1889 when a Chinese official told an audience that a "truly civilized nation should respect the rights of other societies, and refrain from stealing other men's property, or imposing upon others unwelcome beliefs."

YELLOW PERIL

Although the worst violence against Chinese in America lapsed by the late 1880s, the anti-Chinese mindset survived to spawn a virulent genre of literature. Warnings of a "yellow peril" coincided, oddly enough, with China's growing weakness from the 1870s on. The ambivalence of sympathy and suspicion toward Chinese could be found in many places. For example, the journal of the Salvation Army, *War Cry*, referred to Chinese in China by their formal names and spoke respectfully of them as men and women. But *War Cry* routinely condemned decadent "Chinamen" living in the United States as drug dealers and white slavers, corrupting innocent Americans. President Theodore Roosevelt felt no need to temper his language when he characterized the Chinese as an "immoral, degraded and worthless race."

In the final decades of the nineteenth century and through the 1930s, the most common image of China and its people came from popular culture, including

---

[3]Selections from many of these now lost church films, as well as Hollywood depictions of China from the 1920s through 1940s, can be found in Irv Drasnin's documentary, *Misunderstanding China*, cited previously.

comic strips and pulp magazines. The "pulps," which sold as many as 20 million copies per month, serialized tales of mysterious and dangerous "Orientals" such as the saga of "Mr. Wu Fang" who lusted after the "blonde maiden, Tanya."

Fear of a race war, yellow against white, appeared in England as early as the mid-nineteenth century, some of it in the writings of Charles Dickens. He and his imitators described white women lured by Chinese into opium dens at a time when perhaps 200 Chinese lived in London. The genre spread to the United States by the 1870s with the appearance of H. J. West's *The Chinese Invasion* (1873), followed by Atwell Whitney's *Almond Eyed* (1878), Pierton W. Dooner's *Last Days of the Republic* (1880), and Robert Wolter's *A Short and Truthful History of the Taking of California and Oregon by the Chinese in the Year A.D. 1899* (1882). America's most popular adventure writer and self-proclaimed socialist, Jack London, joined those prophesying race war in 1910 when he published *The Unparalleled Invasion* in *McClure's*, a leading progressive magazine. London imagined a China that by 1976 had become the most populous and powerful nation in the world. After overrunning most of Asia, it threatened Europe and North America. With the fate of the world at stake, a global alliance of white nations crushed China by launching a preemptive strike. The United States and its European allies flew airplanes over China that dropped glass vials containing "every virulent form of infectious death" to obliterate the "chattering yellow populace." Western armies massed on China's borders slaughtered those trying to flee. Ultimately, 500 million Chinese perished, and "then began the great task, the sanitation of China . . . according to the democratic American program." In London's account, the alliance against China ended the mistrust among traditional rivals such as Germany and France and secured world peace, minus half the world's population.

The most influential race war narrative came from the pen of British writer (and later American resident) Arthur Henry Ward. In 1913, now calling himself Sax Rohmer, he published *The Mystery of Dr. Fu Manchu*. A largely self-educated man, Rohmer found inspiration from the stories of Edgar Allan Poe and Arthur Conan Doyle. He moved to the United States in 1931 after he became a global publishing phenomenon. Over five decades, ending with his death in 1959, he published 15 Fu Manchu novels (along with many other mystery books) and wrote or supervised the production of dozens of comic books, radio plays, feature films, and television shows featuring his arch villain. "Imagine," Rohmer wrote of his protagonist, "a person tall, lean and feline, high shouldered with a brow like Shakespeare and a face like Satan, close shaven skull and long magnetic eyes of a true cat green." Then, "invest him with all the cruel cunning of an entire eastern race, accumulated in one giant intellect with all the resources science past and present, with all the resources if you will of a wealthy government—which however already denied all knowledge of his existence—imagine that awful being and you have a mental picture of Dr. Fu Manchu, the yellow peril incarnate in one man." Quite a description from an author who late in life boasted, "I made my name on Fu Manchu because I know nothing about China."

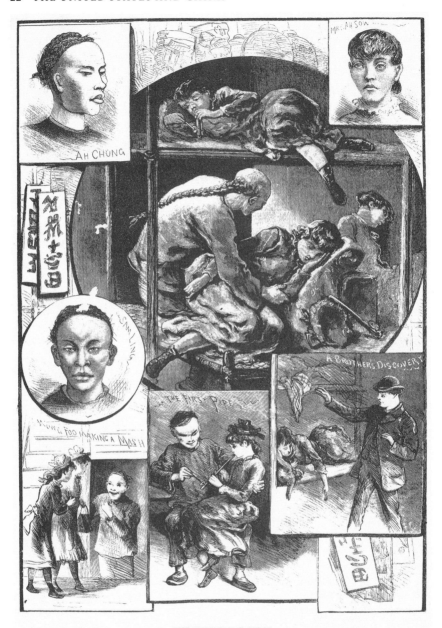

THE MONGOLIAN CURSE.

BLIGHTING EFFECTS OF THE INTRODUCTION OF A DEBASING CELESTIAL HABIT AMONG THE YOUNG GIRLS OF NEW YORK—
SCENES IN AND AROUND THE CHINESE OPIUM JOINTS IN MOTT STREET.

A Police Gazette comic book of the 1880s warns of girls lured into Chinese opium dens in American cities. (The Granger Collection, New York)

The formulaic novels and stories typically began with the murder of a pillar of the British Empire by Asiatic plotters under the control of Fu Manchu. Rohmer's fictional hero, Nayland Smith, bravely battled the "fiendish, yellow dragon of death." The "price of failure," Smith warned readers, might be the "swamping of the white world by the Yellow Hordes." Six Fu Manchu films were released during the 1960s and the villain's echo appeared as "Dr. No" in Ian Fleming's James Bond novel (1958) and film version in 1962. After Frankenstein's monster, Fu Manchu became Hollywood's most popular villain. Actor Boris Karloff played both roles. His characterization of Fu Manchu added yet another cliché to American slang, "Chinese torture."

Hollywood, as noted later, occasionally depicted heroic or at least sympathetic Chinese. These included the peasants of the 1937 film version of *The Good Earth*. The Honolulu-based detective (based on an actual cop), Charlie Chan, appeared in dozens of films released by several studios over four decades. Of the half dozen actors playing the title role, none was actually Chinese and all spoke English, as one historian noted, "as if they learned it in a fortune cookie."

Americans taking stock in the 1890s prided themselves for not having gone to war against China as had other Western powers. They boasted of their effort to bring to China Christianity, good health, and education. After 1900, several prominent American universities established branches in China and others brought thousands of Chinese scholarship students to the United States—often with funds initially provided by the Chinese government as part of the penalty they paid after the Boxer uprising. But whether a Chinese attended Yale-in-China or Yale in New Haven, Connecticut, the underlying goal was to make him or her more like an American. In film, as in real life, a good Chinese at the end of the nineteenth century meant one who converted to Christianity and worked to make over China in the American image.

SELECTED ADDITIONAL READINGS

Among the many valuable books detailing the history of late imperial and early twentieth-century China are four studies by Jonathan D. Spence, *The Gate of Heavenly Peace: The Chinese and Their Revolution, 1895–1980* (New York, 1981), *The Chan's Great Continent: China in Western Minds* (New York, 1988), *God's Chinese Son: The Chinese Heavenly Kingdom of Hong Xiuquan* (New York, 1996), and *The Chinese Century: A Photographic History of the Last 100 Years* (New York, 1996); John K. Fairbank and Merle Goldman, *China: A New History* (Cambridge, Mass., 1998); Mary C. Wright, *The Last Stand of Chinese Conservatism: The T'ung–Chih Restoration, 1862–1874* (Stanford, Ca., 1957); Philip Kuhn, *Rebellion and Its Enemies in Late Imperial China* (Cambridge, Mass., 1974); Orville Schell and Franz Schurmann, eds., *Imperial China: The Decline of the Last Dynasty and the Origins of Modern China, the 18th and 19th Centuries* (New York, 1967); and Odd Arne Westad, *Restless Empire: China and the World since 1750* (New York, 2012).

Studies of the Western impact on China, foreign trade, missionaries, and immigration include Irv Drasnin, *Misunderstanding China* (a documentary film produced for CBS in

1972); John K. Fairbank, *Trade and Diplomacy on the China Coast: The Opening of the Treaty Ports* (Cambridge, Mass., 1953); Julia Lovell, *The Opium War* (London, 2011); Peter Fay, *The Opium War, 1839–42* (Chapel Hill, N.C., 1975); Jacques M. Downs, *The Golden Ghetto: The American Commercial Community at Canton and the Shaping of American China Policy, 1784–1844* (Bethlehem, Pa., 1997); Eric J. Dolin, *When America First Met China: An Exotic History of Tea, Drugs, and Money in the Age of Sail* (New York, 2012); Michael Hunt, *The Making of a Special Relationship: The United States and China to 1914* (New York, 1983); Akira Iriye, *Across the Pacific* (New York, 1967); James C. Thomson, Peter W. Stanley, and John C. Perry, *Sentimental Imperialists: The American Experience in East Asia* (New York, 1981); Harold Isaacs, *Scratches on Our Minds: American Images of India and China* (New York, 1958); R. David Arkush and Leo Ou-fan Lee, *Land without Ghosts: Chinese Impressions of America from the Mid-19th Century to the Present* (Berkeley, Ca., 1989); John K. Fairbank, ed., *The Missionary Enterprise in China and America* (Cambridge, Mass., 1974); Paul Varg, *Missionaries, Chinese and Diplomats: The American Protestant Missionary Movement in China, 1890–1952* (Princeton, N.J., 1958); Jane Hunter, *The Gospel of Gentility: American Women Missionaries in Turn-of-the-Century China* (New Haven, Conn., 1984); Ronald Takaki, *Strangers from a Different Shore: A History of Asian Americans* (New York, 1989); Stuart Miller, *Unwelcome Immigrant: The American Image of the Chinese, 1875–1882* (Berkeley, Ca., 1969); Robert McClellan, *The Heathen Chinee: A Study of American Attitude toward China, 1890–1905* (Columbus, Oh., 1971); Maxine Hong Kingston, *China Men* (New York, 1980); David L. Anderson, *Imperialism and Idealism: American Diplomats in China, 1861–1898* (Bloomington, Ind., 1985); Jonathan Goldstein, *Philadelphia and the China Trade, 1682–1846* (Philadelphia, Pa., 1978); Stephen Ambrose, *Nothing Like It in the World: The Men Who Built the Transcontinental Railroad, 1863–1869* (New York, 2000); Marilyn B. Young, *The Rhetoric of Empire* (Cambridge, Mass., 1969); Ernest R. May and John K. Fairbank, eds., *America's China Trade in Historical Perspective: The Chinese and American Performance* (Cambridge, Mass., 1986); Robert G. Lee, *Orientals: Asian Americans in Popular Culture* (Philadelphia, Pa., 1999); and Eileen Scully, *Bargaining with the State from Afar* (New York, 2001). Gordon H. Chang, *Fateful Ties: A History of America's Preoccupation with China* (Cambridge, Mass., 2015).

CHAPTER 2

Asia in Disorder, 1890s–1936

During the 75 years that elapsed between the end of the American Civil War and the outbreak of World War II, the United States and China followed vastly different paths. Whereas the United States began a period of accelerated economic development that resulted in its becoming the world's largest economy and a nation with global influence, China continued its slide into poverty, rebellion, and foreign domination. The increasingly feeble Qing Dynasty survived on life support and the forbearance of the Great Powers who found it more convenient to leave the Manchus on the throne than to assume for themselves the burden of direct rule. Like the Europeans and then the Japanese, American missionaries and merchants, and eventually a small contingent of soldiers and sailors, enjoyed the benefits of the unequal treaties that allowed them to pass through China's open doors. Most of the time, however, the U.S. government hardly bothered about China as long as no one impeded American commercial and religious activities.

Until 1899, the United States deferred to Great Britain on most China policy matters. Elsewhere in the Pacific, Americans acted more forcefully. By the early 1890s Americans had taken control of the Hawaii as well as Wake and Midway Islands and parts of Samoa. The U.S. Navy played a key role in compelling Japan to open itself to foreign contact. In 1853–1854, Commodore Matthew Perry led a naval expedition to Tokyo Bay, with orders to make the Tokugawa Shogun (hereditary military ruler) sign a trade agreement similar to the pacts recently imposed on China. Perry's steam-powered warships and the miniature railroad and telegraph system he displayed on shore convinced the Japanese they must at least temporarily bow to foreign pressure. A writer in the *Presbyterian Review* observed that with China following the West's lead, "Christian civilization and commerce had closed upon the Japanese Empire on both sides."

Japan, however, avoided China's fate. For nearly 15 years after Perry's visit, the outside powers were absorbed in their own conflicts. The British and French fought Russia and Ottoman Turkey over Crimea. The Americans were consumed by the issue of slavery in the late 1850s and then fought a bloody civil war from

1861 to 1865. By the late 1860s, Japanese nationalists saw China as an object lesson in everything that could go wrong in a country that remained weak and disorganized. Determined to avoid this fate, Japanese elites used this interim to depose the Tokugawa shogun and to organize a new government under the symbolic leadership of the formerly ceremonial emperor. This so-called Meiji Restoration (named for Emperor Meiji) in 1868 ushered in a period of centralized control that promoted rapid economic growth and social change. Japanese reformers embraced Western technology, science, and organizational skills in their quest to build a powerful, modern, and independent Japan. By the 1890s Japan had become a regional military and economic power and had rid itself of unequal treaties. Chinese nationalists initially admired Japan's success, but by the 1890s saw the newly empowered Japan as another greedy nation hoping to carve up China.

THE COLLAPSE OF THE ASIAN POWER BALANCE

Since the era of the Opium Wars, an equilibrium of sorts had existed in China and East Asia that sustained a balance among the world's powers. By the 1890s, that balance shattered as events inside and outside China altered the landscape. Inside China, popular resentment against foreign domination and the inept Qing grew more prevalent. Outside, the Europeans, the United States, and Japan intensified their efforts to dominate underdeveloped parts of the world. Between the 1860s and 1910, nearly 25 percent of the surface of the earth was seized as new colonies. This included most of Africa, much of Southeast Asia, parts of the Middle East, numerous Pacific Islands, and provinces on China's periphery. Late-industrializing nations, such as Germany, Japan, and Czarist Russia, in addition to England and France, were especially motivated to "earn" their great power stripes by building new empires. During the 1880s and 1890s, many American opinion leaders, including politicians, the business community, popular writers, and religious thinkers, asserted that national purpose and prosperity required that the nation play a more active role in global affairs. The Pacific coast no longer seemed a limit to expansion but a threshold to transcend. A large naval building program begun in the late 1880s reflected this concern.

Japan's rapid defeat of China in their war of 1894–1895, fought over influence in Korea and Manchuria,[1] precipitated a race by other nations to divide China into "spheres of influence." After thrashing China, Japan demanded control over several provinces. When France, Germany, and Russia threatened retaliation, Japan backed off. Instead, Japan joined the Europeans in seeking informal control of key ports, mines, and railroad routes. Although these spheres were not formal colonies,

---

[1]Since the 1860s, Qing politics were dominated by the Empress Dowager, Cixi, concubine of the emperor who died in 1861. She gradually extended her reach into foreign and military affairs, both provoking China's neighbors and weakening its defenses. For example, Cixi diverted funds for naval building to construct, instead, elaborate marble ships that decorated a lake near her residence. Some recent accounts portray Cixi as a closet feminist and modernizer.

American business and diplomatic observers voiced alarm that the Europeans and Japanese would discriminate against American trade within them. In 1898, concerned business leaders organized the American Asiatic Association to press the State Department to protect their current and future commercial interests in China. The outbreak of the Spanish–American War in April 1898 thrust the United States into a more active role throughout the Asia-Pacific region.

Cuba, the last major remnant of Spain's new world empire, had been fighting for independence for nearly a decade before America intervened. Concerns over U.S. investments, the island's proximity to Florida, and revulsion over the Spanish army's brutal antiguerrilla campaign that included torture and the forced relocation of civilians aroused American ire. President William McKinley demanded that Spain end its human rights violations (a term perhaps first used at this time) in Cuba and accept U.S. mediation with the rebels. Madrid's rejection of this proposal, followed by the mysterious destruction (probably from an accidental internal explosion, not sabotage) of the U.S. cruiser *Maine* during its visit to Havana in February 1898, prompted McKinley to ask Congress in April for a declaration of war against Spain.

It required several months to organize a largely volunteer invasion force. But once the Americans arrived, Spanish units in Cuba folded quickly. In August, Spain asked for an armistice and what Secretary of State John Hay called a "splendid little war" was over. In the Pacific, the U.S. Navy struck more quickly against Spanish outposts, including the Philippine Islands. In a brief battle, the small Asiatic squadron commanded by Commodore George Dewey sank a decrepit Spanish fleet in Manila Bay. Dewey brought with him from exile in Hong Kong a Filipino independence fighter, Emilio Aguinaldo, who promised to rally Filipino rebels against Spanish land forces. Dewey had promised Aguinaldo that following victory, the islands would be granted independence. However, powerful interests in Washington decided otherwise.

Explaining his decision to annex the Philippines, McKinley claimed that when the war began he had no idea where the islands were located. But over several months he came to share the views of such men as naval strategist Captain Alfred Thayer Mahan and his own former assistant secretary of the navy and Cuban war hero, Theodore Roosevelt. In their writings and speeches, both argued that the United States required Pacific colonies to build its "manly character" and promote commercial opportunities in and around China. McKinley told a delegation of Methodist clergy at the White House that he intended to push for annexation of the entire Philippine archipelago. Speaking in what sounded like bullet points, the president asserted that the Filipinos were too primitive to rule themselves. It would be "bad business" to turn them over to America's "commercial rivals" in the Orient. After much prayer, he resolved to "uplift and civilize and Christianize [the Filipinos— most of whom were Catholics!] and by God's grace to do the very best we could by them as our fellow men for whom Christ also died."

The literary champion of British imperialism, Rudyard Kipling, had written a poem that made similar arguments in favor of annexing the Philippines.

Advanced nations such as the United States, Kipling argued, had a responsibility to "pick up the White Man's Burden" in Asia and Africa. The poet, of course, hoped that by acquiring colonies, the United States would have a stake in defending the British Empire. The notion that American control would provide a better life for backward peoples even found expression in advertisements. A full-page display by the Pears Soap Company featured a likeness of Dewey washing his hands with a clearly marked bar of Pears soap. Surrounding him were groups of missionaries schooling native children and merchants handing out soap to naked, dark-skinned Filipinos. The caption read, "The first step towards lightening the White Man's Burden is through teaching the virtues of cleanliness. Pears Soap is a potent factor in brightening the dark corners of the earth as civilization advances, while amongst the cultured of all nations it holds the highest place—it is the ideal toilet soap."

In February 1899, in return for a token payment, Spain ceded the Philippines, Guam, and Puerto Rico to American control and granted Cuba independence under American guidance. The Senate—and public—engaged in a spirited debate over Philippine annexation. (Few disputed taking Puerto Rico or Guam; separately, Congress annexed Hawaii, which had been under de facto American control since sugar planters overthrew the native monarchy in 1893.)

Democratic presidential candidate William Jennings Bryan, industrialist Andrew Carnegie, and writer Mark Twain criticized annexation as a betrayal of democracy. Several southern senators opposed bringing under American control millions more people of color while the South was in the midst of imposing rigid racial segregation. Senator Albert J. Beveridge of Indiana countered that control of the Philippines, in addition to being part of God's plan for American expansion, would assure access to the islands' resources, and, more importantly, to "China's illimitable markets."

Beveridge and his supporters mustered two-thirds of the Senate in favor of creating a new American empire. Unfortunately, they neglected to consult the Filipinos. In the wake of the Senate vote, Filipinos demanding independence rose in revolt against American colonization. The brutal war to suppress the guerrillas lasted four years, requiring deployment of 70,000 troops and causing the deaths of tens of thousands of Filipinos and more than 4,000 Americans.

Until 1898, most American business leaders and politicians concerned with the China market assumed that the efficiency of American industry and agriculture, along with the acquisition of the Philippines, would assure trade expansion. There were hopes that a new burst of Chinese reform begun that year would also help. Kang Youwei, an advisor to the young emperor, Kuang Hsu, promoted a plan to modernize the government. But after a few months, Empress Dowager Cixi (Kuang Hsu's aunt and the real power behind the throne) struck back. She imprisoned her nephew and killed or exiled most of the reformers. The chaos prompted more talk by Germany, Japan, and Russia of carving up spheres within China.

Pressed to act, Secretary of State John Hay sought guidance from William Rockhill, the State Department's acknowledged China expert. Rockhill feared that any moves to divide China into special zones would be a disaster both for the Chinese and for American commercial interests. Outside pressure might topple the Qing and create a vacuum that foreign powers would fill. To prevent this, Rockhill urged that the United States act to preserve China's territorial integrity.

Hay and President McKinley agreed, but saw limits in the ability of the United States to act forcefully. As Hay told the president, the "inherent weakness of our position is this: we do not want to rob China ourselves, and our public opinion will not permit us to interfere with any army to prevent others from robbing her. Besides, we have no army." [Most U.S. forces were tied down in the Philippines.] Hay dismissed talk about our "preeminent moral position giving us the authority to dictate to the world" as "mere flap-doodle."

Alfred Hippisley, an English friend of Rockhill who worked for the Chinese Customs Service as a revenue collector, worried that if the Europeans and Japanese seized spheres within China, they would block collection of customs receipts that sustained the Qing dynasty, causing it to collapse. He suggested to Rockhill that China's stability could be preserved by getting the foreign powers to agree that even if they seized spheres of influence they would not discriminate against foreign trade or block collection of customs revenues needed by the Chinese government.

Hay liked the idea because it required no force or threats, just tacit consent by other nations. He made this proposal in a series of notes he sent to the European and Japanese governments in September 1899. These so-called Open Door Notes were issued without consulting the Chinese government. Although all the recipients gave evasive or weakly positive responses, none rejected Hay's proposal outright.

What seemed like an easy and cost-free maneuver to protect American trade and block the further division of China threatened to unravel less than a year later when a mass antiforeign campaign swept north China. The so-called Boxer Rebellion was one part of a broad-based antimissionary, antiforeign, anti-Qing movement centered in Shandong province. Since the mid-1890s, a large number of rural labors had joined a sect that blamed foreign influence—especially Christianity—for China's weakness.

The Boxers, or *yihotuan*, wore colorful turbans, robes, and boots, practiced martial arts, and invoked magic as part of their rituals. Although lacking much organizational structure, the sword- and spear-wielding Boxers claimed that their magic made them immune to bullets and that the spirits of innumerable dead Chinese would join them in sweeping out foreign influence. In some ways the Boxers resembled other millennial movements in the 1890s that arose among indigenous peoples in Africa and North America to resist outside pressure. For example, the Ghost Dancers among the Sioux in South Dakota similarly invoked magic spells to conjure the spirits of dead ancestors and to counter modern weapons.

In the spring of 1900 thousands of Boxers entered Beijing shouting slogans to "support the Qing, exterminate the foreigners." They hoped to overrun the foreign diplomatic compounds. Qing officials had ambivalent feelings about this

"A Fair Field and No Favor." This cartoon from Harper's Weekly in 1899 depicts the view held by many Americans: The U.S. was "protecting" and helping China by blocking any one nation from dominating its trade. (Harper's Weekly, Vol. 43, No. 2239)

grass-roots movement. Some saw it as a threat to the dynasty, others as a useful tool to turn against foreigners. Empress Dowager Cixi ultimately gave the Boxers her blessing, declaring that "foreigners infringed upon our territorial integrity, trampled our people under their feet," and "blaspheme our gods."

IS THIS IMPERIALISM?
"NO BLOW HAS BEEN STRUCK EXCEPT FOR LIBERTY AND HUMANITY, AND NONE WILL BE."—WILLIAM McKINLEY

President McKinley and Uncle Sam suppress Boxers, 1900. This cartoon depicts McKinley, who had led the U.S. into war with Spain over Cuba and then opted to annex the Philippines, as playing a leading role in the International Military Expedition that invaded China to rescue diplomats, missionaries, and merchants. (The Granger Collection, New York)

Most officials in south China ignored the court's declaration of war and much of the regular army remained neutral. Nevertheless, after killing the German ambassador in mid-June, the Boxers laid siege to the diplomatic compound in Beijing. Foreign enclaves in Tianjin also came under attack.

The siege in Beijing lasted nearly two months, while eight nations, including the United States, assembled a military force in China numbering about 60,000. The foreign powers described the operation as a humanitarian rescue mission in a failed state that had reverted to barbarism. After at least one abortive attempt, in August about 20,000 foreign troops, including a few thousand Americans redeployed from the Philippines, succeeded in marching from Tianjin to Beijing, a distance of about 100 miles. The relief expedition destroyed more or less everything in its path. The Empress Dowager and her entourage fled the Forbidden City to undertake what she called an "inspection tour" in western China. Casualty estimates included the murder of about 250 missionaries and several thousand Chinese Christians by the Boxers, a few hundred foreign troops killed in combat, and about 100,000 Boxers and Chinese civilians killed by rampaging Western and Japanese soldiers. Chinese historians writing after the Communist victory of 1949 described the Boxers as peasant revolutionaries.

In July, during the siege in Beijing, Secretary of State Hay feared that the Europeans and Japanese might seize Chinese territory as compensation for Boxer attacks. Hoping to prevent this, Hay sent a second round of Open Door Notes, calling on all the powers to respect China's territorial integrity. Should the worst happen, however, Hay and McKinley discussed a contingency plan to "slice the watermelon" and grab a naval base and some territory for the United States. This proved unnecessary because the Europeans and Japanese were too jealous of each other to agree on a division of spoils.

In September 1901 the occupying powers forced the remnants of the Qing government to sign what were called the Boxer Protocols. Qing officials linked to the rebels were executed or exiled. China paid a massive indemnity roughly equivalent to $300 million (with $25 million going to the United States) and agreed that foreign troops could remain on its soil. Japan deployed what it called the Kwantung Army to southern Manchuria, whereas the United States maintained a

U.S. troops on maneuvers near the Forbidden City, Beijing, 1900. (© Bettmann/Corbis)

small force of Marines and infantry in Shanghai and other garrisons. The British and American navies, among others, assigned ships to patrol the rivers and treaty ports. Although nominally intact, China had become a vassal state.

CHINA DIVIDED

Although by 1900 foreigners in China were generally free to live where they wanted, their numbers before 1941 remained small, never going above a half million. Japanese comprised about half the country's foreign residents. After the Bolshevik revolution of 1917, about 100,000 Russians fled to China. A few tens of thousands of European refugees, many of them Jews, arrived during the 1930s. Fifteen thousand British citizens and fewer Americans lived in China before 1941. Shanghai remained the foreigners' capital, with about 70,000 in residence.

The Open Door Notes and Boxer intervention revealed growing, but limited, U.S. interest in Chinese and Asian affairs. China was important, but not worth a direct confrontation with, say, Russia or Japan. Americans remained focused on Europe and Latin America. As for commerce in the early twentieth century, China had "potential," although its $60 million in two-way trade with the United States was small compared with the value of Japanese American trade. Through 1919, American exports to China seldom reached 2 percent of total foreign trade.

Well into the 1930s, American government and public opinion waivered on the relative importance of maintaining strong ties with China or Japan. Policies changed with the mix of personalities and issues. Official American talk of defending the open door remained an abstraction. Philanthropists took pride in using some of the money collected as penalty for Boxer attacks to fund scholarships for Chinese students in the United States and to build a college in Beijing. But since U.S. law barred most Chinese from entering the United States, the open door only swung in one direction.

In 1904 Czarist Russia and Imperial Japan collided in northeast China, or Manchuria. Russian troops had moved into the sparsely populated province and established naval and army bases, whereas Japanese forces occupied Korea and coveted neighboring Manchuria. Each hoped to dominate the resource-rich area. When Japanese troops mounted a "surprise attack" on Russian bases in Manchuria, American observers praised Japanese skill and daring. China, the nominal sovereign of Manchuria, remained a spectator to the conflict.

President Theodore Roosevelt, who succeeded the assassinated McKinley in 1901, considered Russia a bigger threat to American global interests and encouraged New York bankers to provide badly needed loans to Japan. By attacking Russia, Roosevelt wrote to his son, Japan was "playing our game in Asia." After two years of combat, the president mediated a settlement between the rivals for which he received the Nobel Peace Prize. China, however, lost most of its authority in Manchuria.

Roosevelt's grudging respect for Japan contrasted with his low opinion of Chinese, whom he called "chinks" and a "worthless, degraded race." Congress shared this view, voting in 1904 to permanently tighten immigration restrictions that now barred most Chinese from entering the United States. At home, Chinese students, merchants, and political activists expressed outrage at American action and in 1905 organized an effective boycott of American products. The boycott failed to alter U.S. immigration policy but convinced many Chinese that only mass action could defend their rights.

The key issue in Asia, as Roosevelt saw it, was not China, but maintaining good relations with Japan. Anti-Japanese agitation in California in 1907, where school boards moved to segregate Asian children from whites, threatened this equilibrium. Roosevelt cut a deal with state authorities where they would refrain from segregating the Japanese. In return, Japan agreed to voluntarily limit the immigration of unskilled workers to the United States.

Roosevelt's successor, William Howard Taft, squandered much of the goodwill Roosevelt created. During most of his presidency, from 1909 to 1913, Taft, along with Secretary of State Philander Knox, worked to block both Russian and Japanese influence in Manchuria. Arguments by junior diplomats such as Willard Straight oversold Knox on the importance of Manchuria to the United States. This prompted Knox to pursue a policy dubbed "dollar diplomacy," encouraging American investors to finance railroad construction in Manchuria. Japan and Russia both resented American meddling and U.S. investors showed little enthusiasm to take risks. Taft, like several of his successors, overestimated America's material stake in China while underestimating its importance to Japan and Russia.

After the death of Empress Dowager Cixi in 1908, Qing officials instituted a long-delayed series of reforms in an attempt to salvage the dynasty. These included starting a modern school system, replacing the moribund Confucian examination system with merit selection, streamlining the tax collection to encourage enterprise, and even creating provincial assemblies to share governance. They hoped these actions would appease critics at home and abroad.

The reforms, however, came too late to save the dynasty. In 1911, a regional military revolt quickly spread and became focused on deposing the Qing. Fueled by anti-Manchu sentiment, the movement found support among constitutional monarchists, liberal democrats, socialists, and regional military commanders. The last emperor, a five-year-old boy named Pu Yi, abdicated early in 1912. A vaguely organized republic replaced the monarchy, with regional military leaders holding the reigns of power. Sun Yat-sen (Sun Zhongshan), long active in anti-Qing politics, served briefly as a figurehead leader.

Sun had become well known among overseas Chinese for his 20-year effort to depose the Qing. Born in Guangzhou in 1866, he moved to Hawaii at age 13, attended a mission school (where future president Barack Obama enrolled in the 1970s), and moved to Hong Kong in 1882 to study medicine. There he formally converted to Christianity and began organizing anti-Qing activities. His political philosophy blended Christianity, socialism, and nationalism but lacked a practical framework. Sun traveled widely to raise funds among Chinese living abroad. When the 1911 revolt began, he was speaking in Denver and rushed back to China to catch up with events. Sun lasted only a few weeks as titular head of the new Chinese Republic before General Yuan Shikai pushed him aside. Sun spent the next decade searching for a patron and the means to achieve power.

Between 1912 and his death in 1916, Yuan tried to unify China and win foreign acceptance. In 1913, President Woodrow Wilson recognized Yuan's government, but also withdrew U.S. support from an international consortium organized to lend China money. Wilson condemned the consortium as antidemocratic. Although well intentioned, Wilson's decision left the United States with little ability to influence the actions that other nations were undertaking in China.

Several private Americans counseled Yuan's regime. Among the most important was political science professor Frank Goodnow. China's effort at republican rule seemed so dysfunctional that Goodnow urged Yuan to restore the monarchy. The general followed this advice, proclaiming himself emperor of China in 1916. When he died a few months later, the vestiges of central political authority also disappeared.

THE IMPACT OF WORLD WAR I

The outbreak of war in Europe in August 1914 further hindered China's transition to modern nationhood. As the Europeans focused on slaughtering each other and the United States struggled to remain neutral, Japan seized the opportunity to extend its control in China. After nominally allying itself with Great Britain and France, Japan seized German-controlled Shandong province. A year later, in 1915, Tokyo presented Yuan's government with what became known as the "21 Demands." These called for expanding Japan's power in Manchuria, assuming a dominant economic role in much of the rest of China, limiting China's relations with other nations, and installing Japanese "advisers" throughout the Chinese government.

President Wilson, influenced by his minister to Beijing, Paul Reinsch, and many missionaries, weighed in on China's behalf. He criticized the 21 Demands for violating the open door and infringing on Chinese sovereignty. To increase American leverage, Wilson reversed his earlier decision and supported efforts by American banks to lend money to China through an international consortium. In the face of this resistance, Japan backed down.

China nominally supported the Allied cause during the war, hoping to assure friendly treatment in any postwar settlement. Although the Chinese did no fighting, the warring nations recruited Chinese laborers to dig trenches and work in munitions factories. About 150,000 Chinese worked on the western front and about 50,000 on the eastern front. Many Chinese laborers landed in California en route to Europe. But to ensure that none of them lingered in the United States, they were often placed in sealed trains bound for ports on the East Coast. Among those who worked in Europe were future Communist leaders Zhou Enlai and Deng Xiaoping, although they did not pass through the United States.

Although Japan abandoned its 21 Demands, Yuan Shikai's death in 1916 eliminated what remained of a central government. For the next 12 years, regional military strongmen, or warlords, filled the vacuum. They sometimes formed tactical alliances and on occasion cooperated with civilians who nominally exercised authority in Beijing. But no real national government existed. Outlying territories, such as Tibet, Mongolia, and Manchuria, slipped toward quasi-independence or under foreign control.

The onset of the warlord era meant that no one really spoke for China at the Paris Peace Conference of 1919 following the end of World War I. Japan demanded that the victorious Allies and the United States recognize their racial equality. American and British leaders opposed this as a pretext for expanded Japanese immigration. Rebuffed, Tokyo insisted that the Allies approve its retention of Shandong and its claims to special rights within Manchuria and China. Chinese patriots at home, and even the weak Chinese diplomatic mission in Paris, demanded that the peace settlement restore Shandong to Chinese control and limit Japanese claims to special influence.

Within China, a growing number of students enrolled at recently created missionary and secular colleges heard President Wilson's wartime calls for self-determination of subject peoples and the right of every nation to determine its own form of government. These principles, Wilson stressed, should form the core of his proposed League of Nations. The president's words heartened Chinese patriots who anticipated that the United States would stand up for China.

Unfortunately, power politics trumped promises about self-determination and equality for all nations. Wilson considered it vital for Japan to join the League of Nations, even if this meant giving in to its demand to retain Shandong. He hoped that this compromise, like many others he made, could be corrected once the league began to function. Chinese students, intellectuals, and political activists saw the act as a betrayal and condemned both the United States and the weak government in Beijing for sacrificing China.

On May 4, 1919, thousands of demonstrators took to the streets of Beijing to protest the deal over Shandong. Many of these activists, such as the assistant librarian at Beijing University, Mao Zedong, abandoned their faith in American democratic models. Mao, like many nationalists in colonial areas, embraced more radical political and cultural doctrines as the way to transform China. Many who participated in this so-called May 4th Movement soon became active in either Sun Yat-sen's Guomindang (GMD or Nationalist Party) or the Communist Gongchandang (GCD) party founded in 1921.

CHINESE NATIONALISM AND INTERNATIONAL DIPLOMACY: THE 1920s

Although the United States failed to join the League of Nations that Wilson crafted, the peace treaty signed at the Versailles Palace in June 1919 created a veneer of international order that lasted for just over a decade in East Asia. Chinese nationalists continued to agitate against Western and Japanese imperialism as the 1920s began, and central rule in China all but disappeared. Since the United States had not joined the league, it searched for an alternate framework to assure cooperation in East Asia. U.S. officials also wanted to halt Japan's naval buildup and avoid an arms race in the Pacific. Managing relations with Japan was especially important because in the decade after World War I the value of U.S. exports to Japan was about triple the value of trade with China. Japan and the United States had an additional reason to cooperate: both feared the activities of the new Communist regime in the Soviet Union, which had promised to support struggles by the Chinese and other Asians to throw off the yoke of foreign domination.

To resolve these problems, Secretary of State Charles Evans Hughes organized an international conference in Washington at the end of 1921. (The Soviet Union was excluded and the Chinese delegation was granted only observer status.) The conference lasted into 1922 and yielded three major agreements. The five-power treaty put limits on the number of battleships each major power could possess. Two other treaties guaranteed the status of existing colonies in the Pacific and committed the signatories not to interfere with China's political or territorial integrity.

The Soviets complained that the Washington treaties did little more than guarantee imperialist domination of Asia. Chinese nationalists criticized the pacts as merely an agreement among thieves not to steal more from China or each other. All China received from the deals made in Washington was a promise that at some future date the foreign powers would consider the restoration of tariff autonomy.

Chinese nationalists perceived the Soviet Union—itself an outcast since the 1917 revolution—as the one outside power eager to assist their struggle for autonomy. Vladimir Lenin, leader of the new Soviet state, had interpreted Marxism to justify revolutionary activity in preindustrial and colonial societies although they lacked a strong working class. Even if "backward" countries like China were not ready for a true Communist revolution, Lenin argued, small groups of political activists could organize a mass movement of peasants and laborers under the banner of nationalism. By defeating the warlords and their foreign backers, the Chinese would weaken global imperialism and capitalism. Creation of a true Communist China could wait for a later stage. The road to Communist power in Western Europe, Lenin reportedly declared, "ran through Beijing."

In July 1919, an official in the new Communist government issued the so-called Karakhan Manifesto, a promise to renounce many of the special privileges and territory the Czars had stripped from China during the past century. Although the declaration was couched in generalities and, by the time news of it reached China in 1920, had ceased to be Soviet policy, its tone marked a dramatic break with how all the foreign powers had treated China since the Opium Wars. For the first time in nearly a century, a foreign power had offered to give back something to China, not take more away.

During the early 1920s, agents of the Communist International, or Comintern, reached out to several groups of Chinese nationalists. The Moscow-based

Comintern functioned as an arm of Soviet foreign policy and the headquarters of the world Communist movement. Soviet emissaries encouraged formation of a Chinese Communist Party in 1921, but Moscow placed its heavy bets on GMD leader Sun Yat-sen. For nearly a decade, Sun had flitted around China in search of military and financial support. In 1923, Soviet envoy Adolf Joffe made a deal with Sun to provide assistance if he reorganized the GMD along Soviet lines.

As part of the arrangement, Sun sent his military aide, Chiang Kai-shek (Jiang Jieshi), to Moscow to study Soviet military and political organization. Chiang, born in 1887, previously studied military science in Japan. When he returned to China after several months in the Soviet Union, he created the Whampoa military academy, near Guangzhou, to train military officers. In 1924, the small Chinese Communist Party joined the Nationalists in a "united front" that allowed Communists such as Zhou Enlai and Comintern agent Mikhail Borodin to train political organizers at Whampoa. Both parties agreed to launch a Northern Expedition to unify the country.

By the time Sun died of cancer in 1925, shortly before the start of the 1926 military campaign, the United Front began to fray. Sun's successor, Chiang Kai-shek, moved the party in a more conservative direction than his mentor. However, because he needed the support provided by the Soviet Union, Chiang maintained his uneasy alliance with the Communists.

During 1926 and 1927, as the troops of the Northern Expedition moved toward central China, the Europeans, Americans, and Japanese all voiced concern over how the nationalist movement would affect their trade, investments, and privileges. The foreigners mistakenly considered Chiang a "Red General." Despite Chiang's actual antipathy toward his leftist partners, Soviet advisers pressured the Communists to maintain the coalition. In the spring of 1927, after GMD troops entered Shanghai, Chiang struck against his erstwhile allies. In a series of brutal purges, Chiang ordered the slaughter of several thousand Communists. Mao and Zhou narrowly escaped to the countryside. The misguided Comintern agents either fled or were expelled.

Chiang's strike solidified his control of the GMD and helped to convince wealthy Chinese and foreign diplomats that he was the best barrier against Communism. By 1928, after he survived additional domestic challenges to his leadership, Chiang persuaded the foreign powers he was the best hope they had to protect their citizens and property and to work for the gradual revision of the unequal treaties. In return, the Europeans, Americans, and Japanese extended diplomatic recognition and financial support to the newly proclaimed "Republic of China" with its capital in Nanjing. Under Chiang, the regime was essentially a one-party state. But to the world, China appeared more stable and unified than at any time since 1911.

Chiang's personal life also won praise from Americans in China and at home. In 1927 he married into one of China's wealthiest and most prominent Christian families. Charley Soong had visited America, become a Methodist, and made a fortune in China as a banker and printer of bibles. His son, T. V. Soong, received a PhD in economics from Harvard. Charley sent his three daughters, Ching-ling

(Qingling), Ai-ling (Ailing), and May-ling (Meiling), to Wesleyan College in Georgia. The youngest, Meiling, later attended Wellesley College in Massachusetts. Qingling married Sun Yat-sen, Ailing married banker H. H. Kung, and Meiling wed Chiang Kai-shek. The marriage enhanced Chiang's stature both inside China and internationally. As part of his vows, Chiang agreed to become a Christian. The missionaries who instructed him portrayed the event as evidence of their—and America's—growing influence in China. Both the marriage and Chiang's conversion were prominently featured in *Time* magazine, as well as in the weekly newsreel, *The March of Time*. Publisher Henry Luce, born in China to missionary parents, became the couple's most ardent booster in the United States. His publications celebrated their union as "made in the U.S.A."

Chiang's transformation from hostile Red General to friendly Christian democrat was the first of many such makeovers. Over the next four decades, Americans would sequentially perceive Chiang as a victim of Japanese aggression, a noble ally in defense of freedom, an inept crook, a reliable partner in containing Communism, and, ultimately, a historical anachronism.

Despite the positive relationship the United States established with both China and Japan during the 1920s, American public opinion and Congress remained extremely hostile to the notion of Asian immigration. The National Origins Act of 1924 not only imposed strict limits on Eastern European immigration, but also replaced the patchwork of statutes and informal deals that had restricted most Chinese and Japanese immigration with a complete ban on "Orientals." This catchall included Chinese, Japanese, and most Indians and Southeast Asians. With few changes, the racial barrier lasted until 1965.

THE GREAT DEPRESSION AND THE COLLAPSE OF THE WASHINGTON TREATY SYSTEM

To a considerable degree, international cooperation in Asia, especially restraints on Japanese expansion, relied on world prosperity. For example, Japan tolerated incremental efforts by the new Chinese government to expand authority into Manchuria so long as it did not go too far and Japan enjoyed access to other markets and sources of raw materials. Booming world trade during most of the 1920s, much of it financed by American bank loans, private investments, and consumer demand, facilitated good relations between the United States and Japan and gave the Republic of China some breathing space.

The economic crisis that began at the end of 1929, soon known as the Great Depression, shattered world trade and destroyed the economic underpinnings of the Washington treaties of 1922. The consequences to China proved devastating. As world trade and credit shriveled, Japanese exports were frozen out of Europe and the United States. This quickly impeded Japan's ability to purchase the foreign raw materials that fueled its home industry. Now, more than ever, unimpeded access to China, and especially Manchuria, appeared to Japanese leaders as the key to reducing their economic vulnerability.

Since 1929 Chiang had moved slowly to reestablish Chinese authority in Manchuria, long dominated by the Japanese or their local puppets. A divided Japanese government, beset by rivalries among civilian politicians, militarists, and industrialists, debated how to protect its stake. Until 1929, civilian politicians in Tokyo had kept the militarists in line by stressing that cooperation and trade with the United States and Europe outweighed the value of seizing Manchuria. By 1931, however, with global trade in freefall and as new trade barriers shut Japan out of Western markets, the equation changed. Even if breaking the Washington treaties by seizing Manchuria alienated the United States and other Western powers, the gain now appeared to outweigh the risk.

Japan's policies were further complicated by the status of the semiautonomous Kwantung Army, a Japanese force stationed in Manchuria since the Boxer uprising. This Japanese army had extensive economic interests in Manchuria and opposed the extension of Chinese power. When Chiang Kai-shek struck a deal with a Manchurian warlord, Zhang Xueliang, to impose Chinese authority in Manchuria, the Kwantung Army struck back. In September 1931, Japanese armed forces staged a mock Chinese attack on their own units and used this as a pretext for the Kwantung Army to take full control. Once in control, Japan went through the charade of creating an independent, but puppet state called "Manchukuo," nominally ruled by Pu Yi, the Qing child emperor who had abdicated in 1912.

Chinese resistance proved no match for the Japanese army. Chiang Kai-shek found it expedient to retire, temporarily, as supreme leader. Western governments and the League of Nations criticized Japan's aggression as a violation of the Washington treaty and other international pacts, but took no retaliatory action. The American government and public were offended more by the principle of Japan's treaty violations than by the harm done to China.

Secretary of State Henry Stimson prevailed on a reluctant President Herbert Hoover (who, as a mining engineer on his honeymoon in 1900, had experienced the Boxer siege of Tianjin) to take symbolic action. In January 1932, the secretary issued the Stimson, or Non-Recognition, Doctrine, in which the United States refused to recognize the legality of Manchukuo or other territories seized by Japan. But until the late 1930s this remained the limit of America's response. Even an attack by the Japanese navy on Shanghai, which killed several thousand Chinese civilians, elicited only statements of regret by Washington. Amid the hardships of the Depression, the rise of fascism and Communism in Europe, and bitter memories of World War I, a broad-based American peace movement that opposed military intervention persuaded most Americans in and out of government to avoid fighting in a faraway place. Americans wished China well, but would not block Japan's way.

TO THE SINO-JAPANESE WAR

After the loss of Manchuria, Chiang spent the years from 1932 to 1936 fighting domestic rivals and struggling to create a viable government. The GMD, which controlled the Republic of China, represented a fluid alliance of militarists, bureaucrats, landlords, and business interests united mostly by their anti-Communism and conservative nationalism. As head of the military council, Chiang controlled the party and government. Eventually, he held more than 80 government posts simultaneously. American journalist Theodore White, who spent several years in China, observed that "any concept of China that differed from Chiang's own" was "treated with as much hostility as an enemy division." Both in party ranks and in government service, more than honesty, experience, or ability, Chiang demanded "complete, unconditional loyalty to himself."

The progressive ideals expressed by Sun Yat-sen, especially his calls for land and social reform, largely died with him. Adding to Chiang's difficulties, even during the 1930s he never fully governed China. The central government exercised complete control over a handful of provinces, and many more remained under the sway of semiautonomous warlords. In rural China, where most people lived, national policies had little impact on the routine of daily life.

To maintain his dominance, Chiang manipulated the competing factions within the GMD. This blocked any combination of rivals from effectively challenging his authority. But it also kept the army, party, and bureaucracy too divided to govern effectively. During the 1930s, the government in Nanjing enacted many laws to reduce rents, rationalize taxation, control usury, and spur economic development. But local authorities generally ignored these statutes. Since the party depended heavily on the support of landlords and bankers, Chiang was reluctant to move against their interests.

Foreign governments and missionaries were impressed by Chiang's moderate nationalism and sincere professions of faith. He actively cultivated the support of American missionaries by inviting them to participate in government health and education campaigns. The New Life Movement, launched in 1934, typified this. The reform program blended Confucian ideals and Christian precepts about how to live virtuously. To improve their own lives and the nation's well-being, Chinese were urged to "correct their posture, avoid spitting on floors, and pursue right conduct." They were also exhorted to respect authority.

One skeptic described the New Life Movement as the vision of a reformed China held by American Methodist clubwomen. It did, in fact, correspond closely to Soong Meiling's profession of faith. When asked by a religious publication in 1934 to write an article on "What My Religion Means to Me," she delegated the task to an American friend, Geraldine Fitch, who worked for the Young Men's Christian Association in China. Fitch produced a "conversion narrative" showing how Meiling came to Christianity as part of personal and national salvation. Her job as China's "First Lady" was to serve as spiritual aide to her husband.

The flip side of this reform activity was Chiang's increasing reliance on support from a fascist-style police force within the GMD government. The Military Bureau of Investigation and Statistics, known informally as Blue Shirts, was controlled by Chiang's confidante, General Dai Li. With roots in Shanghai's underworld, Dai Li helped Chiang purge Communists in 1927 and remained a loyal henchman till his death shortly after World War II. The Blue Shirts specialized in intimidating, torturing, or killing opponents.

Although the new presidential administration of Franklin D. Roosevelt kept its distance from Chiang before 1937, the Chinese leader enjoyed the patronage of *Time–Life* publisher Henry Luce. In 1931, Chiang first appeared on a *Time* cover, along with a story that praised him for resisting Japanese aggression. He next appeared in 1933, with an account of his efforts to fight Communist guerrillas. Luce put Chiang on two covers during 1936, stressing his key role in resisting Communist and Japanese expansion. The Chinese leader, according to the magazine, responded to threats with "good roads, good morals, and good bombs." *Time* praised him as the "greatest man in the Far East."

As president elect, Franklin Roosevelt paid lip service to the Stimson Doctrine, but once in office did all he could to minimize conflict with Japan. Roosevelt's limited foreign policy initiatives included improving relations with Latin America and recognizing the Soviet Union. In 1934, when Japan declared that its "special responsibilities" in Asia justified its opposition to any American technical, military, or economic aid to China, the State Department issued a perfunctory response but declined to challenge Tokyo.

Aside from Henry Luce, most public figures, business leaders, and diplomats saw more reasons to disengage from China than to expand involvement. Wall Street banker Thomas Lamont, for example, despite his involvement in international finance and humanitarian aid to China, in 1936 told the U.S. ambassador to China, Nelson Johnson, that if China was too weak to protect itself, the United States could not do the job for it. "Certainly," he explained, "America is not going to court trouble by any quixotic attempt to checkmate Japan in Asia." The Roosevelt administration often discouraged private investors from activity in China likely to antagonize Japan.

Before the outbreak of the Sino–Japanese War in 1937, the only major financial initiative undertaken by the United States that affected China proved less than helpful. In 1934, under pressure from domestic silver producers to raise prices, the Treasury increased silver purchases. With more profit to be made selling silver coins to the Treasury than leaving them in circulation, millions of dollars worth of Chinese silver currency flowed into the United States, hurting the Chinese economy. Even when the Chinese government appealed for relief in 1935, Roosevelt declined to act, wary of antagonizing either the Nevada silver industry or the Japanese, who might interpret this as aid to China. Roosevelt declared he would not change his policy "merely because the Chinese were unable to protect themselves."

Despite economic pressures and frequent Japanese military probes south of Manchuria, Chiang focused much of his attention and resources on eliminating domestic rivals. Between 1931 and 1934, the Nationalist armies launched five major "Bandit Extermination Campaigns" against Communist forces that had regrouped in a mountainous area of Jiangxi province. In their assaults on this self-proclaimed "Soviet" zone, Chiang relied heavily on advice provided by

German advisers, such as General Hans Von Seeckt, sent to China with Adolf Hitler's encouragement. The strategy, which relied upon encircling and starving the rebel areas, proved effective and forced the Communists to flee in disarray in 1934. Mao and about 100,000 Communist followers broke through the GMD blockade and began what became known as the Long March. Only about one-third of the original force survived the year-long, 6,000-mile trek that led them to remote Shaanxi province in China's northwest. The hardships endured by the marchers became a legend in revolutionary history. As described in the next chapter, American journalist Edgar Snow chronicled the Long March and helped popularize the Chinese Communist leader, Mao Zedong, in the West.

Since the early 1930s, the Chinese Communists had called for national unity to resist Japan. In 1935, following the lead of the Comintern, the party urged the creation of an anti-Japanese United Front. Mao hoped that if Chiang heeded his call, it would ease pressure on the Communists and enhance the party's stature as defender of the nation. These unity appeals found support among the Manchurian troops of General Zhang Xueliang, who had been driven out of Manchuria by the Japanese and were now confronting the Communists in China's northwest. They preferred to reclaim their lost homeland from Japan rather than killing other Chinese as Chiang demanded.

Despite mounting calls within China to confront Japan, Chiang doggedly pursued his plan to destroy the "Red Bandits." Frustrated by the slow pace of the offensive, Chiang flew to forward military headquarters in the city of Xi'an (Sian) in December 1936. Instead of rallying to him, disgruntled GMD commanders, led by Zhang Xueliang, placed him under house arrest on December 12.

Several of Chiang's captors favored killing him. Ultimately, the Chinese Communists, the Soviet Union, and the United States all pressed to save his life. Both Roosevelt and Soviet leader Josef Stalin believed that whatever his faults, Chiang preserved some degree of unity in China. Without him, everything might fall apart and clear the way for Japanese expansion into all China and beyond. Roosevelt told his ambassador in Nanjing to spread the word that Chiang's survival was of grave concern to "the whole world." Stalin passed word to Communist negotiator Zhou Enlai that only Chiang could create a United Front. Admiral Harry Yarnell, commander of the U.S. Navy's Asiatic Fleet, described Chiang as a "man of destiny" who "personified" resistance to Japan. Although exaggerations, these expressions of concern contained just enough validity to save Chiang. On Christmas day, Chiang and Zhou announced agreement to end the civil war and form a United Front to resist Japan. The biggest loser in the deal was Zhang Xueliang, whom Chiang imprisoned for the next 50 years, first in China and then in Taiwan.

Chiang's two-week ordeal in Xi'an boosted his status both within and outside China. A *March of Time* newsreel shown in thousands of American theaters after the conclusion of the incident implied that Chiang's release (which was attributed to "reading his bible") on Christmas morning should be seen as a sign of divine grace. In the view of many Americans, China had ceased to be an abstraction. Chiang Kai-shek had become China.

SELECTED ADDITIONAL READINGS

Walter LaFeber, *The New Empire: An Interpretation of American Expansion, 1860–1898* (New York, 1963) and *The Clash: A History of U.S.–Japan Relations* (New York, 1997); Thomas J. McCormick, *The China Market: America's Quest for Informal Empire, 1893–1901* (New York, 1967); David S. Healy, *U.S. Expansionism: The Imperialist Urge in the 1890s* (Madison, Wi., 1970); Jung Chang, *Empress Dowager Cixi: The Concubine Who Launched Modern China* (New York, 2013); Diana Preston, *Besieged in Peking: The Story of the 1900 Boxer Rising* (London, 1999); Joseph Esherick, *The Origins of the Boxer Uprising* (Berkeley, Ca., 1987); David J. Silbey, *The Boxer Rebellion and the Great Game in China* (New York, 2012); Paul A. Cohen, *History in Three Keys: The Boxers as Event, Experience, and Myth* (New York, 1997); Michael Hunt, *Frontier Defense and the Open Door: Manchuria in Chinese–American Relations, 1895–1911* (New Haven, Conn., 1973) and *The Genesis of Chinese Communist Foreign Policy* (New York, 1996); Jerry Israel, *Progressivism and the Open Door: America and China, 1905–1921* (Pittsburgh, Pa., 1971); Paul Varg, *The Making of a Myth: The United States and China, 1879–1912* (East Lansing, Mi., 1968); Eileen Scully, *Bargaining with the State from Afar* (New York, 2001); Emily Rosenberg, *Financial Missionaries to the World: The Politics and Culture of Dollar Diplomacy* (Cambridge, Mass., 1999); Akira Iriye, *Pacific Estrangement: Japan and American Expansionism, 1879–1911* (Cambridge, Mass., 1972); Lloyd Gardner, *Safe for Democracy: The Anglo-American Response to Revolution* (New York, 1984); Ernest Young, *The Presidency of Yuan Shih-K'ai: Liberalism and Dictatorship in Early Republican China* (Ann Arbor, Mi., 1977); Noel Pugach, *Paul S. Reinsch: Open Door Diplomat in Action* (Millwood, N.Y., 1979); Chou Tse-tung, *The May Fourth Movement* (Cambridge, Mass., 1960); Erez Manela, *The Wilsonian Moment: Self-Determination and the International Origins of Anti-Colonial Nationalism* (New York, 2007); Sherman Cochran, *Big Business in China: Sino–American Rivalry in the Cigarette Industry* (Cambridge, Mass., 1980); Akira Iriye, *After Imperialism: The Search for a New Order in the Far East, 1921–1931* (Cambridge, Mass., 1965); Roger Dingman, *Power in the Pacific: The Origins of Naval Limitations, 1914–1922* (Chicago, 1976); Dorothy Borg, *American Policy and the Chinese Revolution, 1925–1928* (New York, 1947); Warren Cohen, *Empire without Tears* (Philadelphia, 1987); Jonathan D. Spence, *To Change China: Western Advisers in China, 1920–1960* (New York, 1980); Edgar Snow, *Red Star over China* (New York, 1937); Harrison E. Salsbury, *The Long March: The Untold Story* (New York, 1985); T. Christopher Jespersen, *American Images of China, 1931–1949* (Stanford, Ca., 1996); William C. Kirby, *Germany and Republican China, 1927–1937* (Stanford, Ca., 1984); James C. Thomson Jr., *While China Faced West: American Reformers in Nationalist China, 1927–1937* (Cambridge, Mass., 1969); James Sheridan, *China in Disintegration: The Republican Era in Chinese History* (New York, 1975); Lloyd Eastman, *The Abortive Revolution: China under Nationalist Rule, 1927–1937* (Cambridge, Mass., 1974); Christopher Thorne, *The Limits of Foreign Policy: The West, The League, and the Far Eastern Crisis, 1931–1933* (New York, 1973); Dorothy Borg, *The United States and the Far Eastern Crisis of 1933–1938* (Cambridge, Mass., 1964); Jay Taylor, *The Generalissimo: Chiang Kai-shek and the Struggle for Modern China* (Cambridge, Mass., 2010).

CHAPTER 3

From the Marco Polo Bridge
to Pearl Harbor

The year 1937 promised great things for China. Chiang Kai-shek had clutched victory from the jaws of defeat at Xi'an, emerging as a symbol of national unity. The new United Front promised to end the fighting between Nationalists and Communists and turn the nation's resolve against Japan. In an editorial on January 1, the respected *Ta Kung Pao* newspaper expressed a common hope in declaring, "China will have only the United Front, and never again will there be internal hostility."

Foreign leaders as varied as Franklin Roosevelt and Josef Stalin endorsed Chiang's claim to be China's unifier and defender. In the United States, several popular books, magazine articles, and movies appeared shortly before or during 1937 that provided extremely sympathetic treatment of China and its people. These accounts differed dramatically from the "yellow peril" literature that often dominated depictions of Chinese.

Pearl Buck, a child of American missionaries who grew up in China, published her novel, *The Good Earth*, in 1931. Even at the depths of the Depression, it sold 2 million copies and won a Pulitzer Prize. Buck had returned to north China as a young wife in the late 1920s and described rural life in great detail. Her portrayal of how a husband and wife of the Wang clan struggled to survive amid drought, violence, famine, and plagues of locusts humanized Chinese peasants and made them understandable to Americans. The 1937 film version of *The Good Earth* proved even more popular. Buck's stature increased after 1938 when she won the Nobel Prize for Literature.

Although never reaching Buck's level of fame, several other female writers published articles in "women's" magazines during the late 1930s containing sympathetic accounts of Chinese life. Among the most prolific of these writers were Agnes Smedley, Anna Louise Strong, Helen Foster, Emily Hahn, and Ida Pruitt. Their articles sympathetically portrayed varied aspects of Chinese culture, politics, and peasant life.

Carl Crow, a journalist long resident in Shanghai, wrote frequently about Chinese business conditions. His most popular account, written in 1937, bore the evocative title *Four Hundred Million Customers*. (His count was 100 million low.) Crow offered practical tips on how to conduct business in China and suggested ways to market consumer goods including cigarettes, cosmetics, and automobiles. American manufacturers, he noted, already exported more than 11 billion cigarettes annually to China, more than to the rest of the world combined. Crow's upbeat advice resembled the script of the 1935 film *Oil for the Lamps of China*. In a climactic scene, a petroleum executive tells a group of starry-eyed salesman, "The Company is sending you out to China to dispel the darkness of centuries with the light of a new era. Oil for the lamps of China, American oil!" Building a great corporation, the executive explained, was a way to "expand the frontier of civilization."

Journalist Edgar Snow published the second most influential book on China during the 1930s. Based on his travels into China's distant northwest, *Red Star over China* (1937) introduced Americans to the Chinese Communist movement and its leaders. Snow portrayed Mao Zedong and his followers as a colorful group of patriotic radical reformers, not extremist revolutionaries. Mao, he wrote, had a "certain form of destiny in him." Even in remote Shaanxi province, Snow noted, Communists of all ranks played ping-pong, or table tennis, with gusto. The game had come to China through the British in treaty ports early in the century. Each unit of the Communist Army had a champion. Mao, Zhou Enlai, and Zhu De all played enthusiastically. Several mass-circulation American magazines published excerpts from the book. Even *Life* magazine, which usually disparaged positive accounts of any Chinese other than those allied with Chiang, praised Snow and published some of his photographs.

Also in 1937, Hollywood released a film version of *Lost Horizon*, based on James Hilton's 1933 novel. This utopian fantasy about the valley of Shangri-la in the Himalaya Mountains of western China portrayed a sanctuary of love and reason in a violent world. (In April 1942, when a handful of American planes flying from an aircraft carrier bombed Tokyo, President Roosevelt told curious reporters that they had taken off from Shangri-la.) Although a highly romanticized version of Asian life and philosophy, *Lost Horizons*, like the books and articles described above, depicted Chinese and Tibetans as sympathetic human beings.

The "good press" China received in these books and films affected how many Americans responded to Japan's attack on China in July 1937. Japanese nationalists saw the United Front as a direct challenge to their plans for expansion into and beyond China. On July 7, Japanese troops stationed near the Marco Polo Bridge southwest of Beijing provoked a battle with Chinese soldiers. As the fighting escalated, the Japanese government demanded greater control over north China as the price of a ceasefire. Patriotic fervor among Chinese made it impossible for Chiang to appease Tokyo as he had over Manchuria in 1931/1932. Both sides rushed reinforcements to the battlefield and soon were engaged in a massive war that lasted eight years.

Japan's aggression angered most Americans, who saw China as an innocent victim. Yet neither President Roosevelt nor the U.S. public favored military intervention or doing anything risky to assist China. The national mood reflected a common view that intervention in World War I had been a costly error. That belief spawned an active peace movement during the 1930s, which pressed Congress to enact a series of neutrality laws starting in 1935. These statutes barred most government and private weapons sales and loans to warring nations, regardless of which attacked first. Evidence of German, Italian, and Japanese aggression did little to alter this isolationist or unilateralist impulse. Japan's seizure of Manchuria, Germany's annexation of Austria and threats against Czechoslovakia and Poland, Italy's conquest of Ethiopia, and Italian and German aid to Francisco Franco's fascist revolt against the democratic Spanish government were not caused by U.S. policy, but American inaction did nothing to deter aggression. In 1936, when Japan joined Germany and Italy in the Anti-Comintern Pact, raising the specter of a coordinated effort by the three nations to dominate the world, isolationists found a new reason to avoid helping China.

During 1937–1938, Japanese forces quickly overran most of the major ports and cities along China's coast. Ordinary soldiers, often prompted by their officers, frequently assaulted Chinese civilians. The most notorious incident occurred after the Imperial army seized the Republic of China's capital of Nanjing. Chiang and his government had abandoned the capital city early in December. After the remaining disorganized Chinese defenders were routed, Japanese troops began a six-week killing spree that lasted from mid-December 1937 until late January 1938. Although estimates vary, at least 200,000 civilians were shot, bayonetted, and raped. The Japanese press boasted of a contest in which two officers competed to see which of them could more quickly slice off the heads of 100 captives with their swords. Western businessmen and missionaries established an international safety zone within the city, which offered limited protection to some Chinese.

In the aftermath of what became known as the Rape of Nanking (Nanjing), American missionaries and their supporters wrote and spoke extensively about China's victimization by Japan. These reports spurred the creation of an influential lobbying group, the American Committee for Non-Participation in Japanese Aggression. It counted numerous prominent figures among its membership, including former secretary of war Henry L. Stimson, journalist William Allen White, retired rear admiral Harry Yarnell, and publisher Henry Luce. At the local level, Chinese Americans picketed Japanese ships in American ports and urged shoppers to shun products made in Japan, such as silk stockings.

Nevertheless, by the end of 1938, Japan controlled roughly the eastern third of China and nearly all the coastline. The Nationalist regime traded space for time, retreating steadily westward. Eventually it established a wartime capital in Chungking (Chongqing), beyond the easy reach of Japanese aircraft and infantry. The contest became a war of attrition, as the Japanese awaited the collapse of organized resistance and Chiang held on until, he hoped, the Japanese blundered into war with the United States.

Mounting reports of Japanese brutality deeply impacted American public opinion. Shortly before the Nanjing massacre, 43 percent of Americans expressed sympathy for China and only 2 percent for Japan. A few months later, 59 percent of Americans described themselves as pro-Chinese, 1 percent as pro-Japanese, and 40 percent as neutral. By 1939, the number of Americans supporting China rose to 74 percent, the undecided declined to 24 percent, and those sympathetic to Japan comprised less than 2 percent. Yet as late as 1939, only 6 percent of Americans favored fighting Japan on China's behalf. About half supported trade sanctions against Tokyo. A fourth of the public continued to favor doing nothing.

Like many Americans, President Roosevelt sympathized with China and considered low-risk ways of helping, but had no intention of fighting Japan. By not invoking the neutrality laws, Washington allowed China to buy American munitions and enjoy at least theoretical access to American credit. Japan, of course, had no need for either. In reality, neither loans nor arms were forthcoming to China.

In October 1937, Roosevelt condemned Japan during a speech he delivered in Chicago. The president decried what he called an "epidemic of world lawlessness" that ought to be "quarantined" by civilized nations. But when isolationist newspapers and politicians criticized this as "warmongering," Roosevelt opted to do nothing. Even in December 1937, when Japanese aircraft sank the U.S. Navy gunboat *Panay* while it escorted Standard Oil barges on the Yangtze River (and machine gunned survivors in the water), the United States held back. Polls revealed that most Americans thought the navy was foolish to operate a ship in a war zone. The president accepted Japan's apology and payment of compensation. Prominent Americans in and out of government suggested that the most prudent course of action for Americans in China was withdrawal. In the wake of the attack on the *Panay*, Congress came close to adopting a constitutional amendment requiring a national referendum before the country went to war.

By late 1938, however, the views of many Americans changed substantially. The idea took hold that the U.S. national interest required preservation of an "independent, democratic, and pro-American" China. As Japanese leaders boasted of their plans to create a "new order in Asia," Japan seemed less like a regional bully and more like a global menace in league with Germany and Italy. As much as anything, the gruesome toll of fighting in China gradually altered American opinion. In a world still shocked by modern air war, the bombing of defenseless Chinese cities and the deliberate rape and pillage by Japanese troops seemed especially barbaric. As depicted by American journalists and missionaries, the Japanese resembled "warrior ants" and "faceless fiends" destroying everything in their path.

During the Japanese attack on Shanghai at the end of 1937, a journalist photographed a wounded, abandoned Chinese infant crying amid bombed out and twisted railway tracks. Among the most memorable of war photographs, it was still referred to five years later when Americans sent donations to United China Relief. A woman from New Jersey sent $3.00 with a note saying, "it is from my three daughters and it is for the little guy on the railroad tracks somewhere in China."

A Chinese child amidst the rubble of Japanese-bombed Shanghai, 1937. This photograph was widely circulated in the United States during the 1930s and early-1940s to raise money and support for China. (© Corbis)

A few weeks after the child's picture appeared in *Time*, the magazine published a cover portrait of Generalissimo and Madame Chiang Kai-shek, proclaiming them "Man and Wife of the Year." The magazine praised their courageous defense of China against the onslaught of Japanese who seemed driven by a primal urge to conquer. China, under "one supreme ruler and his remarkable wife," fought in defense of values common to Western civilization. If Chiang prevailed, *Time* speculated, he might become "Asia's Man of the Century."

American missionaries, naval personnel, and diplomats sent word home of Japanese cruelty. Japan, they argued, had aims far beyond merely exploiting China. Ambassador Nelson Johnson predicted the Japanese intended to "eliminate all Western influence among the Chinese." Admiral Harry Yarnell informed Roosevelt that the war in China was fundamentally a challenge to "Western civilization." Unless American stopped Japan, the "white race would have no future in Asia."

As these reports percolated through government and popular circles, an idea formed in the mind of President Roosevelt and his advisers. Although Chinese military forces had little offensive capability, their mere existence tied down more than a million Japanese troops that could not be deployed to attack the Philippines, Indochina, Thailand, Malaya, Singapore, the Dutch East Indies, India, Australia, and New Zealand.

An almost certainly apocryphal but illustrative story was told of a news conference held in mid-1938 in Chongqing by a Chinese commander. "General," an American reporter supposedly asked, "In the last year you lost nearly a million men in battle, while the Japanese lost only one hundred thousand. Given these terrible losses, what is going to happen?" Patiently, the Chinese commander is said to have replied, "Pretty soon there be no more Japanese."

This view of China as a vast punching bag or, more benignly, a shock absorber, on which the Japanese would wear themselves out had a brutal but understandable appeal to the Roosevelt administration. By aiding China, Washington could frustrate and wear down Japan without risking war. China didn't have to win, just not lose.

THE ORIGINS OF THE CHINESE–AMERICAN ALLIANCE

For more than a year after Japan attacked China, members of the Roosevelt administration, like the general public, wavered between sympathy and a desire to do something for China and a determination to avoid conflict with Japan. As early as September 1937, a presidential aide wrote that the "peace of the world is tied up with China's ability to win or prolong its resistance to Japanese aggression." But this remained a minority view. By the end of 1938, however, the world situation had become bleak. In Europe, Nazi Germany had broken the promise it made at the Munich Conference to take only "part" of Czechoslovakia. Instead, it had gobbled up the remains of that democratic nation and took aim at Poland. In November it unleashed massive violence against Jews within Germany. Japan's talk of building a new order in Asia under its control echoed Hitler's claim that Germany deserved "living room" in Eastern Europe. As China's military and economic situation grew more desperate, the prospect of Japan in control of the Asian mainland became more chilling. When some of Chiang's aides spread rumors that he might be forced to end resistance or even reach an accommodation with Japan, key officials in the Roosevelt administration responded.

The most influential advocate of assistance to China among Roosevelt's inner circle was Secretary of the Treasury Henry Morgenthau Jr. The Treasury secretary considered both Germany and Japan grave threats. He judged it critical to sustain Chinese resistance to Japan as a way of buying time for the United States to rearm. Morgenthau believed that economic assistance to Chiang would enable his forces to tie down and perhaps ultimately defeat the Japanese invaders—perhaps without direct U.S. involvement.

In contrast, Secretary of State Cordell Hull shied away from supporting China. Although no friend of Japan, he desperately wanted to avoid a war in Asia. His reluctance to act led Morgenthau to work around, rather than with, the State

Department. The Treasury secretary developed a plan to grant China commercial credits to purchase vital supplies in the United States. The idea of a $25 million credit, although modest in size, had greater symbolic value. State Department China expert Stanley Hornbeck, who favored a more active policy than his boss, urged Roosevelt to approve the loan. Economic aid, he explained, was a first step in America's "diplomatic war plan" against Japan. Both Hornbeck and Morgenthau made the point that in the absence of American aid, the Soviet Union, which also feared Japan, had already granted credits to China and was poised to begin supplying substantial military aid. The absence of American aid might drive Chiang "into the hands of Russia."

In December 1938, while Hull visited Latin America, Roosevelt approved a $25 million credit for China. The press characterized this as a commitment to Chinese independence. One of the Chinese negotiators assured Chiang that the aid was intended as a "political loan." The United States had "thrown in her lot with China and cannot withdraw."

This optimism proved a bit premature because no immediate cascade of American aid followed. But during the next three years, Washington gradually expanded the size and scope of assistance to China. Loans were eventually coupled with the imposition of trade restrictions on American sales to Japan. In 1939, Roosevelt pressed U.S. companies to impose a "moral embargo" on the sales of aircraft parts. In January 1940, the State Department announced that the United States would not renew the 1911 commercial treaty with Japan, allowing Washington to impose effective embargoes on the sale of strategic material, including aviation gasoline, steel, and, in July 1941, petroleum.

Friends of China criticized the president for acting too cautiously in punishing Japan. But Roosevelt and his military advisers recognized that economic warfare against Japan might quickly lead to armed conflict, which the United States was unprepared for. It made more sense, the president explained privately, to "slip a noose around Japan's neck" and every once in a while "give a tug."

U.S. assistance to China was also complicated by competing demands to build up America's own forces and to bolster Great Britain. Strategic planners stressed the primacy of stopping Hitler. Defending China and hobbling Japan were important, but secondary, concerns. In addition, continued factional conflict within China complicated the question of how to distribute aid. Chiang, American officials recognized, used foreign aid not only to fight the Japanese, but also to gain advantage over domestic rivals within the GMD as well as the Chinese Communists. Chiang's American allies lobbied to assure that only he would receive U.S. aid.

In an effort to mute Japan's reaction, initial U.S. credits went to a Chinese government "front," the Universal Trading Corporation (UTC). Chiang approved the plan because the UTC (succeeded by China Defense Supplies [CDS]) was controlled by family loyalists, including his brother-in-law, T. V. Soong. Soong placed several former U.S. government officials on the payroll, where they were expected to plead China's cause with their former agencies. For example, Soong employed lawyer Tommy Corcoran, who had been especially close to Roosevelt, in a lobby-ing position.

Some of those working for the UTC and CDS made fortunes. More import-antly, they solidified the links between the GMD and a wide assortment of former, present, and future American bureaucrats. This arrangement frustrated Treasury Secretary Morgenthau, who complained that when he dealt with Americans on the staff of CDS he never knew whether they were working for "Mr. Roosevelt or T. V. Soong, because half the time they were on one payroll and the rest of the time . . . on the other."

Chiang also went outside the formal structure of intergovernment contact, es-pecially to circumvent Americans whom he believed were not sufficiently support-ive. For example, both Chiang and his wife often communicated with Washington through the naval attaché in Chongqing, James McHugh, whom they considered a personal friend. They would give him "secret" messages to pass on to officials in Washington, including several veiled threats of Chinese surrender unless add-itional aid was forthcoming. Because T. V. Soong coordinated this informal net-work and many of the messages came from the three Soong sisters, Ailing, Meiling, and Chingling, Treasury officials composed a satiric tune entitled "Sing a Song of Six Soongs" to describe their dealings.

Despite confusion and miscommunication, American aid to China in-creased substantially by the end of 1940, impelled in large part by Japan's deci-sion in September to join Nazi Germany and fascist Italy in the Tripartite Pact, or Axis Alliance. Before that, most Americans who favored active measures against aggression focused on threats in Europe posed by Germany. Asia seemed an afterthought and sympathy for China did not translate into determination to punish Japan. But by aligning with Germany and Italy, Japan, in the minds of many Americans, had merged the threats in Europe and Asia. China, ironically, became the chief beneficiary of Japan's new alliance.

Early in 1941 Roosevelt proposed and Congress soon approved a massive Lend–Lease program designed to give the president a nearly free hand in assist-ing any nation whose defense he deemed vital to the United States. Great Britain and China were among the nations designated to receive this economic and mili-tary aid in the spring of 1941. In a strange twist, despite increased U.S. aid to China, American commercial sales of raw materials to Japan surged from 1939 to mid-1941, ending only when Washington imposed a trade freeze in July.

Coinciding with the administration's new support for China, Henry and Clare Luce visited Chiang Kai-shek in his beleaguered wartime capital. Impressed as ever by the Generalissimo, Luce told readers and policy makers in Washington that aid to China was even more important than sustaining Great Britain. During 1941 Luce backed his words with action, helping to organize the private aid or-ganization, United China Relief.

But even as the size and scope of American assistance grew, so did tensions within the United Front. As Chiang become more certain of Washington's support, he appeared both less inclined to take the initiative against Japan and more prone to attack the Chinese Communists. The U.S. effort to keep China fighting Japan had the unanticipated consequence of rekindling the civil war within China.

THE COLLAPSE OF THE UNITED FRONT

The truce negotiated between the Nationalists and Communists in 1937 represented a ceasefire that allowed both sides to concentrate greater resources against the Japanese. Each party intended to resist Japan in a way best suited to maximize its claim to future power. From the end of 1938 through the end of 1941, Chiang generally avoided direct clashes with the better armed Japanese while hoping that American aid would give him an advantage over both his foreign and his domestic rivals. The GMD leader made clear his priority: "the Japanese," he reportedly said, "were a disease of the skin; the Communists a disease of the heart."

The Chinese Communist movement, now centered near the northwest city of Yan'an (Yenan), entered the war against Japan with an army less than a tenth the size of the GMD force. But the Communists, who also avoided, when possible, direct fighting against the Japanese, utilized the struggle as a way to recruit new soldiers and political supporters. Mao downplayed Marxist theory in favor of promoting nationalist resistance to the Japanese invaders. In the countryside, the party promoted moderate land and tax reform. Building a military and civilian base, Mao believed, would best position the Communists to defeat the Nationalists once the Japanese were vanquished.

Chiang and Mao understood each other's strategy. But so long as Japan remained a preeminent threat, both had an incentive to maintain the United Front. Each party stationed some representatives in the other's capital, but otherwise maintained separate military and political organizations. Neither party tolerated much dissent. Chiang's secret police, the Blue Shirts headed by Dai Li, brutally suppressed dissident activity. Meanwhile, a GMD army, commanded by General Hu Tsung-nan, blockaded Yan'an. In Communist areas, the party enforced its own orthodoxy and, especially after 1942, purged those who deviated from Mao's leadership.

Despite these tensions, through the end of 1940, the bulk of foreign military assistance to China came from the Soviet Union and nearly all went to the Nationalists. Stalin, like Roosevelt, feared that a Japanese victory in China would free its troops to expand northward as well as southward. China, Stalin hoped, could be preserved as a buffer. In 1939, Soviet and Japanese troops fought a major battle at Nomohan, along the Mongolian–Soviet border. The Soviets pushed back the Japanese military probe, but recognized the importance of keeping China in the fight against Japan. The continued flow of Soviet aid probably restrained Chiang from launching direct attack against his erstwhile Communist allies.

By early 1941, however, the growing threat of Germany in Eastern Europe led Stalin to shift priorities. In April the Soviets signed a nonaggression pact with Japan and reduced aid to the Nationalists. This coincided with the increase in U.S. aid to China. Chiang had told American diplomats that he intended to move more forcefully against the Chinese Communists once he received more American support. By November, with the start of Lend–Lease aid, he expressed confidence in his ability to handle Japan, but called for increased American assistance to help suppress the "defiant Communists."

Chiang also faced other pressures at the end of 1940 and start of 1941. Japan had bolstered its support for a puppet Chinese government led by Chiang's old rival, Wang Ching-wei. By joining the Tripartite Pact (Axis Alliance) Japan intended, in part, to show China, Britain, and the United States that it stood alongside the dominant powers in Europe. Following his easy victories over France, Belgium, and Holland in the summer of 1940, Hitler praised the Japanese as "honorary" members of the Aryan master race.[1] With the status of French Indochina and the Dutch East Indies now uncertain given Germany's European conquests, it seemed increasingly important, American strategists believed, to stabilize China.

To show support for Chiang amid these developments, Roosevelt approved an increase in assistance levels. In November 1940 he approved granting China a $100 million credit, the largest aid package to date. A few weeks later, in January 1941, Chiang ordered his forces to attack the Communist New Fourth Army in disputed territory along the Yangtze River. This civil strife deeply alarmed Americans, who counted on a stable China to tie down the Japanese. Eager to avert full-scale civil war, the United States began a mediation effort between the Communists and Nationalists that continued in one form or another until 1947.

American diplomats and military intelligence officials knew little about the Chinese Communists. Between the late 1920s and early 1930s, many American diplomats in China doubted that an organized Communist movement had survived the debacle of 1927. They speculated that rural bandits and local political insurgents used Communist slogans in attacks on government outposts and foreign property but lacked any connection to Moscow. In fact, even these conservative American representatives voiced a measure of sympathy for social bandits in the countryside. As Ambassador Johnson wrote in 1933, "the shadow of Bolshevism will lie over parts of China until" meaningful rural reform "has improved the lot of the masses and an efficient administration has produced a sense of security in the interior."

Following creation of the United Front in 1937, both the Communists and the Nationalists played down their differences in public, stressing their common anti-Japanese program. Edgar Snow's widely read and sympathetic 1937 portrait of the Chinese Communist movement was the most extensive source of information to outsiders.

During 1937 and 1938, two U.S. military attachés in China, Joseph W. Stilwell and Evans Carlson, reported extensively on Communist military performance. Based on their personal travels and observations, Stilwell and Carlson (who had

---

[1] In private, Hitler was less accommodating of Japan. He told an aide that after defeating Britain and the Soviet Union he would turn against the "little yellow monkeys" and take Asia for himself.

made special arrangement to send his reports directly to Roosevelt) praised the Communists as skilled organizers and effective guerrilla fighters. Both doubted that Communist political dogma would appeal to China's "individualistic peasants."

By the time the New Fourth Army incident occurred in January 1941, officials in Washington were still uncertain what approach, if any, the United States should adopt toward the Communists. But Roosevelt worried that civil conflict in China could only help the Japanese. With Congress poised to approve Lend–Lease, military aid to China could begin in earnest. It would be a disaster, he believed, if Chiang turned American weapons against fellow Chinese. With this concern in mind, the president dispatched a personal emissary, Dr. Lauchlin Currie, to China.

Before becoming a White House advisor, Lauchlin Currie earned a doctorate in economics at Harvard and served in several New Deal agencies, including the Treasury Department and Federal Reserve. He had popularized the idea of deficit spending as a way to stimulate economic growth and helped introduce the theories of British economist John Maynard Keynes to Americans.[2]

After spending several weeks in Chongqing in February and March 1941, Currie returned to Washington with a plan to preserve the United Front while increasing American aid. The envoy urged Chiang to "follow Roosevelt's example" of undercutting radical opponents by enacting reforms. Currie persuaded Roosevelt to send Chiang a group of "liberal" advisers who would work to improve transportation, tax collection, and government efficiency. Currie hoped this would alleviate tensions and enhance GMD popularity. Meanwhile, the U.S. government would work to improve Chiang's image by placing "inspired stories" in the American press. If journalists said "nice things about him," Chiang's stature would improve at home and abroad. Currie assured Roosevelt that Chiang considered the president the "greatest man in the world" and this gave him leverage over the Generalissimo.

In his full report, Currie outlined the broad parameters of what became Roosevelt's China policy until the final stages of the war. The Nationalist regime should be treated as a "great power." Chiang should be given more economic and military support and encouraged to reform. Washington should promote, but not compel, cooperation among the Chinese to ensure a more effective struggle against Japan.

Currie sugar-coated his recommendations, suppressing his own doubts about Chiang's willingness or ability to reform. He also exaggerated the level of American influence over Chinese affairs. Chiang remained an intense, proud, and often stubborn nationalist who barely concealed his contempt for Western

---

[2]Congressional investigators during the early 1950s accused Currie of spying for the Soviet Union during World War II. He denied the charges and left the United States to work in Colombia as an economic adviser. In the 1990s, when historians examined decrypted Soviet wartime cables, it became clear that Currie provided some information to the Soviets. However, Currie made his most important contribution to China policy in 1941 and 1942 when he advocated expanding U.S. aid to Chiang Kai-shek, not the Chinese Communists.

culture and advice. He would never surrender meaningful power to a Chinese rival, no less an American. Currie also failed to recognize the risk of inflating Chiang's image and importance. The wildly pro-Nationalist accounts that appeared in the American press after 1941 provided Chiang with an exaggerated sense of his own importance to the United States. Although Currie's approach paid some immediate dividends, such as preserving the skeleton of the United Front, in the long run it served neither the United States nor China well.

Determined to solve immediate problems, neither Currie nor Roosevelt considered these long-term risks. The recommendations, combined with passage of the Lend–Lease aid program, solidified the American connection to the GMD. Of course, when Roosevelt followed Currie's plan and dispatched a group of technical specialists to advise Chiang, he ignored them.[3] But the White House barely noticed. Chiang now had several powerful advocates around the president, and he had received a promise that 30 of his infantry divisions would be equipped with American arms. Despite production and shipping bottlenecks and the need to arm America's own troops and to assist Great Britain, aid to China began increasing during the last half of 1941. The more aid that arrived, the greater the American stake in China's success. The greater the stake, the more pressing the need to protect it. As the historian Barbara Tuchman wrote about this burgeoning alliance, "a silver chord attached the American to the Nationalist government." There was "no more entangling alliance than aid to indigent friends." This silver chord pulled the Nationalist regime and the United States farther along the road to joint military operations, to the growing alarm of Japan.

A SECRET AIR WAR PLAN
AND THE PEARL HARBOR ATTACK

As the United States committed itself to the defense of Great Britain and China, American military planners conceived of several unusual methods to hinder the war-making power of Germany and Japan. Among the most elaborate of these was a plan for ostensibly private American pilots, employed by a Chinese company, to initiate air strikes against Japanese forces in China and on cities in Japan. These attacks, it was hoped, would bolster Chinese morale and deter Japan from expanding its war beyond China.

Advocates of this secret air war plan claimed it could achieve major benefits with minimal risk. The bulk of Lend–Lease supplies were destined for Britain and, after the German invasion of June 1941, to the Soviet Union. Nearly all U.S. strategists agreed that keeping Britain and the Soviet Union fighting was a top priority. Supporters of the air war plan argued that the deployment of a small

---

[3]Among the advisers sent was Professor Owen Lattimore, an expert on Mongol culture and a popular writer on Asia. Like Currie, but with less evidence, Lattimore was later accused of Communist affiliations. But also like Currie, he was a strong advocate of aid to Chiang in the early 1940s.

number of fighter planes and bombers to China for use against Japan would complement this Europe-first strategy. Striking Japan indirectly, they believed, minimized the risk of Japanese retaliation against the United States.

This concept originated with Claire L. Chennault, a retired army air force pilot. After he left the service in 1936, Chennault worked as a private military adviser to both General and Madame Chiang. He was especially close to Madame Chiang, fondly addressing her as "princess." The GMD regime hoped that Chennault's ties to the American military would help secure aid. In the summer of 1940, Chennault and T. V. Soong were sent to Washington to promote the idea of creating a secret Chinese–American air force to attack Japan.

In November 1940, they submitted to Treasury Secretary Morgenthau plans to create a 500-plane force supplied by the United States and flown by American pilots employed by a Chinese company. They envisioned not only harassing enemy forces in China, but also "attacking Japan proper." Soong argued that attacks on Japanese factories and cities would undermine morale as well as Japan's war-making ability. Morgenthau, then the key figure in U.S. aid to China, urged adopting the idea in discussions he held with aides to Roosevelt and representatives of the State, Navy, and War Departments. Encouraged by their initial response, Morgenthau told Soong that although 500 planes were not available, "what did he think of the idea of some long-range bombers with the understanding that they were to be used to bomb Tokyo and other large cities?" This, both men agreed, might "change the whole picture in the Far East."

By December Morgenthau, Chennault, and Soong discussed specific targets and weapons. The Treasury secretary urged the use of incendiary bombs because "Japanese cities were all made of just wood and paper." Chennault agreed, adding that even if some planes were lost, such an attack "would be well justified." None of the participants seemed concerned that despite the ruse of using "Chinese" planes and contract pilots, the Japanese would certainly know who was behind the attacks.

Secretary of War Henry Stimson and Army Chief of Staff General George C. Marshall vigorously opposed the scheme. They resented any diversion of scarce aircraft from the buildup in Britain and for American forces in the Philippines. They criticized military planning outside the normal chain of command and worried that any attack on Japan would provoke a counterstrike against U.S. interests in the Pacific. Roosevelt suggested a compromise. Instead of the requested bombers, he would divert 100 fighter aircraft to China, where they could be used against Japanese ground troops and coastal shipping, but not against the Japanese home islands.

Since China lacked trained pilots, Chennault, Soong, Morgenthau, Currie, and other officials devised a solution. The president would issue a secret executive order permitting army pilots to resign their commissions and sign contracts with the Chinese Central Aircraft Manufacturing Corporation, whose funds came through Lend–Lease. The pilots, newly designated as the American Volunteer Group, would fly the fighter planes transferred to the Chinese government under Lend–Lease.

By May 1941, many of the key decisions on aid to China were being run out of the White House, specifically by Lauchlin Currie. Since his mission to China, Currie worked closely with Chennault and Soong and became a key booster of their air war plan. He urged Roosevelt to go beyond the fighter-plane scheme and approve the earlier idea of bombing Japan. This, he stressed, would give American pilots valuable combat experience, bolster Chinese morale, and likely deter, not provoke, Japanese attacks elsewhere in Asia.

As Roosevelt considered this, the military balance in Europe and Asia shifted once again. In June, Germany invaded the Soviet Union. In late July Japan occupied southern French Indochina, putting it in a position to attack and seize the oil-rich Dutch East Indies, the Philippines, and British Burma, Malaya, Hong Kong, and Singapore. On July 26, immediately after Japan seized southern Indochina, the U.S. government imposed a freeze on nearly all trade with Japan, including petroleum. This left Tokyo with a 12- to 18-month stockpile. At the same time, Roosevelt signed a secret order sending American bombers to China to be flown by the American Volunteer Group against Japan.[4]

During the final months of 1941, U.S. and Japanese negotiators in Washington engaged in futile efforts to postpone, if not avert, war. The Japanese insisted that any withdrawal from Indochina be preceded by a resumption of U.S. oil sales and a peace settlement in China dictated by Tokyo. Secretary of State Hull demanded that Japan pull its forces out of Indochina, end the war in China, disavow armed expansion, and sever its alliance with Germany *before* the resumption of oil sales. At various times each side considered a short-term deal to delay a showdown, but neither gave in on key demands. Late in November Chiang warned Roosevelt that any softening of the oil embargo—Japan's minimum condition—would represent a "sacrifice" of China and might lead to a military "collapse." From London, Prime Minister Winston Churchill also warned of dire consequences if Chinese interests were ignored. The president's aides cautioned him about accepting a "sellout" to Japan.

Another factor adding to American mistrust was the content of electronic intercepts of Japanese messages. During 1941, naval cryptologists had "broken" several high-level Japanese diplomatic codes. Similar in some ways to the British breakthrough reading German codes ("Enigma"), the Americans had built a coding machine, dubbed *Purple*, which matched the sophisticated coding device used by the Japanese. Given the codename *Magic*, these intercepts of Japanese communications allowed the president and his top advisers to read many of the messages exchanged between the Japanese leaders in Tokyo and their diplomats in Washington.

From these sources, American policy makers concluded that Japanese diplomats might not be negotiating in good faith and that even if they were, military

---

[4]War between the United States and Japan broke out on December 7, before the bombers and their crews became operational. However, the Japanese picked up reports of the plan, designed to begin by late December. This probably added to the factors that went into the decision to attack the U.S. fleet. As discussed later, Chennault played a controversial role in wartime China and then in Cold War operations in Asia.

leaders in Tokyo might well ignore any agreement. Unfortunately, the codebreakers had not yet deciphered Japanese military codes. Thus, although U.S. officials knew by the end of November that war was likely, they could not determine exactly when, where, and how it might begin.

In a final exchange, on November 26, Hull told Japanese negotiators that the United States, the British, and the pro-American government in the Dutch East Indies would not resume oil sales until Japan withdrew from Indochina, stopped the war against China, and pledged no further aggression in the Pacific. Hull knew these terms were not acceptable to Tokyo. The War and Navy Departments notified U.S. commanders in the Pacific that Japan might attack at any time. With their oil reserves rapidly depleting, and with the United States augmenting its air power in the Philippines and China, Japanese leaders resolved to implement their war plan, beginning with a strike on the Pacific fleet at Pearl Harbor.

The war between the United States and Japan resulted in large part from the U.S. determination to resist Japanese expansion by enhancing China's ability to fight. President Roosevelt came gradually to believe that with the help of a strong China, Japan could be contained and defeated. A strong China meant a strong Chiang Kai-shek. More than a military calculation, in American eyes Chiang became a symbol of China's resistance and future value as a postwar ally. Even as the war began, Roosevelt's thoughts turned to building a new order in Asia based on an alliance with a strong, stable, and democratic China, the defeat of Japan, and the gradual decolonization of the region. That vision both energized and frustrated Americans as they entered the bloodiest war in world history.

SELECTED ADDITIONAL READINGS

Karen Leong, *The China Mystique: Pearl S. Buck, Anna May Wang, Mayling Soong and the Transformation of American Orientalism* (Berkeley, Ca., 2005); Iris Chang, *The Rape of Nanking: The Forgotten Holocaust of World War II* (New York, 1997); S. Bernard Thomas, *The Season of High Adventure: Edgar Snow in China* (Berkeley, Ca., 1999); John Maxwell Hamilton, *Edgar Snow: A Biography* (Baton Rouge, La., 2003); Michael Barnhart, *Japan Prepares for Total War: The Search for Economic Security, 1919–1941* (Ithaca, N.Y., 1987); Dorothy Borg and Shumpei Okamoto, eds., *Pearl Harbor as History: Japanese American Relations, 1931–1941* (New York, 1973); Warren I. Cohen, *The Chinese Connection: Roger S. Greene, Thomas Lamont, George E. Sokolsky and American East Asian Relations* (New York, 1978); Robert J. C. Butow, *Tojo and the Coming of the War* (Princeton, N.J., 1961) and *The John Doe Associates: Backdoor Diplomacy for Peace* (Stanford, Ca., 1974); Herbert Feis, *The Road to Pearl Harbor: The Coming of the War between the United States and Japan* (Princeton, N.J., 1950); Jonathan Utley, *Going to War with Japan, 1937–1941* (Knoxville, Tenn., 1985); Eri Hotta, *Japan 1941: Countdown to Infamy* (New York, 2013); Rana Mitter, *Forgotten Ally: China's World War II, 1937–1945* (Boston, 2013); Robert Dallek, *Franklin D. Roosevelt and American Foreign Policy, 1932–1945* (New York, 1979); Waldo H. Heinrichs, *Threshold of War: Franklin D. Roosevelt and American Entry into World War II* (New York, 1988); Frederick Wakeman, *The Shanghai Badlands: Wartime Terrorism and Urban Crime, 1937–1941* (New York, 1996); Michael Schaller, *The U.S. Crusade in China, 1938–1945* (New York, 1979).

CHAPTER 4

The Chinese–American Alliance

Japan's air attack on the American fleet at Pearl Harbor on December 7, 1941, followed by the rapid conquests of the Philippines and all colonial Southeast Asia, erased any hope that aid to China would deter Japanese aggression. When Germany entered the war against the United States a few days later, America's war became global. Stunned by Japan's early victories, Americans found comfort in their alliance with a "battle-tested" Chinese army. An editorial in the *New York Times* declared that the two nations were "partners in a larger unity. . . . We have as our ally China, with its inexhaustible manpower—China, from whose patient and untiring and infinitely resourceful people there will now return to us tenfold payment upon such aid as we have given."

Washington's official view of a faithful ally found expression in an episode of the U.S. Army's widely circulated film series, *Why We Fight*. In the *Battle Cry of China*, the narrator explained how the "oldest and youngest of the world's great nations, together with the British Commonwealth, fight side by side in the struggle that is as old as China herself. The struggle of freedom against slavery, civilization against barbarism, good against evil."

America's allies reacted to Japan's attack on the United States with an overwhelming sense of relief. British Prime Minister Winston Churchill declared, "So we had won after all! Hitler's fate was sealed, Mussolini's fate was sealed. As for the Japanese, they would be ground to powder." In Chongqing, government officials celebrated what they considered China's salvation. Novelist Han Suyin, wife of a GMD general, recalled the reaction to news that the United States had entered the war.

> Almost immediately there were noises in the street . . . people surging out of their houses to buy newspapers . . . the military council was jubilant. Chiang was so happy he sang an old opera aria and played Ave Maria all day. The Kuomintang government officials went around congratulating each other as if a great victory had been won. From their standpoint it was a great victory. . . . At last, at last, America was at war with Japan. Now China's strategic importance

would grow even more. American money and equipment would flow in; half a billion dollars, one billion dollars. . . . Now America would have to support Chiang, and that meant U.S. dollars into the pockets of the officials, into the pockets of the army commanders, and guns to General Hu Tsung-nan for the coming war against [the Communists in] Yenan.

Japan's attack not only brought the United States fully into China's corner, but also quickly altered the political balance in Asia. With startling speed, the colonial bastions of the Philippines, Dutch East Indies, Malaya, Singapore, and Hong Kong fell. Relatively few Asians were eager to exchange Japanese masters for Europeans, but the power and speed of Japan's armed forces tremendously impressed other Asians who had seen Western armies as invulnerable.

In China, between 1942 and 1945, despite increased American aid and advice, Chiang proved unable or unwilling to fight the Japanese more effectively. As GMD authority declined, that of the Communists expanded. Although Communist forces fought only limited engagements against the Japanese, their ability to project themselves as nationalist heroes against the invaders provided momentum and political cover that carried them through the war and into the civil war that followed.

Until his death in April 1945, President Roosevelt struggled both to win the war and to secure the peace by harnessing the forces of nationalism unleashed by Japan in Asia.[1] Roosevelt looked beyond Japan's defeat to ask who would eventually control the East Indies, the Philippines, Indochina, etc. After Japan had been "ground to powder," what would restrain Soviet expansion in Asia? How would China, with a fourth of the world's population, influence events? Would postwar China be pro-American, antiforeign, or pro-Soviet? The president and other policy makers grappled with the challenge of steering these forces of change in the least dangerous directions.

Ideally, postwar China (and, hopefully, Asia) would be governed by moderate nationalists in tune with American political and economic values. Gradual reform, not violent social upheaval, held the key to progress. A stable, united, pro-American China, Roosevelt believed, could become the linchpin of Asian security—replacing Japan, restraining the Soviet Union, and acting as guide and protector to its neighbors emerging from colonialism. Even if China played only a modest role in defeating Japan, it might well become a dominant force in postwar Asia. The president voiced these beliefs frequently, as when he told skeptical British allies that China, with its vast population, would be "very useful twenty-five years hence, even though China cannot contribute much military or naval support for the moment." At the very least, simply by staying in the war, China tied down nearly 2 million Japanese troops.

---

[1] Shortly after Japan's attack on Pearl Harbor, Roosevelt told his son Elliott that the legacy of European imperialism in Asia was a primary cause of the war. "Don't think for a minute," he explained, "that Americans would be dying in the Pacific tonight if it hadn't been for the shortsighted greed of the French, and the British and the Dutch."

Roosevelt envisioned China as a critical partner in stabilizing postwar Asia. He hoped that the major wartime allies—the United States, Great Britain, the Soviet Union, and China—would act as "Four Policeman" to cooperate in enforcing regional peace. As the policeman in Asia, China would be America's proxy or, as Winston Churchill complained, America's "faggot vote."

Whatever he thought of wartime China, the fact remains that Roosevelt's attention—along with U.S. aid, troops, and supplies—was focused heavily on the

Uncle Sam feeding a Chinese child, by Ed. Hunter. This poster was one of many similar depictions circulated in the U.S. by United China Relief, Inc. during World War II.

(B. A. Garside Collection, Hoover Institution Archives)

war in Europe. The naval campaigns in the Pacific and army and Marine assaults on south Pacific islands took second place. China placed a distant third in strategic priority. Yet, for a variety of practical and romantic reasons, Roosevelt insisted on including China in the front ranks of the wartime Grand Alliance. A circle of like-minded enthusiasts convinced the president that he could link American power to the GMD to create a moderately effective wartime ally and a powerful postwar friend. As Harry Hopkins, Roosevelt's closest aide remarked, after the war, "in any serious conflict of policy with Russia," Chiang's government "would line up on our side."

Whatever his other priorities, Chiang and his inner circle hoped that by cleaving closely to the United States, China could recover its "lost territories" (Manchuria, Taiwan, Hong Kong, Outer Mongolia). They, too, worried about Soviet expansion and whether Stalin would promote Chinese unity or push Mao toward conflict with the GMD.

Before any of Roosevelt's wartime plans or postwar visions could be realized, however, new life had to be breathed into the GMD. Despite his professed interest in China (consisting mostly of references to his merchant grandfather), Roosevelt never fully realized that, as with Germany and Austria in World War I, the United States had allied itself to a corpse. Despite increasing infusions of money (a half billion dollars in 1942) and arms, the GMD's hold on power steadily diminished.

Warning signals reached Washington even before the smoke cleared from the burning vessels sunk at Pearl Harbor. General John Magruder, a military observer in China, warned the War Department that Chiang intended to hoard as much American aid as he could, "largely with the idea of postwar military action." Chinese strategists, he wrote, lived in a "world of make believe," and Chiang considered his troops and weapons "static assets" to be preserved for fighting against "fellow countrymen for economic and political supremacy." Ambassador Clarence Gauss described Chiang as "suffer[ing] from a touch of unreality derived from a somewhat grandiose or ivory tower conception of his and China's role."

Roosevelt hated hearing these negative reports. Like most people, he interpreted information in ways that confirmed his beliefs and hopes. When it failed to do so, he often blamed the messenger and sought out conduits that would provide him more compatible information. Once again, Lauchlin Currie—a strong advocate of aid to China before Pearl Harbor—delivered the assurances Roosevelt wanted to hear. After a mission to China in 1942, Currie informed the president,

> We have a unique opportunity to exert a profound influence on the development of China and hence Asia. It appears to me to be profoundly in our national interest to give full support to the Generalissimo both military and diplomatic. I do not think we need to lay down any conditions nor tie any strings to this support . . . we can rely on him so far as lies within his power to go in the direction of our wishes in prosecuting a vigorous war policy and in creating a modern, democratic and powerful state.

Not only Roosevelt, but also much of the American public bought into the romantic view of China as a vital ally. Madame Chiang (Soong Meiling) toured the United States from November 1942 through the following May, including a prolonged stay in the White House.[2] American educated, articulate, and glamorous, she epitomized hopes for China's future. One administration official described the importance of her visit as "counteracting" Japanese propaganda that their war aim was to liberate Asians from white rule. Japan's rhetoric, he feared, had found a following among some Chinese, Filipinos, Indians, and Malaysians and "it even reaches our own Negroes."

In February 1943 Madame Chiang delivered an address to both Houses of Congress that was broadcast nationally on the radio. China, like the United States, she declared, fought for a "better world, not just for ourselves but for all mankind." Her subtext, that the war in China against Japan should take priority over other battlefronts, contradicted American strategy. During a cross-country tour ending at the Hollywood Bowl, the "first lady of China" told large audiences that China was America's foremost ally and deserved more aid, not closer scrutiny. Henry Luce's *Time* and *Life* magazines provided especially generous coverage to the tour.

Despite her effort to link Chinese and American aspirations Madame Chiang's speeches often left audiences puzzled. She packed her presentations with obscure words and syntax. For example, in a speech on "Democracy vs. Ochlocrasy," she explained that "ochlocracy . . . is but the inchoate rococo of mob rule bred on febrile emotions and unrestraint." What she meant was anyone's guess. To some it seemed incongruous that she discussed China's plight while hosting extravagant receptions in luxury hotels. Overall, however, her tour generated positive impressions of China. In the wake of her visit, Congress began the process to amend the hated "unequal treaties" and repealed the near total prohibition on Chinese immigration. In place of exclusion, 105 Chinese would be permitted to immigrate annually to the United States.[3]

THE REAL WAR IN CHINA

Beyond the favorable news stories generated by the White House and *Time* magazine lay the tragic dimensions of wartime China. Wartime censorship—and sometimes self-censorship—blocked the American public from receiving

---

[2]Most Americans, with a prod from Henry Luce's publications, believed that Soong Meiling was a Chinese equivalent of First Lady Eleanor Roosevelt—a political partner and close adviser to her husband. In fact, she was often estranged from Chiang and frequently lived separately. For example, she spent nearly all of 1943 in the United States and Canada, returned briefly to China, and then left for an extended tour of Brazil.

[3]American military personnel in China during and shortly after World War II married about 9,000 Chinese women. Congress passed special legislation in 1945 and 1946 to permit them to follow their husbands home.

accounts by journalists and diplomats in China about the despair, corruption, and defeatism in Nationalist China. Theodore White, a young *Time* reporter and unlikely protégé of Henry Luce, wrote incisively about real events he witnessed. But most of what appeared under his byline was edited to reflect Luce's high regard for Chiang. White published many of his original reports in a postwar compilation, *Thunder out of China* (1946). His description of famine in Henan province during 1942–1943 in which about 4 million people died revealed a China unknown to most Americans.

> The peasants as we saw them were dying. They were dying on the roads, in the mountains, by the railway stations, in their mud huts, in the fields. And as they died, the government continued to wring from them the last possible ounce of tax. . . . The government in county after county was demanding of the peasant . . . more grain than he had raised. No excuses were allowed; peasants who were eating elm bark and dried leaves had to haul their last sack of seed grain to the tax collector's office. Peasants who were so weak they could barely walk had to collect fodder for the army's horses. . . . One of the most macabre touches of all this was the flurry of land speculation. Merchants, small government officials, army officers, and rich land owners who still had food were engaged in purchasing the peasants' ancestral areas at criminally low figures. . . . We knew there was fury, as cold and relentless as death itself, in the bosom of the peasants of Henan, that their loyalty had been hollowed to nothingness by the extortion of their government.[4]

Similar tragedies occurred in many regions of China during the war, undercutting Madame Chiang's words about building better worlds and *Time*'s praise of the Generalissimo as a "Christian and scholar first," a soldier "only by necessity." Even the most capable and selfless civilian and military leaders would have struggled under the circumstances of wartime China. But the Americans most knowledgeable about China, especially those in Chongqing, considered the GMD venal at best and criminal at worst.

The chaos and exploitation of civilians were matched by the behavior of the Nationalist armies. A wartime report by American military observers described the formation of a typical army unit.

> Conscription comes to the Chinese peasant like famine or flood, only more regularly—every year twice—and claims more victims. Famine, flood, and drought compare with conscription like chicken pox with plague. The virus is spread over the Chinese countryside. . . . There is first the press gang. For example, you are working in a field looking after your rice [when suddenly] a number of men tie your hands behind your back and take you with them. . . . Hoe and plow rust in the field, the wife runs to the magistrate to cry and beg for her husband, the children starve.

---

[4]The primary cause of the famine was drought, made worse by the policy of collecting taxes in the form of grain. During the war, a famine in British-ruled Bengal killed nearly as many people and was also worsened by military grain requisitions.

The report, which compared Chinese army hospitals to Nazi death camps, recounted how prison officials made money by selling convicts into service. Roped together, peasants and convicts were marched hundreds of miles to training camps. Those caught fleeing were beaten and forced on. Even the death of common soldiers, by disease or wounds, benefitted officers.

> If somebody dies, his body is left behind. His name on the list is carried along. As long as his death is not reported, he continues to be a source of income, increased by the fact that he has ceased to consume. His rice and pay become a long-lasting token of memory in the pocket of his commanding officers. His family will have to forget him.

White, along with many American diplomats and military officers in China, faulted the Nationalist regime for abandoning nearly all principles and replacing them with a determination to fight the Communists and use outside aid to remain in power.

AMERICAN MILITARY STRATEGY IN CHINA

Shortly after the Pearl Harbor attack, Chiang Kai-shek contacted Roosevelt through his brother-in-law, T. V. Soong, to request that a high-ranking American be sent to China as a military adviser. In passing on the message, Soong added that "the officer need not be an expert on the Far East." The Nationalist leaders hoped that the administration would send someone largely ignorant of Chinese affairs and presumably malleable. They were startled when Army Chief of Staff George C. Marshall selected his close associate, General Joseph W. Stilwell. "Vinegar Joe," as his men and journalists called him, was a blunt-speaking, no-nonsense soldier who during the 1920s and 1930s had learned Chinese and as a military attaché had traveled through much of China on foot. His closeness to Marshall and his extensive background in China made him appear to Americans an inspired choice to command the small (around 60,000 at its peak) number of U.S. support, technical, and air force personnel in China. As commander of the newly created China–Burma–India theater, Stilwell was expected to advise Chiang and to oversee the reorganization and use of China's large but unwieldy army.

Almost three years later, in the fall of 1944, a deeply frustrated Stilwell described how political intrigue had undercut all his reform efforts. "American aid," Stilwell complained, "had to take into consideration the domestic side of every move we have undertaken . . . so that the Gimo's (Generalissimo Chiang) own command will get the most benefit from it." All military operations were subordinated to Roosevelt's hope of "preserving China's precarious unity" under Chiang's leadership. Stilwell concluded that the only "cure for China's trouble is the elimination of Chiang Kai-shek."

Stilwell's mission began and ended in rancor. Soon after he arrived in China in March 1942, he tried to assume command of Chinese ground forces in the fight to keep open the Burma Road that linked China to India and the war materials

Generalissimo Chiang Kai-Shek and General Joseph W. Stilwell share an uncharacteristic lighter moment in Chungking, 1942. (National Archives)

stockpiled there. When he tried to exercise command on the Burma front, Stilwell discovered that Chiang frequently undercut and contradicted his orders. When Burma fell, Stilwell found himself behind enemy lines. He spent many weeks leading his men out of the jungles on foot, telling journalists when they reached India, "we took a hell of a beating."

Chiang resented Stilwell's condescension and vigorously opposed committing his own troops and equipment to fighting the Japanese, especially under foreign command. If American transport planes could fly supplies over the "hump" or Himalaya Mountains, why, Chiang wondered, should he squander men and weapons to a fight for a land route? Although air transport was limited, costly, and dangerous, it did not require Chiang to sacrifice his own resources as would the fight to open a route through Burma.

The defeat in Burma convinced Stilwell that only a reformed Chinese army, committed to opening the Burma supply route, could play a part in defeating

Japan. Chiang, he believed, blocked all reforms—in the army, in government, in the tax system, etc. Although the "wasteful and inefficient system of juggling" Chinese armies and commanders might help keep Chiang in power, it emasculated the effectiveness of Chinese troops, did little to combat Japan, and failed to promote long-term U.S. interests.

The Chinese army nominally consisted of 4 million men under arms, organized into 316 divisions. Chiang directly controlled only about 30 divisions. A dozen or so generals commanded the rest, some allied to the Generalissimo and others virtually independent. One powerful army group of 400,000 troops under General Hu Tsung-nan was assigned to blockade Yan'an, the seat of Chinese Communist power.

Nearly everything about this system—from recruitment, to training and equipment, to command—disgusted Stilwell. Despite his contempt for Chiang, Stilwell had high regard for the capabilities of individual Chinese soldiers whom he hoped to shape into an effective fighting force. He called for reducing the size of the army and picking out 30 divisions for special training. Stilwell planned to select a Chinese officer, based on competence, to lead these new divisions in a campaign to reopen a transport route through Burma. Once substantial aid arrived over the Burma road, Stilwell intended to use it to create an efficient national army.

Chiang's resistance to his plans provoked Stilwell to write in his diary, "Why doesn't the little dummy realize that his only hope is the thirty division plan and creation of a separate, efficient and well-equipped and well-trained force?" But Chiang understood the implications of Stilwell's plans. Giving an American general power to select, promote, or sack Chinese officers, as well as to grant or withhold Lend–Lease aid, would gut Chiang's authority. Without power to reward and punish subalterns, how could he retain power? Consequently, Chiang did all he could to delay reform and rid himself of the foreign meddler.[5]

Stilwell grew livid at Chiang's refusal to initiate a Burma campaign or reform the army structure. As he put it, "the stupid little ass fails to grab the opportunity of his life." The Chinese government, Stilwell concluded, was a structure based on fear and favor in the hands of an "ignorant stubborn man." Stilwell came to believe that "only outside influence can do anything for China—either enemy action will smash her or some regenerative ideas must be formed and put into effect at once." In his diary and in casual conversation, Stilwell dubbed Chiang "the Peanut." Many rank-and-file American military personnel in China shared Stilwell's cynical view, referring to the Generalissimo with names like "Cash My Check" and "Chancre Shek."

After a frustrating year, Stilwell decided he must become the "regenerative idea" and began to challenge Chiang for control. Stilwell hoped to force Chiang's compliance by getting Roosevelt to give him (Stilwell) control over Lend–Lease

---

[5]Chiang had a strong, antiforeign streak. His wartime, probably ghost-written, book, *China's Destiny*, blamed the West for most of China's problems and justified authoritarian rule. Chiang's aides feared a backlash and tried to bar its translation or sale to Americans.

distribution. The president delayed giving his support to Stilwell until September 1944 and then withdrew it almost immediately.

CHINESE MANIPULATION OF AMERICAN POLICY

Chiang recognized that he must offer Roosevelt something positive. To assure the uninterrupted flow of aid, he offered a constructive alternative to Stilwell's strategy. Determined to "play the barbarians off against each other," the Generalissimo identified American military commanders who advocated policies that did not threaten his military and political control but still made China appear a useful ally. The antidotes to Stilwell came in the persons of Navy Commander Milton Miles and Army Air Force General Claire Chennault.

Miles, a naval officer searching for a role in landlocked wartime China, hit on the idea during 1942 of creating a "secret" commando-style unit in which American and Chinese personnel fought the Japanese. The idea gained support from admirals in Washington who hoped that wartime cooperation would yield postwar naval bases in China. Miles's Naval Group China allied itself with General Dai Li, often dubbed "China's Himmler," who led Chiang's secret police. The two men formed the Sino–American Cooperative Organization to funnel military aid to loyal Chinese units without Stilwell's oversight. Although only a small number of Americans served in the Sino–American Cooperative Organization, they played an outsized role in building up Dai Li's power and undercutting Stilwell and American diplomats critical of Chiang by leaking critical information to Chiang.

The Generalissimo found an even more influential American partner in Claire Chennault, former head of the American Volunteer Group (Flying Tigers) and now commander of a small air task force in China. Like Miles, Chennault felt a deep bond with Chiang and resented Stilwell's efforts to pressure Chiang into fighting an expanded ground war. Air power, Chennault argued, held the key to low-cost victory and improved Chinese–American relations.

Chiang championed Chennault's call for an expanded air war because it served several needs. If the limited freight capacity flown into China from India, over the Hump, went mostly to fuel and supply Chennault's planes, Stilwell would lack the equipment to grant or deny much of anything. More importantly, a powerful American air force operating from China, especially if commanded by an acolyte such as Chennault, posed no threat to the Generalissimo while making it seem that China was pulling its weight in the war against Japan. In return, the United States might increase its relatively meager aid program.

Chennault worked hard to secure Roosevelt's support. Disliked by the War Department leadership and Army Chief of Staff Marshall—both of whom considered the flier a publicity hound—Chennault established personal links to the president. Among his key allies was Joseph Alsop, an aide to the flier who was a distant cousin of Roosevelt's and a friend of presidential adviser Harry Hopkins. Alsop and T. V. Soong deluged the White House with reports calling Stilwell's activities a "national disgrace." But if Chennault received even a modest number of additional planes, he could cripple Japanese forces in China and bring Japan to its knees. With an expanded air force, Chennault boasted, he could "not only bring about the downfall of Japan," but also "make the Chinese lasting friends of the United States." He would generate such good will that "China will be a great and friendly trade market for generations."

Stilwell despised Chennault personally and professionally. An air campaign, he argued, not only would disperse scarce resources but also made no sense. If and when American air attacks on Japanese troops and coastal shipping had an impact, Japanese forces would simply overrun China's unprotected air bases. The Chinese army, in its current shape, could offer little defense.

The president and his closest civilian aides, such as Hopkins, resented Stilwell's shrill warnings of impending doom in China. Chennault, in contrast, reassured Hopkins that if Roosevelt supported an air war, "there was no doubt of success." Chennault and his supporters chanted their mantra and claimed it would not only kill Japanese but also magically improve the bitter political atmosphere in Chongqing.

Throughout 1943 and the first half of 1944, Stilwell tried in vain to press Chiang and the British (based in India) to begin a military drive to open a land route through Burma. But without presidential backing, nothing happened. In May 1943, Roosevelt attempted to resolve the quandary by inviting both Stilwell and Chennault to present their cases to him in person. The questions Roosevelt

Left-to-right: Chiang Kai-shek, Franklin Delano Roosevelt, Winston Churchill, and Mme. Chiang at Cairo Conference, 1943. (The Granger Collection, New York)

posed to each of them centered more on politics and military logic. What did Stilwell think of Chiang?, asked the president. "He's a vacillating, tricky, undependable old scoundrel who never keeps his word." Chennault thought otherwise. "Sir, I think the Generalissimo is one of the two or three greatest military and political leaders in the world today."

Roosevelt dismissed Stilwell's arguments and embraced Chennault's feel-good assurances. An air campaign promised easy, cheap success with few complications. Stilwell's approach involved protracted, difficult combat, complex negotiations with the British and Chinese, and the likelihood of upsetting the domestic power balance in China. Not surprisingly, the president backed Chennault and decided to allocate the bulk of precious Hump cargo for an air war. Roosevelt came close to recalling Stilwell from China, relenting only when Army Chief of Staff Marshall and Secretary of War Henry Stimson spoke strongly in his defense.

THE RISE AND FALL OF AIR WARFARE IN CHINA

Roosevelt's decision to appease Chiang by shifting support to an air war strategy represented in large part a bet on China's future value as an ally. As the president told General Marshall in 1943, Chiang should not be threatened into reform. It would be counterproductive to bully a man who had created in China "what it took us a couple of centuries to attain." Roosevelt praised Chiang as the "undisputed leader of 400,000,000 people" who could not be dictated to like "the Sultan of Morocco."

This exchange confirmed Marshall's belief of why Roosevelt had accepted Chennault's absurd claim that his small air force could defeat Japan. No one with a grain of military common sense actually believed that air power alone could drive the Japanese out of China. But, "since the Chinese wanted what Chennault wanted, and Roosevelt wanted to give the Chinese what they wanted, all these things fit together very neatly and required no further presidential effort or analysis."

The decision also reflected how little Roosevelt knew about actual Chinese conditions. He possessed a far more sophisticated understanding of European power politics, geography, and history. He had an exaggerated belief in Chiang's ability and willingness to solve China's current and future problems. Also, Roosevelt's glib faith in China's immediate postwar importance led him to placate Chiang and avoid any harsh reckoning.

While Chennault celebrated the go-ahead to begin an expanded air campaign, Stilwell brooded. His diary entries contained tremendous resentment toward Roosevelt, Chiang, and Chennault. Returning to China after the disastrous meeting in Washington, he wrote, "Back in the manure pile after that wonderful trip home" to find "Chiang the same as ever—a grasping, bigoted ungrateful little rattlesnake."

During the next year, through the spring of 1944, Stilwell focused on training and reorganizing a limited number of Chinese divisions while developing plans for a ground offensive in Burma. Chiang continued to interfere with these efforts and came perilously close to an open break with the Communists. The Generalissimo sent regular complaints to officials in Washington about Stilwell's arrogance, while the American commander channeled some Lend–Lease supplies to Chiang's rivals within the GMD. He even dabbled in a few plots designed to remove Chiang from power.

As Chennault launched his air attacks on Japanese forces within China during early 1944, the results proved dramatic—but not in the way he or Chiang anticipated. Japanese military leaders, already on the defensive in the Pacific and Burma, resolved to bolster their position by committing 500,000 troops to finally knocking China out of the war. In the spring the Imperial Army launched ICHIGO in central China, their largest offensive ever, with the aim of destroying American airfields, Chinese armies, and Chiang's government. Over the next several months, Japanese armies overran the poorly defended airfields (as Stilwell had predicted), smashed Chinese resistance, and seemed poised to overrun the GMD footholds in central and western China. As in the past, Chiang made a difficult situation worse by withholding supplies from some frontline commanders whose loyalty he doubted. By the summer of 1944, China again seemed on the verge of collapse.[6]

The impending disaster compelled Roosevelt to re-examine his faith in Chiang. In fact, the process began late in 1943 when the president met Chiang face to face for the first time at the Cairo Conference. Chiang harangued Roosevelt, demanding that he grant China a new billion-dollar loan and additional military support. Yet, Chiang refused to commit to launching an offensive in Burma. Roosevelt left Cairo frustrated by Winston Churchill's priority of recapturing lost colonies and Chiang's determination to do as little as possible.

In contrast, when Roosevelt arrived in Teheran a few days later to confer with Josef Stalin, the two leaders found common ground. Stalin pledged to enter the war against Japan soon after Germany's defeat. This prospect made China's contribution to the war against Japan less consequential. The combined naval, army, and Marine offensive in the Central Pacific, as well as the prospect of a Soviet ground offensive in northeast Asia, reduced China's importance.

When Treasury Secretary Henry Morgenthau Jr. learned of massive fraud carried out by high-level Nationalist officials, he and the president blocked new economic aid to China. Morgenthau fumed that he would not give Chiang's clique "another nickel" and they could all go "jump in the Yangtze." Roosevelt lost even more patience with his ally during the spring of 1944 as Stilwell utilized the several Chinese divisions he controlled to attack the Japanese in Burma. When Chiang blocked the flow of equipment and replacement troops to these units, Roosevelt for the first time suggested he might cut off aid to China. How, many

---

[6]ICHIGO proved a very near thing. But the Japanese ran out of men and supplies before achieving their goal of overrunning all China.

American civilian and military officials asked themselves, could Chiang impede reinforcing Stilwell or the Chinese forces reeling under Japan's ICHIGO offensive while he kept several hundred thousand troops blockading the Communists in northwest China?

ROOSEVELT AND CHIANG: ULTIMATUM AND RETREAT

During the summer of 1944, the liberation of Western Europe began, the Red Army pushed most German forces out of the Soviet Union, and the sea and land offensives in the Pacific steadily reduced Japan's sphere of control and access to raw materials. Only in China were Japanese forces still on the offensive. Frustrated by Chiang's refusal to fight the Japanese in central China and Burma, Roosevelt finally brought down the hammer.

Since Chiang argued that he could not redeploy troops blockading the Communists, the president insisted he try to improve relations with his domestic rivals. If successful, this would free GMD units to fight elsewhere and permit the United States to tap the military potential of the Chinese Communists. Wartime cooperation, Roosevelt also hoped, would boost the prospect of postwar unity. With this in mind, in June 1944 the president dispatched Vice President Henry A. Wallace to China with instructions to press Chiang to make a deal with the Communists.

Roosevelt also insisted that Chiang permit the dispatch of an American observer mission to Yan'an. Their presence, it was hoped, might convince Chiang that the United States could "back more than one horse" in China. It would also provide firsthand knowledge about Mao and his followers. Wallace's report to the president reflected the diminished view of the Generalissimo. Chiang, he wrote, was "at best a short-term investment." Wallace doubted that Chiang possessed the "intelligence or political strength to run postwar China." New leaders would be "brought forward by evolution or revolution, and it now seems more like the latter."

Sensing the changed mood in Washington, Stilwell pressed Roosevelt to order Chiang to give him full control of all Chinese forces. Stilwell sought complete freedom to direct China's war effort and to aid and utilize Communist forces against Japan. On July 4, 1944, the president authorized sending a telegram to Chiang warning that "the future of all Asia is at stake." The air war had failed so now Stilwell must be granted "command of all Chinese and American forces . . . including the Communist forces."

Chiang understood that an outright rejection of this demand might jeopardize American support. Instead, he gave vague assurances of cooperation and asked that Roosevelt send a personal emissary to China to smooth relations. Roosevelt consented and accepted the suggestions of Secretary of War Stimson and Army Chief of Staff Marshall that he send Patrick J. Hurley as mediator. Hurley, a Republican oil lawyer and former secretary of war under Herbert Hoover, had gotten on well with Stilwell during an earlier visit. The president may well have thought it good politics to send a Republican as emissary, especially if the effort failed.

On September 6, 1944, after stopping in Moscow where he received Soviet assurance that Stalin would support Chiang's government and not the Communists, Hurley reached Chongqing. He found Stilwell anxious to command Chinese troops and to get arms to the Communists "who will fight." On September 19, thinking he had Hurley's support, Stilwell personally delivered a message from the president to Chiang. He described the event in his diary.

> Mark this day in red on the calendar of life. At long last, at very long last FDR has finally spoken plain words, and plenty of them, with a firecracker in every sentence. "Get Busy or Else," a hot firecracker. I handled this bundle of paprika to the Peanut and then sank back with a sigh. The harpoon hit the little bugger right in the solar plexus and went right through him . . . but beyond turning green and losing the power of speech, he did not bat an eye. He just said to me, "I understand" and sat in silence jiggling one foot.

Stilwell's victory proved fleeting. As he prepared to assume control over Chinese troops, Hurley collaborated secretly with Chiang to get rid of the meddlesome American. Hurley was convinced that any attempt to circumvent Chiang would open China to Communist and/or Soviet domination. Despite his near total ignorance of China, its people, or politics, Hurley conspired with Chiang and his inner circle to remove Stilwell and prevent American aid from going to Communist forces.[7]

On September 24, 1944, Hurley joined Chiang and T. V. Soong in sending a joint message to Roosevelt. The only real problem in China, they insisted, was Stilwell. His impudence could not be tolerated. But once the troublesome general was removed, Chiang promised to do everything the president asked of him.

As the president pondered what to do, Hurley peppered the White House with additional warnings. On October 10, he asserted that "there is no other Chinese known to me who possesses as many of the elements of leadership as Chiang Kai-shek. Chiang and Stilwell are fundamentally incompatible." Vanity, Hurley argued, motivated Stilwell, who was a fool to attempt to "subjugate a man who has led a nation in revolution and who had led an ill-fed, poorly equipped practically unorganized army against an overwhelming foe for seven years." Playing his ultimate card, Hurley warned Roosevelt that if he "sustained Stilwell . . . you will lose Chiang Kai-shek and possibly you will lose China with him."

The president had to choose between sustaining Stilwell, even at the cost of a break with Chiang, or replacing him with an officer who deferred to Chiang. In effect, this meant writing off China as a potent factor in the defeat of Japan. To further complicate matters, Roosevelt faced an election for an unprecedented

---

[7]Hurley's motives have puzzled historians. After quitting his post in China late in 1945, he harshly criticized President Harry Truman and became a strident anti-Communist on the fringe of American politics. Several diplomats and journalists who observed Hurley in China during late 1944 and 1945 were startled by his erratic behavior. At times he would rant about conspiracies or confuse people he casually met with old friends and family members. At one reception in Chongqing Hurley confused journalist Annalee Jacoby with his wife.

fourth term in less than a month. Running on his record as leader of the Grand Alliance, a break with or collapse of China would be a terrible political burden. Meanwhile, Hurley framed the issue largely as a personality clash, not as a question of Chiang's competence or China's importance. An easy solution presented itself: simply recall the quarrelsome general and bolster the "indispensable" leader of China.

Roosevelt made the expedient decision on October 18, recalling Stilwell. As a replacement, he selected General Albert Wedemeyer, a man Stilwell despised as the "world's most pompous prick." U.S. aid would continue although Chiang denied Wedemeyer command of Chinese troops. Finally, Roosevelt promoted Hurley from personal envoy to U.S. ambassador, replacing career diplomat Clarence Gauss, who shared many of Stilwell's opinions.

Because Stilwell knew China far better than his American rivals, such as Chennault and Miles, it is easy to imagine that if Roosevelt had stood by the general he might have transformed the war effort and averted the civil war that erupted later. If he had the president's backing, some GMD commanders would have followed Stilwell's lead and the Americans probably would have utilized some Chinese Communist troops against the Japanese. But neither Stilwell nor any American could have solved China's chronic problems of poverty, disunity, and political mistrust that transcended the immediate war effort.

In any case, by the end of 1944 the war in Asia and the Pacific was simply passing China by. The U.S. Navy had cut off Japan's home islands from southeast Asian resources; massive air raids mounted from Saipan and other islands would soon destroy 80 percent of Japan's cities; and the Soviets were committed to fight Japan after Germany surrendered. China had moved to the margins of strategic planning. Neither Roosevelt nor his military advisers any longer envisioned China playing a major role in the end stages of the war. Japan would be defeated without China's help, and after Japan's defeat, it seemed clear, China would need to find its own solutions. Following Stilwell's recall, it seemed likely that the path forward, as Vice President Wallace predicted, led directly to civil war.

SELECTED ADDITIONAL READINGS

General Joseph W. Stilwell's wartime diaries are available digitally online from the Hoover Institution, Stanford, California; selections from the diaries can be found in Joseph W. Stilwell, *The Stilwell Papers* (New York, 1948); Theodore White and Annalee Jacoby, *Thunder out of China* (New York, 1946); Theodore White, *In Search of History* (New York, 1978); Han Su-yin, *Destination: Chungking* (New York, 1942) and *Birdless Summer* (New York, 1968); Barbara Tuchman, *Stilwell and the American Experience in China, 1911–1945* (New York, 1971); Rana Mitter, *Forgotten Ally: China's World War II, 1937–1945* (Boston, 2013); Gordon Seagrave, *The Soong Dynasty* (New York, 1985); T. Christopher Jespersen, *American Images of China, 1931–1949* (Stanford, Ca., 1996); Graham Peck, *Two Kinds of Time* (Boston, 1967); John W. Dower, *A War without Mercy: Race and Power in the Pacific War* (New York, 1986); John W. Garver, *Chinese–Soviet Relations, 1937–1945: The Diplomacy of Chinese Nationalism* (New York, 1988);

Christopher Thorne, *Allies of a Kind: The United States, Great Britain, and the War against Japan, 1941–1945* (New York, 1978); Christopher Bayly and Tim Harper, *Forgotten Armies: The Fall of British Asia, 1941–1945* (Boston, 2005); Robert Dallek, *Franklin D. Roosevelt and American Foreign Policy, 1932–1945* (New York, 1979); Lloyd Eastman, *Seeds of Destruction: Nationalist China in War and Revolution, 1937–1949* (Stanford, Ca., 1984); Xiaoyuan Liu, *A Partnership for Disorder: China, the United States, and Their Policies for the Postwar Disposition of the Japanese Empire* (New York, 1996); Ronald Spector, *Eagle against the Sun: The American War with Japan* (New York, 1985); Mark Gallicchio, *The African American Encounter with Japan and China: Black Internationalism in Asia, 1895–1945* (Chapel Hill, N.C., 2000); Karen Leong, *Pearl S. Buck, Anna May Wong, Mayling Soong and the Transformation of American Orientalism* (Berkeley, Ca., 2005); Michael Schaller, *The U.S. Crusade in China, 1938–1945* (New York, 1979).

CHAPTER 5

Americans Encounter
the Chinese Revolution

The antagonism between Stilwell and Chiang comprised only part of a larger Chinese struggle. Throughout the country's vast interior, the Communist–Nationalist rivalry continued, with civil war simmering just beneath the façade of nominal cooperation. Centered in the remote northwestern capital of Yan'an, where many lived in caves carved from the sand hills, the Communists spent the war years building a mass peasant army while skirmishing with the Japanese. When they entered the United Front in 1936, Mao's followers controlled a few thousand square miles of territory, a population of about 1 million, and an army of around 90,000. They appeared to be a negligible force compared to the GMD. When Japan surrendered in August 1945, the Communists fielded 1 million troops and governed 100 million Chinese. Four years later, Chiang had fled to Taiwan and all China was theirs.

By the end of 1938, Japanese invaders occupied the most valuable part of China, roughly the eastern third on a line from Beijing to Guangzhou. When the Nationalist armies and government moved west to Chongqing, they left the fate and loyalty of hundreds of millions of Chinese up for grabs. Chiang traded space for time, waiting for U.S. aid and, he hoped, an American war with Japan. The regime clung to power as best it could, hoarding much of what it received in U.S. aid for later use. Meanwhile, Communist organizers filled the vacuum created by the GMD retreat. In the countryside, often behind Japanese lines, they rallied political support and recruited soldiers.

Chiang was reluctant to initiate any kind of grass-roots mobilization that might challenge landlord control of the countryside as well as Japanese occupation. To win over peasants, he would risk alienating the landed gentry. If he alienated the gentry, who would support and fund his campaign against the Communists? Perhaps a solution lay with the United States. If American forces did most of the fighting against Japan, even as the United States provided military and economic aid to the Nationalist regime, Chiang could marshal the strength for a postwar showdown.

As the Nationalists abandoned much of eastern China, Communist organizers arrived to rally peasants against the Japanese. Although Mao initiated a rectification campaign in 1942 to stifle dissent and promote exclusively his own ideas within the Communist movement, Communist propaganda stressed patriotic themes. A report by U.S. military intelligence chronicled how this operated at the village level. The party's "retinue of propagandists, social and economic workers, school teachers" arrived and they "immediately started organizing the training the peasant masses for resistance through guerrilla warfare." The central motive behind these methods was "that social and economic levels of the peasants had to be improved in order to maintain morale" and "instill among the people a will to resist Japan and support their own armies."

Rather than attacking most land owners or implementing rigid Marxist schemes that might divide the community, the Communists promoted moderate and practical reforms, such as reducing rents and interest rates. The details of the program were less important than the mere fact that the peasants were being treated as human beings. Again, journalist Theodore White described what he saw as the Communists' formula for success.

> If you take a peasant who has been swindled, beaten and kicked about for all his walking days and whose father has transmitted to him an emotion of bitterness reaching back for generations—if you take such a peasant, treat him like a man, ask his opinion, let him vote for a local government, let him organize his own police . . . decide on his own taxes and vote himself a reduction in rent and interest—if you do all that the peasant becomes a man who has something to fight for, and he will fight to preserve it against any enemy, Japanese or Chinese.

The Communists, White reported, helped peasants gather their harvest, taught him "to read and write and fight off the Japanese who raped his wife and tortured his mother." In response, they developed "loyalty to the army and the government and to the party that controls them. Gradually, the peasant votes for that party, thinks the way that party wants him to think, and in many ways becomes an active participant." In countless villages, the Communists organized local defense groups, agricultural cooperatives, schools, and political indoctrination classes. Many peasants believed that the Communists were in the forefront of the struggle to resist Japan and remake China.

The Japanese retaliated against Communist guerrilla attacks in north China during 1941 by waging a terror campaign. The Imperial Army's "Three All Policy" of "Burn All, Kill All, Loot All" led to the destruction of countless villages accused of harboring Communists. Although the savage attacks took a heavy toll, they became a recruiting tool to rally enraged peasants. The Communists harnessed powerful nationalist and revolutionary impulses that formed a wave that eventually carried them to power.

AMERICANS AND THE CHINESE COMMUNISTS, 1942–1944

After the flurry of interest generated in 1937 by Edgar Snow's *Red Star over China,* the U.S. public and government took little notice of the ongoing Communist movement. Although the Communists were part of the United Front, American diplomats and soldiers in China had almost no contact with them.[1] In the late 1930s, a handful of American journalists and adventurers followed Snow's footsteps by sneaking past the GMD blockade into Communist-controlled territory. They included Peggy Snow, Owen Lattimore, T. A. Bisson, Agnes Smedley, Phillip Jaffe, Evans Carlson, and, in 1941, Ernest Hemingway. Nearly all praised the high morale, social reform, and patriotic fervor they observed. Most of these Americans were committed leftists, a fact that diminished their credibility among U.S. government officials.

As larger numbers of American soldiers, diplomats, and journalists entered China after the Pearl Harbor attack, interest in the Communists grew. Among the most curious were a group of Chinese-speaking Foreign Service officers, several of whom had grown up as "missionary kids" in China. These junior diplomats, some of whom also advised Stilwell, joined with journalists to argue for closer scrutiny of the Communist movement. The more frustrated they became with the Nationalists, the more interest they expressed in the Communists.

This new American attention presented both danger and opportunity for the Communists. Mao, like most Chinese, rejoiced when the United States joined the war effort, but feared that Chiang intended to use American weapons against domestic rivals. By participating in the war effort, the Communists hoped, they could restrain Chiang, receive some American aid themselves, and win a measure of legitimacy in American eyes. Zhou Enlai, the Communist representative in Chongqing, took the lead in contacting Americans. Nearly every American who met Zhou, from Lauchlin Currie in 1940 to Henry Kissinger in 1971, came away charmed. Although closely scrutinized by GMD police, Zhou entertained foreign journalists, diplomats, and military officers in his tiny apartment. He extended invitations to visit Yan'an where, he assured them, they would encounter a completely different China.

During much of 1942 and 1943, American diplomats in Chongqing urged their superiors to accept Zhou's invitation. John S. Service, a member of the embassy staff and adviser to Stilwell, feared that not only the Communists but also the Chinese "liberals" of all persuasion deeply resented the policy of exclusive aid to the GMD. The policy might push these groups "toward friendship with Russia." Like most of the embassy staff, Service stressed the importance of learning more about the Communists. What, he asked "is the form of their local government?

---

[1] Under the United Front, the Communists were permitted to maintain a small liaison office in Chongqing, but their base area in the Northwest remained under GMD blockade.

How 'communistic' is it? Does it show any democratic character or possibilities? Has it won the support of the people? How does it compare with conditions" in the parts of China under GMD control? Service wanted to know how strong militarily the Communists were and whether they could be of "value to the Allied Cause."

Service, along with fellow diplomats John P. Davies and Raymond Ludden, feared that the alliance with Chiang would pull the United States into a civil war, almost certainly pushing Mao closer to the Soviet Union. If the United States hoped to influence the direction of nationalism in China and the rest of Asia, Davies wrote his superiors in Washington, American policy must "move with the historical stream rather than fighting it." The Communists, like it or not, were destined to play a major role in China's future and it seemed utter folly to ignore them.

For his own reasons, Stilwell favored cooperation with Yan'an. He wanted to use Communist troops as part of his hoped-for ground offensive. In contrast to the GMD—sunk by "corruption, neglect, chaos, trading with the enemy" and by their "callous disregard for all the rights of men," the Communists, he heard, had "reduced taxes, rents and interest" and "practiced what they preached."

But until the summer of 1944, Roosevelt refused to budge from his blanket support of Chiang. Only when the ICHIGO offensive showed the folly of Chiang and Chennault's air war strategy did the president change course. As China faced collapse, he insisted that Chiang permit official American contact with Yan'an. Roosevelt wanted to explore options for dealing with the Communists, either as a junior partner in a coalition with the GMD or separately. If nothing else, putting out American feelers to to the Communists might frighten Chiang into behaving more responsibly.

In mid-1944 Chiang reluctantly bowed to Roosevelt's request to open American contact with the Communists. A delegation of journalists went first. After three miserable years in Chongqing, these Americans described Yan'an as a "wonderland city." In dozens of articles sent home they described the population as "better fed, huskier, and more energetic than in other parts of China." Peasants described the local government as a friend, not an oppressor. Brooks Atkinson of the *New York Times* considered the soldiers of the Communist Eighth Route Army "among the best clothed and best fed this writer has seen anywhere in China." Another journalist wrote that any American officer would be "proud to command these tough, well-fed, hardened troops." GMD censors gutted much of the praise before the copy reached America, and the reporting so upset Chiang that he forbade nearly all follow-up visits by journalists.

The first group of official Americans reached Yan'an in July 1944. Dubbed the Dixie Mission (in a nod to their presence in "rebel" territory), it consisted of about two dozen military personnel, weather technicians, interpreters, and Foreign Service officers. The mission quickly took on a life of its own, with most of the group sharing John Service's enthusiasm. "We have come into a different country," he wrote, "and are meeting a different people." The Communists were similarly encouraged.

Dixie Mission member John S. Service in Yenan, 1944. Left to right: Zhou Enlai, Zhu De, Service, Mao Zedong, Yeh Jianying. (National Archives)

Between July and November 1944, they feted the Americans as honored guests. Top Communist leaders mixed closely with the group. Mao questioned Service in detail about American policy. Washington had nothing to fear, Mao stressed, because "even the most conservative American businessman can find nothing in our program to object to." However, Mao noted, the Communists were vulnerable and eager to cooperate because "we must have American help." It was important to "know what you Americans are thinking and planning. We cannot risk crossing you, cannot risk conflict with you." These conversations along with what he observed in Yan'an convinced Service that if current trends prevailed, the Communists would soon become the "dominant force in China."

In their talks with the Dixie members, Communist leaders described their efforts to maintain an uneasy truce with the GMD while fighting the Japanese and implementing social reforms. They acknowledged that part of their interest in forging ties with Washington was to restrain Chiang. They did not anticipate much aid from the Soviet Union. The Americans who engaged in these discussions considered Mao both a dedicated Communist and a sincere nationalist determined to restore China as a great power. Mao implied, and the Americans inferred, that he envisioned China as a stabilizing force in Asia and a possible counterweight to Soviet influence. A Communist-ruled China, Mao stressed, need not threaten postwar U.S. interests. In the meantime, he pledged to do what he could to prevent a break with the GMD.

At a more practical level, officers from the Office of Strategic Services in Yan'an offered Communist troops basic instruction in the use of American weapons. They planned to train sabotage squads that could be unleashed against the Japanese. Such small acts of cooperation convinced Mao that U.S. policy might actually shift away from exclusive cooperation with the GMD. As the Communists knew, part of the command crisis between Stilwell and Chiang stemmed from the American commander's desire to get weapons to the Communists who, as he put it, "will fight."

Stilwell, of course, never had the chance to test his belief. In October 1944, Chiang and Patrick Hurley convinced the president to recall Stilwell and continue to exclusively aid the Nationalist regime. From this point on, Hurley, with Roosevelt's tacit consent, pressed the Communists to accept a subordinate role in a coalition led by Chiang. American diplomats who criticized Hurley were gradually removed from China. In February 1945, when Roosevelt and Stalin convened the Yalta Conference, the president pressed the case for dealing only with Chiang.

Earlier, on November 7, 1944, Hurley, now U.S. ambassador, paid an unexpected visit to Yenan. As he stepped off the plane and was greeted by the head of the Dixie mission, a visibly surprised Zhou Enlai yelled, "Keep him here until I can find Chairman Mao." Hurley, who privately called Mao "Moose Dung" and Zhou "Joe N. Lie," then stunned his hosts by bellowing a Choctaw Indian war cry he had learned as a child in Oklahoma. It proved the first of many bizarre outbursts. Soon, the Communist leaders referred to Hurley as "the clown."

The Mercurial and immaculately tailored Patrick Hurley escorting Mao Zedong to peace talks in Chungking, 1944. (© Corbis)

In their initial discussion, Hurley proposed to Mao that the Communists join the GMD in a coalition government. To alleviate Communist doubts, the ambassador promised that it would be a partnership of equals. Washington would distribute aid to both groups. Mao, although skeptical, signed a "Five Point Agreement" to this effect drafted by Hurley. Zhou returned with Hurley to Chongqing to finalize the terms. However, when Zhou met with Chiang and Hurley, the ambassador told him that before entering a coalition the Communists must dissolve their armed forces. This contradicted the provisional agreement and prompted Zhou's return to Yan'an. Mao concluded that Hurley, if not the U.S. government, had deceived him.

Hurley, in turn, blamed the Communists' refusal to surrender their army on backstabbing by pro-Communist American diplomats and military personnel loyal to Stilwell. He resolved to force the Communists to resume negotiations by purging "disloyal" members of his staff and thereby showing Mao and Zhou they had no choice but to accept his terms.

Reluctant to parlay further with Hurley, early in January 1945 Mao and Zhou made a secret offer to meet directly with President Roosevelt in Washington. They asked members of the Dixie Mission to forward their request in a confidential message. Mao and Zhou offered to fly around the world to explain to Roosevelt what a mess Hurley had made. Once he understood what lay at stake, they believed, cooperation with the United States might be possible.

Yet again, however, Hurley blocked their path. The ambassador found out about the plan, probably from a radio operator with Naval Group China attached to the Dixie team. The mole passed the message on to Hurley, General Wedemeyer, and Chiang, rather than to its intended recipient. Hurley then warned the president against any contact with the Communists, accusing them and their American sympathizers of causing all of China's problems. The only solution in China, Hurley insisted, was to force Mao to submit to Chiang.

Encumbered by a thousand problems related to coalition warfare, preparing for the end of the European war and the intensification of the Pacific conflict, and hoping to preserve cooperation with the Soviets, Roosevelt devoted little attention to the latest China flap. Without much reflection, he agreed to spurn Mao's offer and authorized Hurley to purge the ranks of "disloyal" Americans in Chongqing. Hurley promptly removed anyone who challenged his faith in Chiang. At one point he threatened to shoot an embassy staffer who criticized the GMD. Several others were promptly sent home or, as they put it, "Hurleyed out of China."

THE PRESIDENT'S NEW ASIA POLICY: YALTA

Although no longer at the top of his form, the ailing president understood by early 1945 that his dream of fostering a "powerful, united, and pro-American China" was turning into a nightmare. Not only had China failed to add much to the fight against Japan, but also it seemed likely to become a postwar liability.

At best, China might finish the war with a weak GMD government or a fragile coalition. At worst, it could descend into civil war, resulting either in a Communist victory or in Soviet domination. To prevent this, Roosevelt decided to make a deal with the Soviet dictator Josef Stalin who, like Chiang, had added Generalissimo to his impressive list of titles.

Stalin had always felt ambivalence toward foreign Communists, especially those like Mao who established a power base independent of Moscow. Many of Mao's targets in the party rectification campaign during the early 1940s had been Chinese trained in or linked to the Soviet Union. Possibly, Stalin saw Soviet interests best served by a weak GMD in charge of China or a China divided between the two rival parties. Since Stalin intended to reclaim resources, rail lines, and ports in Manchuria once under Czarist but now under Japanese control, he would probably have dealt with any Chinese regime that gave him what he desired.

In February 1945, Stalin, Roosevelt, and Churchill conferred at Yalta, the Black Sea resort on the Crimean peninsula. The "big three" discussed the final stages of the war against Germany and the division of liberated Europe. Stalin insisted on de facto domination of Poland and much of Eastern Europe, areas recently liberated by the Red Army. Roosevelt had little leverage and argued for granting the region at least a measure of autonomy.

Stalin and Roosevelt had an easier time bargaining over Asia. To the relief of U.S. military planners, Stalin pledged to join the war against Japan approximately three months after Germany surrendered. Americans believed this would speed victory and save lives. Stalin promised to support Chiang's regime and not aid the Chinese Communists. But he conditioned these promises on Soviet control over two major ports and two railroads in Manchuria. In addition, Outer Mongolia must remain nominally independent but in the Soviet orbit. Roosevelt quickly agreed, with hardly a thought about how Chiang would react.

The so-called Yalta Far Eastern Agreement, concluded on February 11, 1945, remained secret until the following summer, although details soon leaked out. Both Chinese factions felt betrayed by their ostensible allies. Stalin made clear that his priority was reclaiming strategic interests in Manchuria, not abetting the Communists. Roosevelt proved ready to sacrifice Chinese territory—which Stalin would probably claim anyway—in return for Soviet assistance in defeating Japan. Stalin and Roosevelt may have hoped their bargain would pressure Mao and Chiang to enter some sort of coalition, but this was a secondary consideration. Both Chinese factions recognized the risk of putting too much reliance on their foreign patrons.

In March 1945, John Service, after a visit to Washington, briefly rejoined the fast-diminishing ranks of the Dixie Mission in Yan'an. Mao urged him to push for a change in Washington's policy of supporting Chiang. If Roosevelt followed Hurley's approach, Mao warned, "all that America has been working for will be lost." There was "no such thing," Mao explained, "as American not intervening in China! You are here as China's greatest ally. The fact of your presence is tremendous."

Service and his colleagues tried to alert Washington to Hurley's mischief. On February 28, while the ambassador was in the United States for consultations, nearly the entire embassy staff sent a joint telegram to the State Department warning that he would drag the United States into a civil war. They stressed the "advantage of having the Communists helped by the United States rather than seeking Russian aid or intervention." America's future in Asia, the Treasury Department attaché in Chongqing wrote, must "not be left in the hands of a bungler like Hurley."

The warning fell on deaf ears. In Washington, Hurley and Wedemeyer dismissed all criticism as Communist inspired. The only thing that imperiled China's unity, they told the president, was a weak Communist movement assisted by American sympathizers. Chiang could easily "put down the Communist rebellion" if he received full U.S. support. On April 2, 1945, Hurley emerged from a meeting with the president (who would die two weeks later) to announce that since the Chinese Communists were the main source of disorder in China, they would receive no support from the United States.

AMERICAN–COMMUNIST HOSTILITY, JUNE TO AUGUST 1945

Before Hurley's announcement, the Chinese Communists had muted their public anger with U.S. policy. After April 2, however, they unleashed criticism of Hurley and other "reactionaries" who plotted civil war. When Mao spoke to an assembly of party activists that month, he warned that some Americans were plotting with Chiang to attack the party as soon as Japan surrendered. Mao's suspicion increased in June when he learned that John Service had been arrested in Washington for passing classified reports critical of Chiang and Hurley to the leftist magazine *Amerasia*.[2] His arrest seemed to confirm that the new president, Harry S. Truman, had endorsed the hard-line anti-Communist approach toward China. From Yan'an, the Communists broadcast a radio message beamed to the United States: if the American imperialists did not "withdraw their hands . . . then the Chinese people will teach them a lesson they deserve."

Communist denunciations of U.S. policy became more shrill as the Pacific War drew to a close. Roosevelt's death in mid-April added to the problem. Although he had ultimately declined to support them, Roosevelt remained a symbol of the antifascist alliance. Mao harbored some hope he might reverse his decision to back Hurley and Chiang. But Truman's apparent endorsement of the Hurley line, along with his firing of several liberal New Deal advisers and increased verbal sparring with the Soviet Union, seemed to doom any chance of reconciliation.

---

[2]Service was not indicted for the transgression but it effectively ended his diplomatic career. For much of the next decade he was accused by pro-GMD politicians of helping the Communists gain power in China.

By the time Germany surrendered in May, Truman had fallen further under the sway of several of Roosevelt's more conservative aides, including Navy Secretary James Forrestal and Ambassador to the Soviet Union Averell Harriman. They sharply condemned Soviet moves to dominate Eastern Europe and anticipated that Stalin would grab Manchuria and as much of China as he could unless he was stopped. The Chinese Communists, they argued, would act as Soviet agents. Outside of government, influential voices in foreign affairs, such as future Secretary of State John Foster Dulles, spoke of America's responsibility to protect China from the "predatory designs of an alien power." Chiang had chosen to "rely on the ultimate support of Christian democracies" and must not be abandoned.

Truman's view of China fell in line with those of Harriman and Forrestal. They identified China as one of the flashpoints in U.S.–Soviet relations. If Washington abandoned Chiang, Harriman warned, "we should have to face ultimately the fact that two or three hundred millions of people would march when the Kremlin ordered." The Chinese could become a "red horde."

By the summer of 1945, the Grand Alliance was largely a shell, sustained only by the need to defeat Japan. For the Truman administration the dilemma persisted that although it desired Soviet military assistance against Japan, it feared Soviet expansion in northeast Asia as a consequence of that assistance.

The Potsdam Conference, held in mid-July 1945 in the suburbs of conquered Berlin, revealed these divisions. Soviet and American delegations accused each other of harboring expansionist dreams. The creation of puppet regimes in Poland and elsewhere in Eastern Europe, the Americans argued, showed bad faith. Stalin accused the Americans of breaking promises to provide German reparations and of hatching plots to restore German power. Amid these verbal clashes, Truman learned that scientists in New Mexico had secretly tested an atomic bomb. The new weapon might assure the defeat of Japan without Soviet assistance or a costly invasion. A quick surrender would keep Soviet forces out of Manchuria and prevent them from seeking more privileges or aiding the Chinese Communists. As Truman's new secretary of state James F. Byrnes put it, the atomic bomb might get Japan "to surrender before Russia goes into the war and this will save China." If Russia fought Japan, Byrnes explained, "Stalin will take over and China will suffer." On his way home from Potsdam, Truman told a group of naval officers that with the new weapon, "we did not need the Russians or any other nation."

Most historians agree that Truman's primary motive in using two atomic bombs against Japan was to minimize Allied casualties and end the war quickly. Objectively, it had been clear for months that Japan was defeated, but its military leadership refused to surrender. American strategists hoped that the dramatic impact of a nuclear weapon, combined with a Soviet declaration of war, would stun the Japanese into surrender before a Soviet offensive went far and without the need to invade Japan.

Although not entirely clear, it appears that Stalin's goals in China were fulfilled by the February 1945 Yalta accords. He expected to regain the territory and influence lost to Japan in 1905. He wanted control over Manchuria's two major railroads and the ports of Dairen (Dalian) and Port Arthur (Lushun). If Chiang acquiesced to these demands, Stalin seemed prepared to deal exclusively with the Nationalist regime and forego cooperation with the Chinese Communists. The Soviet leader showed scant enthusiasm for promoting Mao's agenda.

On August 14, 1945, after the United States dropped two atomic bombs on Japan (August 6 and 9) and the Soviet Union declared war on Japan (August 8), Chinese Nationalist and Soviet negotiators in Moscow signed a treaty of friendship that implemented the Yalta accords. Chiang agreed to continued Soviet domination of Outer Mongolia and acquiesced to Soviet control of Manchurian ports and railroads. In return, Stalin pledged "moral, material and military support to China and solely to the Chinese Nationalist Government" led by Chiang. Party leaders in Yan'an, U.S. observers there noted, appeared stunned by the terms, which seemed a sellout.

THE JAPANESE SURRENDER AND ITS AFTERMATH

Japan's surrender came on the same day as the Soviets and Chinese Nationalists reached their agreement. Despite Tokyo's defeat, its wartime conquests had fatally undermined Western colonialism in Southeast Asia. Within a few years the Dutch, British, and French lost nearly all their colonies. (The United States, which before the war had decided to grant independence to the Philippines, did so in 1946.) Japan's defeat also unleashed China's civil war.

On August 14, Stalin sent Mao a message urging him to resume peace talks in Chongqing, along the lines demanded by Hurley. Soviet motives were clear. Negotiations would reduce tensions with the United States and allow the Soviets time to consolidate gains in Manchuria. Under joint pressure from the Soviets, Americans, and Nationalists, Mao dropped his refusal to parlay and agreed to return to Chongqing. But the Communists also resolved to seize territory and expand their influence in Manchuria despite the lack of Soviet support.

Both the Communists and the Nationalists rushed to seize territory and weapons held by the 2 to 3 million or so Japanese and puppet troops in north China and Manchuria. To block Communist gains, on August 15 President Truman issued General Order No. 1. Among other things, it instructed all Japanese commanders in China to surrender their positions and arms only to Chiang's representatives. They were to defend their positions against the Communists until properly relieved. This marked a new level of U.S. commitment to Chiang's survival. The Communists denounced the order as a betrayal of wartime cooperation and insisted on their right to disarm the Japanese.

The U.S. military quickly redeployed by ship and plane GMD military units from the interior and dispatched about 60,000 Marines from the Pacific to secure ports, rail lines, and airfields in north China. During August and September, American and Nationalist units coordinated their movements with the Japanese to block Communist seizures of lines of communication. One disgruntled Marine described these maneuvers in a letter to his senator. His unit was told they were going to China to disarm the Japanese. But the "Chinese had the situation well in hand, and have since gone so far as to re-arm some Japanese units for added protection against Chinese Communists." Once in China, the Marines were told that they needed to remain in north China until Chiang Kai-shek's forces arrived. "In other words, we are here to protect . . . Chiang's interests against possible Communist uprisings. Everything we do here points directly or indirectly towards keeping the Chinese Communists subdued."

Initially, Soviet occupation forces in Manchuria appeared to keep their distance from Chinese Communists. By late October, however, their behavior changed. This reflected several factors, including the large U.S. air and sea lift of Nationalist forces into the area and the general deterioration of U.S.–Soviet relations, especially in Europe. Gradually, Soviet commanders in Manchuria began turning over to the Communists stockpiles of seized Japanese weapons and in some cases blocked the movement of Nationalist troops into ports and airfields. But Soviet behavior remained variable during late 1945 and during 1946, sometimes cooperating with the Communists and sometimes shunning them.

Peace talks resumed in Chongqing during September 1945 but soon deadlocked. Chiang insisted that the Communists surrender their armed forces and territory as a precondition to forming a coalition government. Both Chiang and Hurley believed that Mao would relent, given more or less united Soviet and American support for the Nationalist government. But Mao refused to cave and skirmishes in north China between the rivals grew more frequent during the autumn months. Typically, GMD forces held urban areas, whereas the Communists dominated the countryside. As U.S. military planners in Washington recognized, assuring Nationalist victory would require a major commitment of money, weapons, and perhaps troops.

Undeterred, Ambassador Hurley recommended an open-ended commitment. But his past overconfidence and erratic behavior had eroded his credibility. From China, General Wedemeyer gloomily concluded that Chiang could not unify China without direct American intervention. Given the recent end of the world war, the economic and political challenges in Europe, and the dubious prospect of success in China, neither President Truman nor his chief advisers favored a commitment on this scale. America's large wartime army was rapidly demobilizing and the public had no enthusiasm for fighting a new war in Asia. Sustaining a pro-American China might be emotionally important, but not important enough to justify sending hundreds of thousands of combat troops into battle.

The politics of China policy grew even more confused on November 27, 1945, when Ambassador Hurley, then visiting Washington, abruptly resigned. At a hastily arranged press conference, Hurley gave a rambling account of the administration's alleged mistakes. He condemned the "Hydra-headed direction" of China policy and blasted diplomats who allegedly "sided with the Communist armed party . . . against American policy." Hurley's effort to blame others for his botched approach fueled later charges that traitors had "lost China."

President Truman, who angrily called Hurley a "son-of-a bitch," rushed to contain the damage done by the resignation. He appointed the just-retired army chief of staff, General George C. Marshall, as his personal representative to China. Marshall, a commander held in awe by nearly all Americans, would, Truman hoped, nullify Hurley's libel and perhaps jolt Chinese rivals into serious negotiations. At the least, Marshall might prevent China from become one more flashpoint with the Soviet Union in the emerging Cold War.

SELECTED ADDITIONAL READINGS

Michael Schaller, *The U.S. Crusade in China, 1938–1945* (New York, 1979); Joseph Esherick, ed., *Lost Chance in China: The World War II Dispatches of John S. Service* (New York, 1975); John S. Service, *The Amerasia Papers: Some Problems in the History of U.S.–China Relations* (Berkeley, Ca., 1971); Lynn Joiner, *Honorable Survivor: Mao's China, McCarthy's America, and the Persecution of John S. Service* (Annapolis, Md., 2009); Richard Bernstein, *China 1945: Mao's Revolution and America's Fateful Choice* (New York, 2014); Harvey Klehr and Ronald Radosh, *The Amerasia Spy Case: Prelude to McCarthyism* (Chapel Hill, N.C., 1996); John Patton Davies, *Dragon by the Tail* (New York, 1972); Janice MacKinnon and Stephen MacKinnon, *Agnes Smedley: The Life and Times of an American Radical* (Berkeley, Ca., 1988); Stephen MacKinnon and Oris Friesen, *China Reporting: An Oral History of American Journalism in the 1930s and 1940s* (Berkeley, Ca., 1987); Tracy B. Strong and Helene Keyssar, *Right in Her Soul: The Life and Times of Anna Louise Strong* (New York, 1983); Kenneth Shewmaker, *Americans and Chinese Communists: A Persuasive Encounter* (Ithaca, N.Y., 1971); Carol Carter, *Mission to Yenan: American Liaison with the Chinese Communists, 1944–1947* (Lexington, Ky., 1997); James Reardon Anderson, *Yenan and the Great Powers* (New York, 1980); Mark Gallicchio, *The Cold War Begins: American East Asian Policy and the Fall of the Japanese Empire* (New York, 1988); Ronald Spector, *In the Ruins of Empire: The Japanese Surrender and the Battle for Postwar Asia* (New York, 2008); Odd Arne Westad, *Cold War and Revolution: Soviet–American Rivalry and the Origins of the Chinese Civil War, 1944–1946* (New York, 1993) and *Brothers in Arms: The Rise and Fall of the Sino–Soviet Alliance, 1945–1963* (Washington, D.C., 1999).

Who Lost China? From the Marshall Mission to the Creation of the People's Republic

I n December 1945, President Harry S. Truman sent one more American media-tor to try to avert disaster in China. Although neither the president nor his emissary, General George C. Marshall, considered the prospects for a "united, democratic, and pro-American China" likely, they hoped to avert a worst-case scenario: a civil war between the Nationalists and Communists that dragged in Japanese armies stranded in China, Soviet troops in Manchuria, and U.S. Marines in north China. Meanwhile, the American public and men still in uniform de-manded the rapid demobilization and return home of the vast wartime military. Misguided and gullible public opinion, Time Inc. publisher Henry Luce com-plained, endangered China. Hoping to swing opinion, Luce put Chiang's portrait on the cover of *Time* for a sixth time and published an editorial in *Life* on the importance of standing with the Generalissimo. In the postwar world, he opined, "the safest thing for us to do is rededicate our wartime alliance with China and its government." Luce dismissed criticism of Chiang and his inner circle. "Man for man," he countered, Chiang's advisers were "probably as able and as liberal as Truman's cabinet."

The Truman administration had several goals in China, none as clear cut as those voiced by Luce. U.S. policy makers wanted to remove quickly the ap-proximately 2 million Japanese troops in Manchuria and north China, replacing them with GMD forces. This, they hoped, would speed the Soviet withdrawal from Manchuria, eliminate the need to keep Marines on duty, and prevent the movement of Communist troops into disputed areas. Achieving these goals, the Americans believed, would encourage political compromise in China. In practice, however, U.S. efforts centered mostly on helping the Nationalists, even if it meant temporarily utilizing Japanese troops to do so. This, along with continued military aid to the Nationalists, hindered, rather than helped, political accommodation.

The Joint Chiefs of Staff had informed Truman that keeping Marines in north China was needed to hold back Communist forces and to repatriate the Japanese. If civil war erupted, both Chinese factions were likely to try to enlist the

Japanese. Japanese participation in Chinese fighting would probably prompt greater Soviet intervention. However, if civil war broke out, the Joint Chiefs were uncertain whether the Nationalists could hold Manchuria or north China whether or not the Marines and Japanese departed quickly or lingered.

Since virtually no one in Washington favored sending additional American soldiers to China, Marshall had limited leverage. He decided that the one hope of preventing civil war was to extricate Soviet, American, and Japanese forces as quickly as possible while pressing the Communists and Nationalists to create a coalition government. There were, in fact, moderate elements in both parties who favored a coalition, at least temporarily. But to promote compromise, Marshall needed authority to threaten or reward the contending parties.

On December 9, 1945, Truman and Secretary of State James F. Byrnes told Marshall that if the Communists were prepared to cooperate but the Nationalists balked, he should deal directly with the Communists. If, on the other hand, the Reds were recalcitrant, he could give full U.S. support to Chiang and help move additional armies north. But two days later, Truman reversed himself. No matter what happened or how accommodating the Chinese Communists proved, Truman ordered, Marshall must provide "at least indirect support" to Chiang against the Communists. If the Communists refused to make "reasonable concessions,"

In 1946, Gen. George C. Marshal brings together Communist leader Zhou Enlai with the GMD foreign minister in Chongqing to seek peace. The effort failed. (© Bettmann/CORBIS)

Marshall could assist the Nationalists more fully. Even if Chiang completely blocked a compromise, the United States would not abandon him because this would create a "divided China" or the "resumption of Russian power in Manchuria." As Marshall recognized, no matter what Chiang did, Washington "would have to swallow its pride and much of its policy" and continue to support the GMD.

Whether or not Chiang knew of the one-sided guidelines Truman gave Marshall, the Generalissimo believed that ultimately the United States would support him against Mao. This, as much as anything, probably doomed Marshall's effort. Nevertheless, securing a short-term armistice remained a possibility. As Marshall prepared to travel, for example, Stalin conferred with Jiang Jingguo (the Generalissimo's son) in Moscow. Stalin insisted he would honor his pledge in the recent Sino–Soviet treaty and not support the Communists—so long as the Nationalists maintained their neutrality in the emerging contest between the Soviet Union and the United States. Stalin praised Marshall for trying to work out a peaceful solution in China and promised to withdraw Soviet forces from Manchuria early in 1946.

The Chinese Communists also greeted Marshall's appointment as a positive "change in American policy." Zhou Enlai even agreed to return to Chongqing to participate in a "political consultative conference." But when Communist delegates already in Chongqing arrived at the airport to greet Marshall's incoming flight, a squad of GMD police "started to chase the Communist representatives off the field" and beat them until American diplomats intervened.

As 1946 began, Mao confided to his inner circle the extent of his disappointment with the meager level of Soviet political and material support. The Communists had anticipated strong Soviet backing for their efforts to expand into Manchuria and a more public show of support vis-à-vis the Nationalists. Stalin's tacit cooperation with the GMD, his endorsement of the Marshall Mission, and the refusal of many Soviet commanders in Manchuria to help Communist forces take control of cities and rail lines left Mao no alternative but to seek an American-brokered temporary deal with Chiang.

Within the constraints imposed on him, Marshall tried to be even handed. The Communists insisted on real power sharing and maintenance of a separate armed force. Chiang, convinced he had full American and substantial Soviet support, demanded dissolution of Communist military units and offered his rivals a limited governing role. Talks in Chongqing deadlocked while fighting flared in Manchuria. Soviet cooperation with the GMD eroded after Chiang balked at Stalin's demand for the creation of joint trading companies along the Soviet–Chinese border. Although U.S. ships and planes continued to ferry GMD armies north, Marshall somehow managed to broker a temporary ceasefire during January and February 1946.

The Manchuria truce broke down in April. As Soviet occupation forces withdrew from the region (generally looting all the industrial machinery they could carry), they coordinated their movements with Communist units. This precipitated a scramble among Chinese to take control of strategic locations.

Several local ceasefires were imposed and then broken as battlefield fortunes fluctuated.

As the fighting escalated, U.S. aid, both civilian and military, continued to flow to the Nationalists. In addition to stocks of food, medicines, and raw materials, the U.S. military turned over to Chiang's forces more than $1 billion worth of military equipment already in China. Mao accused the Americans of blatantly encouraging civil war. Reactionaries in Washington, he declared, were attempting to seize what he called the "intermediate zone" of semicolonial countries as a prelude to attacking the Soviet Union. Chiang, bolstered by the influx of American aid, on July 1 ordered a nationwide offensive against the Communists.

Marshall pressed Truman for authority to cut off military aid to the GMD, whom he saw as the more flagrant transgressors. Politics aside, Marshall argued that even with his new American weapons Chiang would most likely lose a civil war. The best way to stem a Communist victory, he believed, was to force Chiang to offer the Reds a meaningful compromise. Truman reluctantly agreed and on July 29, 1946, Marshall imposed an embargo on the transfer of arms to China. Stunned by this move (which lasted a year), Chiang agreed to establish joint truce teams to prevent further fighting. This slowed, but failed to stop, the spread of civil war. The partial halt in combat created an opportunity to withdraw most of the Marines and the surrendered Japanese from battle zones, although a few thousand Japanese soldiers fought alongside the GMD until 1949.

As Marshall tried to stop the fighting out of concern the Communists would win, Stalin pressed the Communists to accept a compromise. The Soviet leader worried that Mao's forces might lose in a full-scale war. Alternatively, their success might provoke U.S. military intervention. Stalin publicly condemned U.S. aid to the Nationalists, but privately suggested that the United States and the Soviet Union adopt what he called a "common policy" (presumably some sort of truce based on a coalition government or partition) to stabilize China.

Chinese public opinion placed most of the blame for renewed fighting on Chiang and his American enablers. A local crime in December 1946 galvanized anti-American opinion. That month several young Marines raped a Beijing college student named Shen Chong. The attack and subsequent court martial, in which U.S. authorities dealt lightly with the Americans, provoked anti-U.S. demonstrations around the country. Students and other activists demanded harsh punishment for the Marines, the withdrawal of foreign troops, and cessation of military aid to the GMD.

The anti-American demonstrations coincided with the collapse of peace talks and the ceasefire at the end of 1946. Both sides launched offensives when local conditions appeared favorable. Despite the arms embargo, Chiang believed that Washington would eventually turn the aid spigot back on. In January 1947, after a year in China, Marshall was called home by Truman to become secretary of state. As he departed, Marshall condemned both sides for betraying peace.

The end of the Marshall Mission coincided with a broader review of American foreign policy. The Truman administration in effect acknowledged that it had no solution for China and that control of China was not central to American security. Influenced by the ideas of George Kennan, head of the State Department's Policy Planning Staff, Truman and his key advisers refocused their strategic thinking. In the contest with the Soviet Union, Kennan argued, certain areas mattered more than others Western Europe and Japan, for example, were valuable because of their industrial–military potential; the Middle East had critical oil resources; but China, economically speaking, was a vast poorhouse. If the United States focused its attention and aid on holding those three contested zones, it would enjoy a vast advantage over the Soviet Union, even if Communism triumphed in China.

Kennan and his supporters stressed that harnessing the economies of Western Europe, Japan, and the Middle East to that of North America would effectively isolate and "contain" the Soviet Union. China was simply too weak and poor to justify a major commitment of American economic or military resources. In Asia, tiny Japan, with a fraction of China's population , could quickly become a pillar of U.S. regional influence and trade—once rebuilt. China, under any regime, would require decades before it became a substantial friend or foe.

As Navy Secretary James Forrestal remarked, "to have a run for our side in competition with the Soviet Union," the "time had come to put Germany, Japan, and the other affiliates of the Axis back to work." In the spring of 1947, Undersecretary of State Dean Acheson declared the United States would "rebuild the two great workshops of Europe and Asia," Germany and Japan.

CIVIL WAR TO LIBERATION

Three violent years elapsed between Marshall's departure from China and the creation of the People's Republic. During 1947, GMD forces captured the initiative. *Time* magazine congratulated Chiang on his "brilliant victories" over the rag-tag Communists. But the tide of battle soon reversed. By 1948, the GMD suffered from what an American military observer described as the "world's worst leadership." Ill-equipped but highly motivated and well-led Communist troops routed GMD armies from positions they could have "defended with broom sticks." A French military observer remarked that as much as anything, GMD corruption destroyed civilian morale and undermined support for and quality of Nationalist troops. A typical soldier serving in Chiang's armies was

> generally considered to be the scum of humanity. Except in elite divisions, such a conception could not be changed and morale remained low despite promised reforms. The soldier of Chiang Kai-shek knew not why he fought. Against the Japanese he could fight for his country and his people; but in this civil war a peasant soldier from Kwangtung province had no idea why he should be fighting in Shansi or Manchuria. Poorly fed, poorly paid, poorly clothed, poorly cared for, poorly armed, often short of ammunition—even at decisive moments— unsustained by any faith in a cause, the Nationalist soldier was easy prey for the clever and impassioned propaganda of the Communists.

During the civil war, the Nationalists not only squandered their initial military advantage, but also alienated almost all segments of society. Early on, as they reoccupied territory held by the Japanese, GMD civil and military leaders indulged in an orgy of personal aggrandizement. They seized for their personal use land and factories, made deals with Chinese collaborators, ignored the people who had suffered under Japanese occupation, and spent much of their time hunting real and alleged Communists. In rural areas, GMD officials often helped landlords collect past rents. Reconstruction proved a low priority.

The Communists adopted more flexible and popular approaches to governing areas that came under their control. In addition to military combat, they fought to transform village life. Communist organizers stoked the fury of the poorest peasants against large landowners, of debtors against creditors, of the exploited against the exploited. By pushing land and social reform, the Communists created a mass base and a pool of military recruits. During 1948, in massive battles in Manchuria and the north China plain, the GMD lost more than a million troops through death, disease, and desertion. Communist ranks expanded and seized the offensive.

As the tide of battle turned, the Communists showed less inclination to seek American favor and moved closer to the Soviets. Apparently surprised by Mao's rapid success, Stalin agreed to assist the Communists, especially in Manchuria. During 1948, Soviet technicians helped repair and maintain railroad lines and Soviet advisers trained some Communist troops. This aid was not wholly altruistic since the Soviet leader intended to maintain special privileges in Manchuria, whoever won the civil war. Yet, even while providing limited aid, Stalin still counseled restraint. For example, in January 1949, the Soviet leader urged Mao to halt his troops' advance at the Yangtze River, effectively creating a divided China. Mao ignored the advice and pushed south.

Stalin approved high-level contacts with the Chinese Communists only when their triumph appeared inevitable. In February 1949 he sent a top aide, Anastas Mikoyan, to confer with Mao. Mikoyan promised that once the Communists created a national government, the Soviet Union would promptly recognize and assist the new regime.

As civil war raged in China, the conflict became a partisan issue in American politics. In 1948, a group of mostly Republican members of the House and Senate criticized Truman's past efforts to promote a coalition government in China and accused him of doing too little to help Chiang. Many Republicans, along with Henry Luce's publications, repeated the accusation made by Patrick Hurley when he resigned as ambassador in 1945, blaming disloyal diplomats for the Communists' success.

Because it had succeeded so well in selling the Containment doctrine to the public, the Truman administration's stance on China seemed defensive. During 1947–1948, the president had successfully promoted the Greek–Turkish aid bill (Truman Doctrine) and the multi-billion-dollar European and Japanese recovery programs (Marshall Plan), launched the Berlin airlift, and created the Central

Intelligence Agency and unified Department of Defense. The administration had also implemented an internal security program. Together, these initiatives were designed to bolster key allies and safeguard the nation from subversion. Chiang's supporters in and out of Congress questioned why so much *less* had been done to help fight Communism in China. The answer, of course, was that few foreign policy or military experts thought China mattered much in the global power balance and concluded that Communism there could *not* be stopped at a reasonable cost. But the failure of the Truman administration to answer or address this question directly left critics free to snipe with impunity.

The make-believe world of many of Chiang's American allies showed in a May 1947 *Time* story describing Ch'en Li-fu, one of Chiang's most notoriously reactionary advisers. The magazine portrayed him as a modern Confucius—wise, modest, and struggling to build a democratic China. Millions of subscribers to *Time* and *Life*, two of the most popular weekly magazines during the late 1940s, read frequent flattering portraits of GMD officials and barbed attacks on the failure of the Truman administration to help America's friends and resist its foes in China.

Between 1931 and 1949, Chiang's portrait appeared on at least eight *Time* covers, more than any other foreign leader. In October 1947, after General Albert Wedemeyer returned from a fact-finding trip to China (where Secretary of State Marshall had sent him to placate Republican critics), *Life* endorsed the general's recommendation to increase military aid and denounced the administration for shelving it. *Life* also carried a sensationalist article by former ambassador to Russia, William Bullitt. A liberal turned arch-conservative, Bullitt insisted China must be "kept out of the hands of Stalin." Washington could do so "at a cost to ourselves which would be small compared to the magnitude of our vital interest in the independence of China."

Bullitt popularized the claim that Roosevelt had betrayed China at Yalta and that Truman perpetuated the outrage. He called for sending $1 billion to China and appointing General Douglas MacArthur, occupation commander in Japan and the Republican's favorite general, to supervise its distribution. The triumph of Communism in China, Bullitt warned, would ensure that "all Asia, including Japan, sooner or later, will fall into [Stalin's] hands." Bullitt predicted that U.S. the independence would "not live a generation longer than the independence of China."

Accounts in *Time* warned that Stalin planned to turn China against the United States, much as Japan had intended earlier. On March 29, 1948, the magazine published maps depicting a blade jutting out of a Communist China and slicing through Southeast Asia and Japan. Soviet bombers operating from China, *Time* warned, could threaten Alaska and the rest of North America.

In July 1949, a story in *Life* focused on the effort by retired Flying Tiger hero General Claire Chennault to revive his wartime unit to fight again on Chiang's behalf. "Last Call for China" proposed upgrading Chennault's Civil Air Transport freight service by granting it a number of fighter planes that could secure a sanctuary for the Nationalists in south and west China. This "fighting American," in *Life*'s words, could save a "third of the Good Earth and 150,000,000 people from Red Domination." In October 1949, *Reader's Digest*, the most widely circulated magazine in the United States, reprinted Chennault's plan under the title "Hold Em! Harass Em! Hamstring Em!" Unknown to the American public, the Central Intelligence Agency had secretly acquired control of Chennault's airline and used it to supply a variety of anti-Communist groups in Asia during the 1950s.

Some congressional Republicans recognized that China was a hot-button issue that they could use against Democrats. Since most Americans knew little more than that Chiang had been a wartime ally and that he was fighting Communists, it proved simple to accuse the administration and its supporters of weakness or even betrayal. Charging Truman with a "sellout" of China also undermined his Cold War achievements such as the Marshall Plan and the Berlin airlift. Many of Chiang's most ardent supporters in Congress cared little about China one way or the other. Senators William F. Knowland (later dubbed the Senator from Formosa), Styles Bridges, Owen Brewster, Kenneth Wherry, and (Democrat) Pat McCarran fell into this category. Others, such as Senator H. Alexander Smith and Congressman Walter Judd (a former medical missionary in China), believed sincerely in Chiang's cause. Richard Nixon, an ambitious young representative from California, straddled both camps.

Some members of this so-called China bloc were remarkably obtuse. Senator Wherry, for example, had declared that "with God's help we will lift up Shanghai, up and up, ever up, until it is just like Kansas City." Pat McCarran of Nevada enthusiastically promoted aid to Chiang's government, so long as it came in the form of silver mined in his state. When the State Department instead proposed food and medical relief, McCarran's interest flagged.

In 1949, Massachusetts Congressman John F. Kennedy, one of a handful of Democrats who focused on China, delivered a bitter attack on Truman's policies. He accused the president and his advisers of deserting China, "whose freedom we once fought to preserve." "What our young men had saved," he lamented, "our diplomats and president have frittered away."

Despite these pressures, the Truman administration resisted calls to intervene substantially in China's civil war. Although a strong anti-Communist, Truman also loathed the Nationalist leadership. He told aides that Chiang, his wife, the Soong family, and their ilk "were all thieves, every last one of them." Even Senator Arthur Vandenberg, the Republican's leading foreign policy spokesman, admitted privately that despite his sympathy for China, "there are limits to our resources and boundaries to our miracles." Democratic Senate Leader Tom Connally spoke more bluntly: "Any more aid to Chiang would be money down a rat hole." By the end of 1948, nearly all Americans who actually knew anything about China—diplomats, academics, business leaders, missionaries, journalists— opposed more than minimal aid to the Nationalist regime. Most had lost all confidence in Chiang and some even believed that a Communist regime might be better than prolonged chaos. They worried that sending more aid to the Nationalists would only drive a triumphant Mao closer into Stalin's embrace.

George Kennan, the so-called Father of Containment, typified the administration's "new thinking" about China. Even if the Communists triumphed, Kennan reasoned, China would remain a "vast poor house" for decades. It would drain Soviet resources, not enhance Soviet power. Eventually, Kennan and others in the State Department hoped, "nationalistic elements" among the Chinese Communists might, like the Tito regime in Yugoslavia, sever ties to the Soviet Union. The worst thing the United States could do was adopt policies that pushed Mao closer to Stalin.

A Gallup survey of April 1948 revealed that 55 percent of Americans approved giving some form of aid (military, economic, or humanitarian) to the Chinese government. A third of the public opposed additional aid, and 13 percent voiced no opinion. A year later, in the summer of 1949, less than 10 percent of Americans favored giving more aid to China, and only one in five still had a favorable opinion of Chiang.

Despite mixed public sentiment and Chiang's grim prospects, during 1948 the Truman administration agreed to a small assistance package for China. (This was in addition to nearly $2 billion in "surplus" military equipment transferred to China during 1945–1946.) The administration consented when Republicans threatened to delay funding for the Marshall Plan targeting European and Japanese recovery. Truman approved the allocation of $125 million for the China Aid Act. The funds could be used in any way the Nationalists wanted. But before most of the cash or supplies reached China, the Communists seized control. In 1949 some of the remaining funds, along with supplementary money, were repurposed to a vaguely worded assistance program specified for use "in the general area of China."

This language demonstrated that even those officials opposed to intervention in China had not given up on containing Communism elsewhere in Asia. For example, the term "in the general area of China" allowed the administration to redirect much of the aid to the French war effort in Indochina during 1949–1950. The Truman administration also stressed the importance of bolstering Japan as an anti-Communist bulwark. During 1948–1949 the State Department ordered many of the early Occupation reforms curtailed. As with policy in occupied Germany, the so-called Reverse Course in Japan stressed industrial recovery, political stability, and anchoring the former enemy to a Western military alliance.

The clearest vision of America's future priorities in Asia appeared in a policy approved by Truman at the end of December 1949. Known by its acronym, NSC 48/2, it reflected the new Secretary of State Dean Acheson's determination to "block further Communist expansion in Asia." This required the United States to build up Japan and to give "particular attention . . . to the problem of French Indochina." In fact, the first American funds given directly to the French war effort in the spring of 1950 came from money originally earmarked for China.

When most of the Nationalist government and army fled the mainland to the island of Taiwan (sometimes called Formosa) in mid-1949, Truman's advisers, including Acheson and Kennan, urged that the United States maintain nominal ties to the Nationalist regime while leaving the door open to possible ties with the emerging Communist government.[1] During 1949 Truman agreed to permit limited trade between the United States and its allies and Communist-held parts of China. He also rebuffed proposals to provide substantial military aid to anti-Communist guerrillas on the mainland or to pledge to defend Taiwan from invasion.

These decisions reflected realities on the ground. By mid-1949 the Communists controlled most of China, Nationalist troops were defecting en masse, and Chiang had decamped to Taiwan, leaving a caretaker government in south China. For obvious political reasons, the administration hoped to avoid delivering a "knock-out blow" to the Nationalists. Some of the president's advisers considered it better to keep the "facts from the American people and thereby not be accused later of playing into the hands of the Communists." But Dean Acheson told members of Congress that Chiang had been doomed by his own mistakes, not by Soviet intervention or American inaction.

To make this point, in August 1949 the administration released a massive "China White Paper," an official review of China policy over the past decade. Secretary of State Acheson hoped the document would clear the air and show the tawdry record of GMD corruption and incompetence. But in an effort to dispel charges that the administration had "stabbed China in the back," Acheson appended a cover letter to the White Paper that ignored or contradicted many of the report's major conclusions. For example, the preface condemned Mao and his followers as brutal thugs who had "foresworn their Chinese heritage and have publicly announced their subservience to a foreign power, Russia." This echoed what Henry Luce and congressional Republicans had been saying for several years, undermining the evidence in the White Paper.

As the likelihood of Communist victory became apparent at the end of 1948 and the chances of American intervention diminished, Mao Zedong began speaking and writing more critically of the United States. He accused American diplomats in China of organizing an "imperialist conspiracy" to mobilize anti-Communist elements inside China. To an extent, Mao and other party leaders argued, the mere presence in China of American diplomats, missionaries, educators, and businesses encouraged counterrevolutionaries. At the end of 1948, Communist authorities in Shenyang (Mukden), a city in Manchuria, placed the staff of the U.S. consulate under house arrest for several months, accusing them

---

[1]Eventually, about 3 million mainlanders crossed the 150-mile Taiwan Strait, where they joined 10 million Taiwanese who had originally migrated from south China over the past few centuries. A small number of non-Chinese indigenous people lived in the mountainous parts of the island. Japan had colonized Taiwan after it defeated China in the Sino–Japanese war of 1895. The island province reverted to Chinese control in 1945.

of espionage. But a few months later, in May 1949, several of Mao's aides approached Ambassador Leighton Stuart, who had remained in Nanjing after the Communist takeover. They invited Stuart, a former educator in Beijing, to return there for a visit during which he would have an opportunity to confer with Communist leaders. Stuart and some State Department officials favored accepting the invitation, considering it a sincere effort to explore avenues of cooperation. But Truman vetoed the idea, arguing forcefully that "under no circumstances" should Stuart go to Beijing. The president feared a Republican backlash and cited the ongoing detention of the consulate staff in Shenyang as reasons to spurn the offer. A dispirited Stuart soon left China, leaving a handful of American diplomats, missionaries, businessmen, and educators behind.

Communist motives for approaching Stuart are uncertain and still debated. Some historians have argued the Communists merely wanted to deflect any last-minute American military intervention. Other have speculated that although Mao was a committed Communist suspicious of the West and anticipating a close relationship with the Soviet Union, as a Chinese nationalist he was reluctant to subordinate China to any foreign power. Maintaining some diplomatic and trade links with the United States and its allies might provide China with valuable assets and give it some leverage with Stalin. Whatever the motives behind the approach, the rejection of this and other feelers from the Communists appeared to reinforce anti-American sentiment within Mao's inner circle.

In June 1949, Mao ordered that all contacts with American diplomats be severed and declared that henceforth, in the struggle against the forces of imperialism, China would "lean to the side" of socialism and the Soviet Union. At some time in the future, after the new China had established itself, he would be ready to open diplomatic and trade contacts with the West. But, as he put it, China needed to "clean house before entertaining guests." Mao then dispatched his deputy, Liu Shaoqi, to Moscow. He had hoped to go himself but Stalin declined to meet Mao before the formal creation of a new Chinese government.

Liu remained in the Soviet Union for most of July and August. In discussions with Stalin he pledged Chinese Communist loyalty to Soviet policies, while Stalin promised future economic and military assistance. He also urged Mao to be cautious about establishing diplomatic ties with the Americans and British. It might be better, Stalin added, to postpone any assault on Taiwan lest it provoke U.S. military intervention. When Liu raised the question of revising the "unequal" 1945 treaty Stalin had signed with Chiang, the Soviet leader gave no indication he intended to relinquish Soviet privileges in Manchuria, even to a Communist government.

On October 1, 1949, Mao stood atop Tiananmen to proclaim creation of the People's Republic of China (PRC). Shortly after, he took his long-delayed trip to Moscow, spending nearly two months in the Soviet Union, from late 1949 into February 1950. During his prolonged visit, he played a waiting game with Stalin. After postponing a meeting with the new Chinese leader, Stalin came around to offer the PRC a loan valued at $300 million, trade credits, and technology transfers. He also promised to assist China if it were attacked by Japan or a country allied with Japan, in other words, the United States. However, the Sino–Soviet Friendship Treaty signed on February 14, 1950, denied China immediate restoration of full sovereignty in Manchuria and other border regions. Stalin privately indicated he would eventually surrender some of the rail and port privileges and control over Outer Mongolia he had extracted from the Nationalists in 1945, but not yet. Perhaps this disappointment led to Mao's grim expression in the official photograph taken to mark the treaty's signing. It looked as if someone had forgotten to tell Mao and Stalin to smile.

The events in Moscow coincided with a growing Chinese–American rivalry in French Indochina. From Mao's perspective, U.S. support for the French colonial war along with assistance to Japan, South Korea, and even limited aid to Taiwan revealed an effort to isolate and encircle China. To counter this encirclement, in January 1950 the PRC recognized the Communist Democratic Republic of Vietnam, led by Ho Chi Minh, and began providing logistic support to Ho's Viet Minh guerrillas. As detailed in the next chapter, China provided assistance to the Communist regime in North Korea, pushed forward a planned invasion of Taiwan, and condemned U.S. talk of keeping military bases in Japan and promoting Japanese rearmament.

Before China recognized Ho's regime, U.S. officials had criticized France's effort to cloak its colonial war in nationalist garments by ruling through the "playboy" emperor, Bao Dai. But in February 1950, the Truman administration held its nose, recognized Bao Dai's puppet government as legitimate, and that spring began providing military aid to him and his French masters. With Chinese support for Ho, the war in Indochina began to resemble a proxy battle between China and the United States.

During Mao's extended visit to Moscow, U.S.–China relations deteriorated. The U.S. consulate in Beijing had continued to function as an informal contact point between the two countries following Ambassador Stuart's departure. In January 1950, the PRC announced it would soon seize the consular property of any foreign government that had not recognized the Communist regime. Mao may have provoked this showdown either to impress Stalin or, alternatively, to pressure the Truman administration into cutting all ties with Taiwan and recognizing the PRC. (Stalin's intention was difficult to fathom, since at different times he urged the Communists to shun contacts with the West and Japan or to build bridges to the outside. Mao may have guessed that while in Moscow it was safer to show Stalin his anti-Western face.) When the State Department refused to close the consulate or extend recognition, the Chinese seized the property. The handful of American officials in Beijing left for home and official contact between the two governments ceased.

Previously, Secretary of State Acheson had told Congress that before the United States took any dramatic new initiatives in China, it should "wait for the dust to settle." He implied that once the PRC began governing and after the expected collapse of the rump Nationalist regime on Taiwan, there might be an opportunity for the two sides to reach a diplomatic accommodation. In January 1950, Acheson and Truman issued what they hoped was their epitaph on China's civil war. The United States would cease all military aid to Taiwan and not shield the island from an anticipated invasion, at least while Chiang remained in power.[2] As the clock ran down on Taiwan, most American China experts voiced quiet hope that with the end of the civil war, Beijing and Washington would resume a dialogue and perhaps maneuver their way into a live-and-let-live relationship. Events in both countries and in East Asia soon confounded this possibility.

SELECTED ADDITIONAL READINGS

Robert E. Herzstein, *Henry R. Luce, Time, and the American Crusade in China* (New York, 2005); Suzanne Pepper, *Civil War in China, 1945–1949: The Political Struggle* (Berkeley, Ca., 1978); James Reardon-Anderson, *Yenan and the Great Powers* (New York, 1980); Steven I. Levine, *The Anvil of Victory: The Communist Revolution in Manchuria, 1945–1948* (New York, 1987); Odd Arne Westad, *The Chinese Civil War, 1946–1950* (Stanford, Ca., 2003) and *Brothers in Arms: The Rise and Fall of the Sino–Soviet Alliance, 1945–1963* (Stanford, Ca., 1998); Mark Gallicchio, *The Scramble for Asia: U.S. Military Power in the Aftermath of the Pacific War* (Lanham, Md., 2008) Ronald Spector, *In the Ruins of Empire: The Japanese Surrender and the Battle for Postwar Asia* (New York, 2008); John Melby, *The Mandate of Heaven: Record of a Civil War in China, 1945–1949* (Toronto, 1968); Nancy B. Tucker, *Patterns in the Dust: Chinese–American Relations and the Recognition Controversy, 1949–50* (New York, 1983) and *China Confidential: American Diplomats and Sino–American Relations, 1945–1966* (New York, 2001); E. J. Kahn, *The China Hands: America's Foreign Service Officers and What Befell Them* (New York, 1976); Gary May, *China Scapegoat: The Diplomatic Ordeal of John Carter Vincent* (Washington, D.C, 1983); Robert P. Newman, *Owen Lattimore and the Loss of China* (Berkeley, Ca., 1992); Lynn Joiner, *Honorable Survivor: Mao's China, McCarthy's America, and the Persecution of John S. Service* (Annapolis, Md., 2009); John N. Thomas, *Institute of Pacific Relations: Asian Scholars and American Politics* (Seattle, Wa., 1974); Harvey Klehr and Ronald Radosh, *The Amerasia Spy Case: Prelude to McCarthyism* (Chapel Hill, N.C., 1996); Harvey Klehr and John Earl Haynes, *Venona: Decoding Soviet Espionage in America* (New Haven, Conn., 2000); Allen Weinstein and Alexander Vassiliev, *The Haunted Wood: Soviet Espionage in America: The Stalin Era* (New York, 1999). Robert M. Blum, *Drawing the Line: The Origin of American Containment Policy in East Asia* (New York, 1982); William W. Stueck, *The Road to Confrontation: American Policy toward China and Korea, 1947–1950* (Chapel Hill, N.C, 1981); James I. Matray, *The Reluctant Crusade: American Foreign Policy in Korea, 1940–1950* (Honolulu, 1985); Dorothy Borg and Waldo Heinrichs, eds., *Uncertain Years: Chinese–American Relations, 1947–1950* (New York, 1980); John L. Gaddis, *Strategies of Containment* (New York, 1982); Gary R. Hess, *The United States*

---

[2]The administration left itself some wiggle room. If a reformist group drove Chiang from power, the United States might reassess its hands-off policy and defend the island.

Emergence as a Southeast Asian Power, 1940–1950 (New York, 1987); Michael Schaller, *The American Occupation of Japan: The Origins of the Cold War in Asia* (New York, 1985); Qing Simei, *From Allies to Enemies: Visions of Modernity, Identity, and U.S.–China Diplomacy, 1945–1960* (Cambridge, Mass., 2007); Chen Jian, *Mao's Road to the Korean War* (New York, 1985) and *Mao's China and the Cold War* (Chapel Hill, N.C., 2001); Michael Hunt, *The Genesis of Chinese Communist Foreign Policy* (New York, 1998); Zhang Hong, *China Perceived: The Making of Urban Images of the United States, 1945–1953* (Santa Barbara, Ca., 2002).

CHAPTER 7

Red Scare and Yellow Peril

Despite their wariness of the new Communist regime in China, President Truman and Secretary of State Acheson hoped to avoid conflict with the PRC. While waiting, as Acheson put it, "for the dust to settle," the United States focused its energies in Asia on developing a secure arc, or "great crescent," of allies that stretched from Japan through Okinawa, the Philippines, and Southeast Asia. This "defensive perimeter," as it was called, would contain possible Chinese expansion while waiting for the PRC's revolutionary fervor to mellow. Unfortunately, regional events frustrated any hope of early Sino–American compromise.[1]

By 1950 anti-American sentiment in China ran deep among both Communist leaders and rank-and-file party members. Mao found it useful to mobilize support by stoking this anger. He probably believed that severing most contact with Americans would also make it easier to secure assistance and protection from the Soviet Union. In a parallel way, some American politicians discovered political advantages in fomenting fear about the "loss of China." Just one year after Mao proclaimed creation of the PRC, Chinese and American soldiers were locked in brutal combat in Korea. Assistant Secretary of State Dean Rusk (later secretary under Presidents John F. Kennedy and Lyndon B. Johnson) declared that the "peace and security of China" had been "sacrificed to the ambitions of a Communist conspiracy." China had been "driven by foreign masters into . . . foreign aggression." Rusk insisted that "Red China" (as American officials called it until 1971) was a "colonial Russian government . . . not the government of China." The slaughter in Korea lasted three years, but Chinese–American hostility continued for two decades.

Looked at objectively, by 1950 the United States had made great strides in achieving the security goals outlined by George Kennan in 1947. Marshall Plan

---

[1]As described separately by both Secretary of State Dean Acheson in Washington and General Douglas MacArthur in Tokyo, this perimeter excluded *both* South Korea and Taiwan.

aid had jump-started European and Japanese recovery, undermining the domestic appeal of Communism. A strong Federal Republic of Germany had emerged in the heart of Europe. Bountiful and inexpensive oil poured from wells in friendly Middle Eastern kingdoms. By most relevant measures, "containment" had blunted the Soviet threat in regions vital to U.S. security and prosperity. Soviet conventional military power in Europe continued to outweigh that of the United States and its allies in the North Atlantic Treaty Organization, but few strategists expected Stalin to resort to war.

Despite holding a winning hand, many ordinary Americans remained skeptical of the balance of power. The public agonized over news released on August 31, 1949, that the Soviets had tested an atomic bomb, breaking the American monopoly. This was followed in October by creation of the PRC and in February 1950 by the signing of a Soviet–Chinese friendship pact. American public opinion was further rattled starting in January 1950 by several revelations of widespread Soviet atomic espionage dating back to World War II. Despite the emotional impact of these events, none altered the global power balance that favored the United States. Nevertheless, a growing number of Americans worried that an aggressive China, backed by a nuclear-armed Soviet Union, might soon dominate Asia. Communism, in this view, was a unified threat that subordinated any expression of nationalism.

RED SCARE

Developments during early 1950 made it difficult for the Truman administration to calm the public and Congress, both of which lost faith in official explanations. Much of the controversy swirled around placing the blame for "who lost China" through deceit and betrayal, who compromised atomic secrets, and who could be trusted to safeguard national security in the wake of these failures.

Accusations of disloyalty and treason regarding China erupted first in November 1945 when Ambassador Patrick Hurley resigned and accused State Department officials of aiding the Communists. The controversy subsided after a brief Senate inquiry and Truman's dispatch of Marshall to China. The issue exploded again early in 1950 in the wake of the PRC signing its alliance with the Soviet Union and several espionage cases that questioned the loyalty of government officials and scientists.

In January 1950, after being accused in earlier testimony before Congress of being both a Communist and a Soviet spy, former State Department official Alger Hiss was convicted in federal court of lying about his past affiliations. (The statute of limitations blocked the government from charging him with espionage.) Although Hiss's work in the State Department during World War II had little to do with China, his conviction gave traction to charges of subversion. That same month, British police arrested Klaus Fuchs, a German émigré scientist, who confessed to participation in a wartime spy ring that passed atomic secrets to the Soviets, which he gathered while working at the Los Alamos laboratory during

World War II. Fuchs provided evidence that led to the arrest in June of an American couple, Julius and Ethel Rosenberg, as "atomic spies" who passed secrets to Moscow. Reacting to these events, Senator Homer Capehart, an Indiana Republican, asked, "How much more are we going to have to take? Fuchs and Acheson and Hiss and hydrogen bombs threatening outside and New Dealism eating away at the vitals of the nation. In the name of Heaven, is this the best America can do?"

Capehart's Republican colleague from Wisconsin, Senator Joseph McCarthy, expanded on these accusations in a speech delivered on February 9, 1950, in Wheeling, West Virginia. McCarthy, whose name became synonymous with the era's anti-Communist crusade, claimed to have uncovered a vast Communist conspiracy inside the federal government. The United States, he asserted, faced defeat in Asia because Dean Acheson, "a pompous diplomat in striped pants with a phony British accent," had turned policy making over to a subversive clique. "I have in my hand," the senator ranted, "a list of two hundred and five [names] known to the Secretary of State as being members of the Communist Party and who nevertheless are still working and shaping policy of the State Department." These diplomats were "loyal to the ideal and designs of Communism rather than those of the free, God-fearing half of the world. . . . I refer to the Far Eastern Division of the State Department and the Voice of America."

In fact, McCarthy had no actual evidence linking the State Department's China experts to espionage. He relied on recycled rumors from earlier inquiries or groundless accusations that had appeared in the press. He took special aim at diplomats who had criticized Chiang Kai-shek. Although the senator later pilloried some individuals the Federal Bureau of Investigation (not he) had linked to espionage, they had no role in making China policy. As one cynical journalist remarked at the time, McCarthy "couldn't find a Communist in Red Square. He didn't know Karl Marx from Groucho." But McCarthy's seemingly endless stream of accusations, as well as the encouragement he received from fellow Republicans and newspaper headline writers, stoked fear among many Americans and paralyzed the Foreign Service. Two of the senator's favorite targets were Foreign Service officer John S. Service and Professor Owen Lattimore of Johns Hopkins University. Service, who had advised Stilwell and participated in the Dixie Mission, and Lattimore, who briefly served as an adviser to Chiang, had both criticized the GMD and predicted its defeat. In McCarthy's telling, this certified them as members of a "Communist conspiracy." The senator accused the bookish Lattimore, an expert on Mongol culture, of being the "number one Soviet agent" in America.

At a raucous Senate hearing in 1950, McCarthy demanded that Service explain why three suspect China specialists (Service, John Paton Davies, and John Carter Vincent) all shared a first name. Was it "mere chance," McCarthy bellowed, that "three Johns lost China?" Service retorted that actually "four Johns lost China." Who was the fourth?, the senator demanded to know. "John K. Shek," Service answered wryly, to the delight of the audience and McCarthy's fury. The diplomat won the verbal joust, but soon lost his job.

Senator Joseph McCarthy, who had blamed American diplomats for "losing China" to the Reds, shares a joke with one of his chief targets, John S. Service. (National Archives)

Other unscrupulous politicians joined McCarthy's witch hunt. Senator Pat McCarran, a Nevada Democrat, played nearly as destructive a role as his Republican colleagues. As chair of the Senate Internal Security Subcommittee beginning in 1951, McCarran devoted several years to hounding diplomats, journalists, and scholars who had been affiliated with groups such as the Institute of Pacific Relations, a respected nongovernment organization concerned with Asian affairs. By the time his crusade against what he called "interlocking subversion" ended in the late 1950s, one official described the Far Eastern Division of the State Department as a "disaster area," filled with "human wreckage."

Security investigations that began under Truman and expanded during the Eisenhower administration targeted several of the most talented and experienced China specialists in government. Typically, they were accused of bad judgment in criticizing the Nationalists or predicting a Communist victory. Some who were stationed in Yan'an as part of the Dixie Mission were criticized for "consorting with Communists," which, of course, was their assignment. Many were forced to resign or were simply fired. Service, Davies, Vincent, and O. Edmund Clubb, for example, were all judged "security risks" or "insufficiently loyal." Owen Lattimore was exonerated after two federal trials in which he was accused of lying about Communist affiliations. With his American academic career in ruins, he took a teaching job in England. Those Asia specialists who remained in the State Department learned to mute their views, whereas others switched to less controversial geographic areas,

During the spring of 1950, prodded in part by Senator McCarthy's escalating charges of treason, the Truman administration inched back toward supporting the GMD in Taiwan. In January, Truman and Acheson had publicly washed their hands of Taiwan. By April, however, they authorized small amounts of assistance to the Nationalist regime. Several of Truman's advisers suggested that the United States encourage one of Chiang's non-Communist rivals in Taiwan to depose him as a prelude to the restoration of full U.S. support and protection. During the spring of 1950 the administration also provided direct assistance to the French military campaign in Indochina and increased its support for President Syngman Rhee's government in South Korea.[2]

In Tokyo, Occupation Commander General Douglas MacArthur joined the debate over Taiwan's status. Bored by his work in Japan and eager to capture public attention, MacArthur issued private advice and public calls for extending his authority to Taiwan, which he described as an "unsinkable aircraft carrier" that could anchor operations to resist Communist expansion. Occupation officials looked the other way and allowed several dozen former Japanese Imperial Army officers to go to Taiwan as military advisers. MacArthur's idea of renewing a commitment to Chiang found support from Acheson's deputy, Dean Rusk, and John Foster Dulles, the State Department's special adviser on Japan. The Joint Chiefs of Staff also expressed interest in resuming efforts to defend Taiwan. In April, a special interagency task force issued an alarming report, NSC-68, that described the Soviet atomic bomb and to a lesser degree the Communist victory in China as presenting grave threats to the nation's security. Predicting new challenges from the Soviet Union and China, the report called for a sharp increase in military spending and a more muscular foreign policy.

Despite these pressures, Truman declined to authorize the huge weapons outlay envisioned in NSC-68. Nor would he fully recommit to defending Taiwan. Only a crisis, it appeared, would convince the president, Congress, and the public to rally behind intervention on Taiwan and enacting major increases in defense spending. As Acheson recalled the tumultuous summer of 1950, "we were sweating over" what to do "in June 1950 and then, thank God, Korea came along."

---

[2]Washington justified aid to the French colonial war by noting that since February 1950 the PRC had recognized Ho Chi Minh's guerrilla movement and begun supplying military assistance to the Viet Minh.

THE KOREAN WAR AND THE CHINESE-AMERICAN CONFRONTATION

North Korea's invasion of the south on June 25, 1950, pulled American combat forces back into Northeast Asia. Within a week of the war's beginning, President Truman committed the United States to defend South Korea, ordered the navy to protect Taiwan, and increased aid to the French in Indochina. These decisions reinforced Mao's belief that the fighting in Korea was largely a pretext for the U.S. intention to encircle, undermine, and perhaps attack the PRC. This fear, along with his desire to demonstrate China's emergence as a major Communist state, prompted Mao to send a "volunteer" army to defend North Korea. By the end of 1950, Chinese and American troops were locked in a brutal war that lasted until July 1953.

Korea, a Japanese colony since 1910, had been split along the 38th parallel at the end of World War II. Soviet forces occupied the north, Americans the south. What began as a temporary division hardened as the Cold War set in. Ignoring most Koreans' hope for unity, each occupying power established a client regime. In the north, a former anti-Japanese guerrilla leader and Communist, Kim Il-sung, ruled with Soviet support. American authorities, with some misgivings, created a southern government ruled by Syngman Rhee, a conservative nationalist long resident in the United States. By July 1949, occupation troops had left the peninsula and the rival Democratic People's Republic of Korea (North) and Republic of Korea (South) each claimed to be the sole legitimate national government. Both regimes were repressive and relied on aid from their patrons to survive. During the three years leading up to the war, as many as 100,000 Koreans perished in internal fighting and border skirmishes along the 38th parallel.

Both Moscow and Washington were wary of their respective clients. Syngman Rhee often threatened to march north, whereas Kim spoke of forcefully taking the south. During late 1949 and early 1950, the military balance on the peninsula changed. China released from military service about 33,000 Koreans who had fought alongside the Communists during the civil war. In meetings with the Soviet leader, Kim pressed Stalin to authorize and support an invasion of the south. He insisted his army, assisted by a popular uprising against Rhee in the south, could finish the job quickly, before effective U.S. intervention. Both Kim and Stalin thought the likelihood of direct American involvement was minimal, in part because a variety of American civilian and military officials, ranging from Secretary of State Acheson to General MacArthur in Tokyo, had described Korea as outside the defense perimeter that the United States would unquestionably defend.

Stalin appears to have considered unification of Korea a low-risk operation that could pay important benefits. A victory by Kim would eliminate any threat of a South Korean thrust to unify the peninsula and would counterbalance the threat posed by a potentially resurgent Japan. The United States had already committed to rebuilding Japan's economy, planned to maintain military bases after the Occupation, and was encouraging some degree of Japanese rearmament.

In addition, under the recently signed treaty with China, Stalin anticipated losing access to some of the Manchurian ports used as naval bases. Access to several new Korean ports would bolster the security of the Soviet Far East. Both Stalin and Kim worried that South Korea was becoming stronger and less susceptible to internal subversion, making a delay in an attack from the north more risky. Stalin was prepared to support Kim's plan, so long as it did not lead to a direct Soviet–American confrontation.

Late in their planning for an attack, Stalin instructed Kim to solicit Mao's approval for the invasion. Possibly, the Soviet leader hoped that by involving China in Kim's war plan, it would eliminate any near term prospect for Sino–American cooperation. In the spring of 1950, the Chinese leader gave his blessing to the venture but kept his own focus elsewhere. Mao's main interest remained liberating Taiwan and he had committed most of China's military resources to that anticipated operation. The Chinese leader expressed some concern that if Kim's invasion failed, China might need to rescue him.

Kim Il-sung's claim that his Soviet-supplied army could quickly overrun southern defenses proved accurate, even without the predicted popular uprising. But his calculation that the United States would or could not react proved disastrously wrong. Truman and his advisers interpreted the attack not as an isolated event but as "part of a global challenge directed by Moscow at American collective security systems." The relationship between Stalin and Kim, one presidential aide quipped, was the same as that between "Walt Disney and Donald Duck." Truman and Acheson were especially concerned that abandoning South Korea would destroy American "credibility," causing major allies like West Germany and Japan to lose faith in U.S. security guarantees.

Within days of the North Korean attack, Truman ordered U.S. air, sea, and land forces to defend the south. He sent the Seventh Fleet to protect Taiwan from an invasion from the Chinese mainland and substantially boosted the level of military and economic aid to fight Communist insurgencies in the Philippines and Indochina. These actions, Washington hoped, would persuade both foes and friends of American determination to resist aggression. The attack on Korea, Truman declared, "makes it plain beyond all doubt that Communism has passed beyond the use of subversion to conquer independent nations and will now use armed invasion and war."

Although he was prepared to act unilaterally, Truman requested and received from the United Nations (UN) support for American action. Some 15 nations answered the call to send troops to defend South Korea, although the vast majority of foreign troops were American and General MacArthur served as both U.S. and UN commander. The UN resolution authorizing force to defend the Republic of Korea passed the Security Council only because the Soviets were boycotting meetings to protest the organization's refusal to expel the Nationalist representative and to seat the PRC as China's legitimate government. This ill-timed absence allowed the United States to claim to be acting as an international peacekeeper. When the Soviets returned in early August, the United States relied on support from the UN General Assembly where no veto existed and Washington could rely on a strong majority.

Mao, Stalin, and Kim all seemed stunned by the quick U.S. decision to defend South Korea and resume protection for Taiwan. On June 28, Chinese foreign minister Zhou Enlai declared that U.S. intervention in Taiwan and Korea constituted "aggression against the territory of China." As Zhou feared, shielding Taiwan marked the first step in a series of decisions to resume full support for the GMD. Naval protection soon led to military assistance and eventually to cooperation in GMD raids on the mainland. Ultimately, the United States assumed treaty obligations to protect Taiwan. Faced with American actions, Mao first delayed, and then postponed indefinitely, plans to conquer the island.

However, the more immediate threat to the PRC came from the several hundred thousand American soldiers and Marines who arrived in South Korea under the command of General Douglas MacArthur. Even if these forces conducted operations south of the 38th parallel, Mao worried that their proximity would destabilize Manchuria and embolden "reactionary" elements still active in China. Even before American troops approached the North Korean–China border in November 1950, Mao and his fellow leaders felt acutely threatened.

As of mid-September, the North Korean invaders overran nearly all the south. American and South Korean forces held only a pocket of land around the far southern port of Pusan. But Chinese strategists and intelligence sources guessed that MacArthur planned to send a large invasion force to overwhelm the northern attackers. As a precaution, early in July, Mao canceled the Taiwan operation and began moving forces from the south to the northeast. Many of the troops were organized as a special "Northeast Border Defense Army" of 300,000 men. As part of the effort to prepare China for battle, Mao initiated a mass anti-American campaign among Chinese civilians. He stressed the need to "Beat American Arrogance" by defending the North. The "Resist American, Aid Korea" movement also provided a patriotic justification for Communist moves to seize control over and shut down most American cultural, religious, and business organization that remained in China. Ironically, many Chinese educated in the United States were stigmatized as potential traitors at the same time as American diplomats who had served in Yan'an were fired as security risks and hundreds of Chinese currently studying at American universities were placed under scrutiny.

As the Chinese anticipated, MacArthur launched a bold amphibious invasion at the South Korean port of Inchon in mid-September. North Korean forces were too weak to resist and Chinese forces were not yet in place. U.S. troops broke out of their encirclement near Pusan and quickly joined the new amphibious units to retake nearly all of South Korea. As shattered North Korean units fled, South Korean and U.S./UN troops retook Seoul and restored the 38th parallel as a boundary. By late September, the United States had fulfilled the UN mandate.

Even before U.S./UN and South Korean forces had recaptured Seoul, powerful civilian and military voices in the Truman administration had indicated a desire to go beyond the defense of South Korea. MacArthur had told his colleagues he planned to destroy completely the North Korean army, even if this required moving north of the prewar boundary. In Washington, President Truman and Secretary Acheson believed that Korean unification would allow the United States to seize the offensive in the Cold War, punish the Kremlin, and force Mao to question the value of his alliance with Stalin. It would also bolster the confidence of Japan and other American allies.

In addition, the success at Inchon and beyond proved intoxicating to both General MacArthur and President Truman. Victory, both felt, had come almost too easily. Repulsing North Korean aggression had cost China and the Soviet Union little. To teach Stalin and Mao a lesson and deter future aggression, the Truman administration decided to invade North Korea and unify the country under southern leadership. Several of America's European allies worried about committing too many resources to Korea but ultimately voted to support a U.S.-sponsored resolution in the UN General Assembly sanctioning the plan.

Domestic politics influenced this decision to escalate. The large-scale rearmament called for in NSC-68 had barely begun. Ending the war quickly, administration officials worried, would short circuit the buildup. The president saw the expanded war plan as a foolproof way to demonstrate his anti-Communist credentials, especially in the one area of his vulnerability, Asia. With midterm elections scheduled for November, it seemed to him good politics and good strategy to fight for Korean unification. MacArthur made a similar calculation. He had twice explored running for president (in 1944 and 1948) and hoped to run in 1952. Although his success in South Korea was impressive, rolling back Communism in North Korea would be the first such victory in the Cold War. Thus, both the commander in chief and the theater commander saw invading the north as a winning strategy.

Anticipating success at Inchon, Truman approved a plan (NSC-81) on September 11 to conquer North Korea. The easy victory at Inchon four days later made an expanded war virtually inevitable. In late September Truman authorized MacArthur to send his forces into North Korea and destroy enemy forces as they fled toward the Yalu River border with China. MacArthur was free to move north unless he encountered Soviet resistance. In the case of Chinese intervention, he should continue to advance if he determined his forces could still prevail. The consensus among U.S. defense and intelligence analysts held that Soviet forces were unlikely to fight directly in Korea unless Stalin had decided to launch a global war anyway. Chinese intervention was considered more likely, but still not probable. Neither Truman's advisers not MacArthur seemed to have given much thought as to how Mao and his government would respond to an American army approaching Manchuria, China's industrial heartland.

The official policy of the Truman administration specified that American troops halt at the Yalu River, confining combat to Korea. But in both private communications and public statements, MacArthur sent mixed and provocative signals. In the run-up to the Inchon landing, he frequently called for greater operational freedom, often taking controversial stands without Washington's approval. For example, in July he flew to Taiwan, embraced Chiang as an ally, and called for Nationalist troops to invade south China. The general told visitors to his headquarters in Tokyo that although Truman hoped to avoid war with China, he (MacArthur) "got down on my knees and prayed nightly" that the Chinese would intervene in Korea or attack Taiwan so he would be able to "deliver such a crushing defeat" against Communism that it would prove "one of the decisive battles of the world." At other times he described Taiwan as essential to the goal of rolling back Communism in China. After Defense Secretary George C. Marshall told him to feel "unhampered" as he moved his forces north of the 38th parallel on September 27, MacArthur told a colleague he now felt prepared to "to take on the Chinese or even Russians."

These statements, along with other developments, must have alarmed the Chinese. For example, Truman had already reversed course and decided to protect and aid Taiwan. The United States was rebuilding Japan and boosting aid to French Indochina and had switched its goal from defending South Korea to destroying the northern regime. U.S. strategy appeared aimed at encircling China and "rolling back" Communism. What would prevent Truman or MacArthur from deciding, once U.S. forces reached the Yalu, to stop and *not* attack Manchuria?

During August and September Chinese leaders pondered how to respond to the American march north. After hesitating to invite Chinese troops into North Korea, Kim Il-sung pleaded for help. After initially opposing direct intervention, Stalin, too, urged Mao to send forces. The PRC leadership waivered in early October, concerned about the domestic costs of intervention (it would, they informed Stalin, delay "our entire plan for peaceful reconstruction") and the lack of sufficient arms and air support to counter the far better equipped Americans. Stalin warned Chinese leaders that they faced a greater threat from the Americans if they failed to intervene in a timely way and then had to allow Kim to establish a government-in-exile in Manchuria. After the Soviet leader promised to help equip numerous Chinese divisions, train Chinese pilots, and provide limited air support along the Yalu River, Mao gave approval on October 8 to send troops, dubbed Chinese People's Volunteers, into Korea. Large-scale movement began about 10 days later.

This decision should not have entirely surprised American civilian and military leaders. Since mid-September Chinese officials in Beijing and elsewhere had issued warnings that China would not stand "idly by" if American troops (as distinguished from South Koreans) entered North Korea. U.S. intelligence sources reported that large numbers of Chinese troops were, in fact, moving toward North Korea. Truman was nervous enough to fly halfway around the globe on October 15 to meet MacArthur at Wake Island. The general glibly dismissed all Chinese threats as bluffs and assured the president that if the Chinese intervened, they would be "slaughtered." Truman pinned a medal on MacArthur's chest and returned to Washington.

Initial Chinese plans to halt the American advance just north of the 38th parallel were confounded by problems in transportation and supply. Instead, their troops made contact with Americans about midway through North Korea during the last days of October. When Truman and the Joint Chiefs issued some half-hearted appeals to MacArthur to slow his advance until Chinese intentions became clear, he leaked stories to the press accusing the president of lacking a backbone and undermining victory. A supreme egoist, he complained that as in World War II, rivals in Washington would "rather see America lose a war than MacArthur win a battle."

MacArthur's determination to push north appeared justified when Chinese troops broke contact after a sharp attack on November 7. Chinese strategists later suggested they had initiated and broken off contact with a twofold purpose. Either the Americans would see the danger and withdraw or, if they moved north, they would be lured into battle, far from their own supply chain, against a much larger Chinese force. Although MacArthur insisted that he faced no more than 30,000 to 60,000 Chinese troops, at least 300,000 were already in place. Undaunted, at the end of November he ordered an "end-the-war" offensive. In a reckless maneuver, he sent two armies east and west of a rugged mountain range toward the Yalu River, unable to communicate with one another. The war would be won and American boys would be "home by Christmas," he boasted. Privately, MacArthur worried that North Korean and Chinese resistance might continue even after his forces reached the Yalu and he would have to "begin bombing key points in Manchuria."

China's *People's Daily* explained what occurred on November 25: 300,000 People's Volunteers launched a counteroffensive against advancing Americans. The volunteers would "check them with force and compel them to stop" because for China there was "no alternative." Soviet planes and pilots provided some air cover along the Yalu, and Stalin eventually approved the sale, on credit, of substantial military equipment to Chinese troops. The Soviet leader was determined, however, to avoid being drawn into a war with the United States. During the next month the Chinese badly mauled U.S. Army and Marine units, who suffered more than 11,000 casualties as they staged a fighting retreat south. It was, a stunned MacArthur admitted, "an entirely new war."

Just five years earlier, Chinese and American soldiers had been allies against Japan. Now, U.S. press headlines described "Red Chinese Hordes" slaughtering GIs. By January 1951, Chinese troops had driven the Americans south of the 38th parallel and threatened to overrun South Korea. Americans, one newsreel reported, were being "routed by Red Army legions, treacherously forced into this war by the unscrupulous leaders of international Communism." With U.S. forces in full retreat, "the Communist perfidy in Korea makes the picture grim."

The reversal in Korea put the Truman administration in a bind. Most strategists feared getting trapped in a war against the "second team" (China), although the greater danger remained a Soviet threat to Western Europe and Japan. A U.S. counterattack on China might also provoke Soviet intervention. MacArthur insisted that China, not the Soviet Union, represented the greater threat to global security. He, along with his Republican backers in Congress, urged Truman to widen the war by unleashing air and naval attacks on China and sending Nationalist troops from Taiwan into Korea and south China. To force Truman's hand, MacArthur orchestrated a campaign in the press and among Congressional Republicans to characterize Truman and Democrats as weak willed and defeatist. Forbidding him to expand the war, MacArthur indicated, risked defeat not only in Korea, but also in efforts to stop Communism everywhere.

President Truman, Secretary of State Acheson, and members of the Joint Chiefs suspected that part of MacArthur's bluster was an effort to shift the blame for his failure to predict or blunt the Chinese attack. Once China intervened, they recognized the futility of trying to unify Korea by force and were prepared to accept a solution to the war based on restoring the 38th parallel. MacArthur insisted this was impossible because Chinese forces were poised to overrun all South Korea. In fact, no such threat existed. Mao, like the Americans, had succumbed to the euphoria of early success and rejected his initial strategy of stopping at the 38th parallel once the Americans were pushed out of the North. Instead, he ordered his army to unify Korea under Communist leadership. But as his field commander, Peng Dehuai, predicted, the Chinese volunteers had outrun their supply lines. This, along with U.S. air superiority and more effective leadership by a new field commander, Lieutenant General Matthew Ridgway, halted the Chinese offensive just south of the 38th parallel. Despite MacArthur's dire prediction of doom, by March 1951 the war had become a stalemate.

Several UN members now called for a ceasefire in place and giving China a provisional voice in the world body. The PRC objected, calling this a ruse to maintain U.S. control of South Korea and protection of Taiwan. In return for a ceasefire, China demanded the immediate withdrawal of U.S. troops from South Korea and Taiwan and giving the PRC a UN seat. Anything less, Mao believed, would undermine China's stature as a revolutionary model. Still imagining that a complete victory was possible, Mao's rejection of a compromise settlement brought enormous costs to China over the following two and a half years of war.

Some U.S. officials urged Truman to consider a deal to abandon both South Korea and Taiwan while giving China a UN seat in return for its support for a peace settlement with Japan. Advocates such as George Kennan, the original strategist of containment, thought this might promote tension between Mao and Stalin while stabilizing East Asia. Fearing a political backlash, Truman insisted that any ceasefire must leave South Korea intact without abandoning Taiwan. Mao rejected an armistice that did not include the withdrawal of U.S. troops from all of Korea. With no compromise in sight, the United States convinced the UN General Assembly to adopt a resolution condemning China as the aggressor in Korea.

In March 1951, the Truman administration shifted course again by considering a plan to offer China a ceasefire in place followed by negotiations on regional problems. Specifically, the United States would suggest a willingness to discuss with China the future of Taiwan and formal UN membership. The prospect of a compromise without victory appalled MacArthur. He sabotaged the peace plan on March 24 by broadcasting a garbled version on the radio before it was presented to the Chinese. The general declared that because he had beaten the Chinese, he was now prepared to accept their surrender! He called on Chinese military commanders in Korea to surrender to him personally. If they refused, he threatened to attack China's "coastal and interior bases." MacArthur's bluster sabotaged Washington's peace initiative, outraged China, and convinced the president that the "Big General in the Far East must be recalled."[3]

MacArthur likely preferred political martyrdom to presiding over a deadlocked war. During March and April he took several actions that virtually ensured his removal. For example, early in April Republican Congressman Joseph Martin, the House minority leader, read in public a letter he received from MacArthur. In it, the general endorsed Martin's earlier call to support a Nationalist Chinese invasion of the mainland and agreed with Martin's inflammatory claim that Truman's refusal to "win" the war in Korea made the president responsible for the "murder" of thousands of Americans. Simply put, MacArthur declared, there was no "substitute for victory." On April 11, with the backing of the Joint Chiefs, Truman sacked MacArthur and appointed Matthew Ridgway both occupation commander in Japan and theater commander in Korea.

MacArthur claimed his firing was part of a plot to sell out Taiwan, Korea, and even Japan to "Red China." Conservative newspapers, such as the *Chicago Tribune* and New York *Journal American*, denounced Truman as "unfit to be president." With MacArthur's firing, California Senator Richard Nixon announced the "happiest group in America are the Communists." Senator Joseph McCarthy demanded that "the son-of-a-bitch ought to be impeached." The Gallup Poll revealed that two-thirds of Americans supported MacArthur and only one-third backed the president.

MacArthur, who had not visited the United States since 1937, returned to a series of gala parades. In a dramatic address to both houses of Congress, he condemned those who would "appease Red China." The United States, he insisted, must achieve nothing short of victory in Korea. To falter in the Far East, he warned, would endanger America's survival. Although he brought some members of Congress to tears with his closing line drawn from an old ballad that "old soldiers never die, they just fade away," MacArthur had no intention of going quietly.

During a week of testimony before a special Senate committee, the general bitterly criticized the administration's military and diplomatic policies. But to his apparent surprise, the Joint Chiefs of Staff supported Truman. Joint Chiefs of Staff chair General Omar Bradley fired off the most memorable line, declaring

---

[3]Truman and his advisers had an additional motive in sacking MacArthur. They feared a renewed Chinese and perhaps Soviet offensive in and around Korea and wanted to give the theater commander maximum authority to respond, perhaps even using atomic weapons in an emergency. However, they did not trust MacArthur. His successor, General Ridgway, received wider permission to engage in hot pursuit of Chinese or Soviet attackers.

that MacArthur's fixation on widening the war in Korea would entrap the United States in the "wrong war, at the wrong place, at the wrong time, and with the wrong enemy." General Dwight D. Eisenhower, once MacArthur's deputy and now commander of the North Atlantic Treaty Organization in Europe, compared MacArthur to Senator McCarthy: both were "opportunists, seeking to ride the crest of a wave." Undeterred, MacArthur launched a nationwide speaking tour (funded by Texas oilmen) designed to promote his presidential prospects for 1952. But when the crowds grew smaller, he canceled future appearances.

Developments in Korea explain why the MacArthur boom faded. General Ridgway quickly rallied dispirited American troops. Without widening the war, using Nationalist troops, or dropping atomic bombs (as MacArthur sometimes hinted he might do), U.S. forces beat back a Chinese offensive launched in the spring of 1951 and stabilized the battlefront. Finally recognizing the PRC's military limits, Mao decided he had proved his ability to stand up to American imperialism and could now accept an armistice based on restoration of the 38th parallel, without consideration of other issues that divided the United States and China. With Stalin's approval, armistice talks began in Kaesong, Korea, on July 10, 1951.

To the surprise of both sides, the talking—and the fighting—dragged on for two more years. Both sides tacitly agreed to restore the north–south division near the prewar boundary. The major hurdle proved to be prisoner repatriation. Previously, at the end of a conflict, the United States returned the prisoners of war (POWs) it held to their country of origin, regardless of personal preference. However, of the approximately 116,000 Chinese and North Korean POWs, 30,000 to 40,000 did not want to return home. (These included some South Koreans dragooned into the North Korean army and former Chinese Nationalist troops who had surrendered in 1949 and been sent to fight in Korea.) Truman, who saw this as both a human rights issue and a useful propaganda weapon, refused compulsory repatriation. He could only imagine how Republican critics would respond to his forcing POWs back to China and North Korea.

Washington's claim to the high moral ground was clouded by the fact that many prisoners were intimidated by American, South Korean, and Chinese Nationalist prison camp guards. Some were threatened with punishment and some were even tattooed with political slogans to force them to request asylum. Early in 1952, when American negotiators explained that prisoners would not be repatriated against their will, China condemned this as a ploy to keep the war going. Beijing attempted to recapture the moral heights by charging that U.S. aircraft had dropped biological weapons over North Korea and Manchuria.[4]

---

[4]The United States did not use biological weapons, but Chinese officials may have linked epidemics that afflicted livestock and people to germ attacks. Suspicions were also raised when American occupation officials in Japan made deals with members of Unit 731, a notorious Japanese chemical and germ warfare group active in wartime China. In return for their experimental data, several members of the unit were given immunity from prosecution and assumed prominent positions in industry.

When U.S. negotiators spoke of prisoner rights, the Chinese responded with false confessions of biological warfare wrung from captured Americans. During the resulting 18-month impasse, both sides continued to launch limited but costly offensives in Korea. More soldiers died after the truce talks began than during the first year of the war.

Stalin's death in March 1953 broke the deadlock. The Soviet dictator had seemed comfortable with continuing a war that tied Americans down in Korea and forced China to do most of the fighting. The group of leaders who succeeded Stalin all favored improving relations with the United States. Kim Il-sung, after three years of warfare, was ready to make peace. Mao also recognized that fighting in Korea paid diminishing returns. China had proven its ability to resist U.S. power, but along with North Korea suffered a million battlefield casualties. Among the Chinese killed was Mao's son. The war retarded Chinese economic growth, interfered with its ability to trade with U.S. allies in Western Europe and Japan, and put China ever more in debt to the Soviet Union. When Zhou Enlai attended Stalin's funeral in Moscow, he and the new Soviet leadership agreed on compromises to end the war, especially accepting the principle of nonforcible repatriation of POWs.

The American public was also disillusioned with the stalemated war that had resulted in around 140,000 casualties, including nearly 37,000 deaths. The war's unpopularity had been a factor in Truman's reluctant decision not to seek re-election in 1952. It also assured Republican candidate and World War II hero Dwight D. Eisenhower an easy victory over Democratic nominee Adlai Stevenson. Eisenhower's campaign promise to "go to Korea" and end the war quickly had resonated with millions of voters.

Eisenhower and his new secretary of state, John Foster Dulles, adopted a two-track plan to break the stalemate in Korea. They issued thinly veiled threats to expand the war, possibly by using atomic weapons against China, unless peace talks made rapid progress. (In fact, for both moral and practical reasons, Eisenhower decided against using nuclear weapons. He also dismissed a proposal by the now-retired MacArthur to seal off North Korea from China by sowing the boundary with nuclear waste.) The administration also announced that the Seventh Fleet would no longer "shield" the Chinese mainland from attacks by Taiwan. Washington, as journalists put it, "unleashed" Chiang Kai-shek. But even as they issued these threats, Eisenhower and Dulles hinted to the Chinese that once the war in Korea ended, they were prepared to deal flexibly with many of the issues dividing China and the United States.

At the end of March, China accepted a U.S. proposal for an interim exchange of sick and wounded POWs. Zhou Enlai then suggested a deal where prisoners who objected to returning home would be transferred to a neutral state, which would then establish their true preference. This would permit both sides to save face. Serious armistice talks resumed during late April 1953 and a commission of neutrals was created to screen POWs held in Korea. By mid-June, just as it appeared, all hurdles had been cleared, South Korean president Syngman Rhee attempted to derail a settlement (since it did not call for unifying Korea) by suddenly releasing 18,000 North Korean POWs whose fate had yet to be determined. The Chinese responded by launching attacks on South Korean military units, undermining later claims by Eisenhower and Dulles that U.S. atomic threats had intimidated China. Nevertheless, Rhee's actions outraged Eisenhower, who considered ordering his overthrow. But even this provocation did not dispel Chinese or American determination to make a deal. On July 27, all participants signed an armistice that left Korea divided along a line slightly north of the 38th parallel that Americans considered more defensible than the prewar boundary. Technically, a state of war continued (as it still does) and Chinese (until 1958) and American troops (to this day) remained on the peninsula.

The dreadful loss of Korean, Chinese, and American lives was only one consequence of the war. By the time of the armistice, the United States had implemented the NSC-68 rearmament program, expanding military expenditures nearly fourfold, from $13 billion annually on the eve of the Korean War to nearly $60 billion in 1953. Most of the funds went to a military buildup in Western Europe and Japan. Defense spending came down a bit after the Korean ceasefire, but remained at historically high levels for the rest of the decade.

Policies and attitudes formed during the war in Korea embittered Chinese–American relations for two decades. Americans overwhelmingly considered China the aggressor in Korea, responsible for the deaths of thousands of Americans. The fighting revitalized popular support for the discredited Nationalist regime on Taiwan and its leader, Chiang Kai-shek. These sentiments made it difficult for any American politician to support recognition of the PRC. By 1953, the Central Intelligence Agency was actively assisting guerrilla raids by Nationalist forces from Taiwan along the China coast. The United States also provided support to a Nationalist-backed force fighting on the China–Burma border. The policies adopted to isolate China economically, diplomatically, and culturally drove the PRC even closer to the Soviet Union.

When China entered the Korean War, the United States not only suspended its own small trade with the PRC, but also organized an embargo among its allies. Congress passed the Battle Act, which threatened American economic retaliation against any country that sold a wide variety of products to China. After the Korean armistice, the United States retained its near total embargo and pressured its European and Japanese allies to severely restrict trade with China. The United States exercised leverage through the China Committee of the Paris-based Coordinating Committee for Export to Communist Areas. Following the American lead, these groups set guidelines for what manufactured goods could be sold and also restricted China's access to credit. The restrictions imposed on China were far more stringent that those limiting trade with the Soviet Union and Eastern Europe. As part of the deal ending the U.S. occupation in April 1952, the United States forced Tokyo to impose even more stringent limits on exports to China.

Although these restrictions were resented by many Japanese, the Korean War had been exceptionally profitable for Japan. A flood of American war orders spurred industrial production and provided access to new technology. By 1954 Japan had earned nearly $4 billion from war contracts, surpassing the level of post–World War II reconstruction aid. As the American ambassador in Tokyo, Robert Murphy, observed, these orders turned Japan into "one big supply depot without which the Korean War could not have been fought."

The war also prompted Washington to sign long-delayed peace and security treaties with Japan. The U.S.-drafted settlement, signed at a ceremony in San Francisco in September 1951—from which Japan's main victim, China, was excluded—linked Japan's security closely to the United States. In a separate security pact, Japan provided the United States nearly unlimited base rights on the home islands and Okinawa. These facilities, together with those in the Philippines, South Korea, Thailand, and Taiwan, provided the infrastructure for most American military activities in Asia for nearly three decades. The United States also pressured Japan into recognizing the Nationalist regime on Taiwan as the government of China and limiting commercial contact with the PRC. Partly to compensate Japan for the loss of its "China market," Japanese exports were permitted to enter the United States on extremely favorable terms.

Among the unintended consequences of the Korea War was the growing U.S. involvement in Indochina. Both the Truman and the Eisenhower administrations worried that China would use Communist Vietnam to control the rest of resource-rich southeast Asia and place an economic stranglehold on Japan. Mao, in turn, feared that the Americans would make Indochina a powerbase from which to threaten China.

Republican foreign policy expert John Foster Dulles, hired by the Truman administration to negotiate an end to the occupation of Japan, articulated this view. Speaking to French officials in Paris in May 1952, Dulles described the wars in both Korea and Indochina as a single struggle to contain China. French Indochina, or Vietnam, he explained, was the "key to Southeast Asia upon the resources of which Japan is largely dependent." If Communism triumphed in Vietnam, Dulles argued, the remainder of Southeast Asia would quickly succumb. From then on, the economically desperate "Japs would be thinking on how to get to the other side." Japan's loss, like that of Germany, would tilt the world's power balance in the Soviet's favor.

As the armistice took hold in Korea, the United States was paying about three-fourths of the cost of the French colonial war in Indochina. By the time the French quit fighting in 1954, Washington had provided more than $2 billion in aid. Every president from Truman through Nixon built on this Korean War legacy to "hold the line" in Southeast Asia against Communism and a perceived Chinese threat.

SELECTED ADDITIONAL READINGS

E. J. Kahn, *The China Hands: America's Foreign Service Officers and What Befell Them* (New York, 1976); Gary May, *China Scapegoat: The Diplomatic Ordeal of John Carter Vincent* (Washington, D.C, 1983); Lynn Joiner, *Honorable Survivor: Mao's China, McCarthy's America, and the Persecution of John S. Service* (Annapolis, Md., 2009); John N. Thomas, *Institute of Pacific Relations: Asian Scholars and American Politics* (Seattle, Wa., 1974); O. Edmund Clubb, *The Witness and I* (New York, 1974); Daniel M. Oshinski, *A Conspiracy So Immense: The World of Joe McCarthy* (New York, 1985); Robert P. Newman, *Owen Lattimore and the Loss of China* (Berkeley, Ca., 1992); William W. Stueck, *The Road to Confrontation: American Policy toward China and Korea, 1947–1950* (Chapel Hill, N.C., 1981), and *The Korean War: An International History* (Princeton, N.J., 1997), and *Rethinking the Korean War: A New Diplomatic History* (Princeton, N.J., 2002); James I. Matray, *The Reluctant Crusade: American Foreign Policy in Korea, 1941–1950* (Honolulu, 1985); Bruce Cumings, *The Origins of the Korean War, 1947–1950* (2 vols.; Princeton, N.J., 1981–1990) and *The Korean War: A History* (New York, 2011); Chen Jian, *China's Road to the Korean War* (New York, 1996), and *Mao's China and the Cold War* (Chapel Hill, N.C., 2001); Steven Casey, *Selling the Korean War: Propaganda, Politics, and Public Opinion in the U.S., 1950–1953* (New York, 2008); Shen Zhihua, *Mao, Stalin and the Korean War: Trilateral Communist Relations in the 1950s* (London, 2012); Thomas Christensen, *Worse Than a Monolith: Alliance Politics and Problems in Asia* (Princeton, N.J., 2011); Robert Accinelli, *Crisis and Commitment: The United States Policy toward Taiwan, 1950–1955* (Chapel Hill, N.C., 1996); Rosemary Foot, *The Wrong War: American Conflict and the Dimensions of the Korean War, 1950–53* (Ithaca, N.Y., 1985), *A Substitute for Victory: The Politics of Peacemaking and the Korean Armistice Talks* (Ithaca, N.Y., 1990), and *The Practice of Power: U.S. Relations with China since 1949* (New York, 1997); Qing Simei, *From Allies to Enemies: Visions of Modernity, Identity, and U.S.–China Diplomacy, 1945–1960* (Cambridge, Mass., 2007); Sergei Goncharov, John Lewis, and Xue Li-tai, *Uncertain Partners: Stalin, Mao and the Korean War* (Stanford, Ca., 1993); Allen S. Whiting, *China Crosses the Yalu* (New York, 1960); Michael Schaller, *Altered States: The U.S. and Japan since the Occupation* (New York, 1997), and *Douglas MacArthur: The Far Eastern General* (New York, 1989); Qiang Zhai, *The Dragaon, the Lion and the Eagle: Chinese–British–American Relations, 1949–58* (Kent, Oh., 1994), and *China and the Vietnam Wars, 1950–1975* (Chapel Hill, N.C., 2000); Zhang Shuguang, *Deterrence and Strategic Culture: Chinese–American Conflicts, 1949–1958* (Ithaca, N.Y., 1992) and *Mao's Military Romanticism: China and the Korean War, 1950–1953* (Lawrence, Kan., 1995); Thomas Christensen, *Useful Adversaries: Grand Strategy, Domestic Mobilization, and Sino–American Conflict, 1949–1958* (Princeton, N.J., 1996); Odd Arne Westad, ed., *Brothers in Arms: The Rise and Fall of the Sino–Soviet Alliance, 1945–1963* (Washington, D.C., 1999).

CHAPTER 8

Chinese–American Estrangement, 1953–1960

Failure to win or even fully explain the objectives of the war in Korea discredited the Truman administration with a public already concerned with its alleged loss of China and penetration by Communists. During the 1952 presidential campaign, Republicans coined the slogan K-1, C-2, signifying Democratic responsibility for "Korea, Communism, and Corruption." Since Roosevelt's election in 1932, Senator Joe McCarthy bellowed, Democrats had perpetrated "twenty years of treason." Republican nominee Dwight D. Eisenhower and his running mate, California Senator Richard M. Nixon, rode a wave of voter discontent into the White House. Over the next 15 years, Eisenhower and his two Democratic successors, John F. Kennedy and Lyndon B. Johnson, excoriated China as a threat to world peace. Although they voiced a more nuanced understanding of the PRC in private, their public rhetoric and unbending policies appeared to drive Sino–American relations from crisis to crisis.

Each of these three presidents pursued four related goals in Asia. They sought to isolate China, protect Taiwan, maintain a prosperous Japan linked to the United States, and keep Communism out of Southeast Asia. To achieve these ends, they supported the Nationalist regime on Taiwan, gradually deepened U.S. military involvement in Vietnam, allowed Japan favored access to U.S. markets, and forged security pacts with most of the nations in an arc or semicircle around China.

From the start, it appeared as if the Eisenhower administration had fully restored American ties to Chiang Kai-shek on Taiwan. In his inaugural speech of January 1953, the new president declared that the U.S. Seventh Fleet that patrolled the Taiwan Strait since the start of the Korean War henceforth would protect Taiwan but would no longer "shield" the PRC from Nationalist attack. It was an open secret that with tacit American approval, Nationalist forces from Taiwan and those operating in Burma routinely launched raids along China's coast and southwest border.

After the Korean armistice in July 1953, the United States maintained a "Europe-focused" foreign policy but intensified its level of involvement in Asia.

The efforts to contain China, build up Japan, protect Taiwan, and stabilize South Korea and Southeast Asia transformed what had been a backwater of American policy into a major theater of the Cold War. Washington's policies toward China and Southeast Asia between 1953 and the late 1960s often antagonized its European and Japanese allies who considered the U.S. approach too moralistic, militaristic, and reflexively anti-Communist.

THE EISENHOWER ADMINISTRATION AND CHINA

In contrast to his grandfatherly affect, President Eisenhower exercised full control over his foreign policy apparatus. The new administration imposed strict controls on trade with China, forged new or expanded security pacts with Japan, Korea, Thailand, the Philippines, Australia, New Zealand, and Taiwan, and helped create an anti-Communist state in the southern half of Vietnam. Although the president and his top aides occasionally voiced private misgivings about their support for Taiwan, their public condemnation of China remained almost as unwavering as the actual policies they pursued.

Despite his highly publicized talk of "unleashing" Chiang Kai-shek, China was never a central element of Eisenhower's foreign policy. More of a geopolitical realist than ideologue, Ike believed that defending European and Japanese security and resisting Communist challenges in the Middle East and Latin America were far more consequential than what transpired in or with China. At the same time, Eisenhower and his secretary of state, John Foster Dulles, recoiled at the misery inflicted on Truman and Dean Acheson by the so-called China Lobby, the pro-GMD alliance of journalists, lobbying organizations, and strident anti-Communists in Congress. Ike and Dulles often accommodated these groups by parroting their rhetoric and even by appointing some of their supporters to high positions in the military and diplomatic corps. To assure support for administration priorities in Europe and Japan, they resolved to keep these "China-firsters" appeased.[1] However, the president and secretary of state usually ignored the more bellicose advice of figures such as Joint Chiefs of Staff chairman Admiral Arthur Radford Defense Secretary Charles Wilson, and Assistant Secretary of State for the Far East Walter Robertson.

The president understood that the PRC was not going to disappear anytime soon and the United States had to accommodate this reality, however unpleasant. Officials in Washington sometimes echoed GOP hard-liners' calls to rollback Chinese Communism, but Eisenhower seldom followed these words with actions. For example, right after he announced that the navy would no longer shield the PRC from attacks by Taiwan, he slowed delivery of weapons to the island until Chiang promised to "play ball" and not act "recklessly."

---

[1] Polling data suggested that both the public and the many Democratic members of Congress were more flexible on the issue of China than Eisenhower recognized. But he hesitated to openly defy Republicans or the China Lobby.

⌊Eisenhower approved small-scale raids against the PRC but opposed opera-tions likely to escalate⌋ He agreed to assist Taiwan in a variety of ways and stood by the Nationalists during several military confrontations with the PRC, but Ike scoffed at Chiang's talk of recovering the mainland. In private, he ridiculed some of Chiang's boosters, such as California Republican Senator William Knowland, as monumentally "stupid." The president's toughest anti-Communist rhetoric, especially toward China, was a kind of camouflage and antivenom against his own party's hard-liners. Until the fighting in Korea ended, Eisenhower felt he had little room to maneuver. But after 1953, he broached the idea with his inner circle about allowing regulated trade with China, contemplated eventual UN member-ship for the PRC, and even envisioned U.S. recognition of "two" Chinas.

Secretary of State John Foster Dulles brought a particularly strident moralism to discussions of foreign policy. As an accomplished international lawyer and lay activist in the Presbyterian church who had helped the Truman administration negotiate the treaty ending the Japanese occupation⌋ Dulles initially showed some flexibility over how to deal with the PRC. But once the Korean War began and he observed the political attacks inflicted on Dean Acheson, Dulles concluded that he must appease GOP conservatives if he were to succeed as secretary of state⌋ His frequent bombastic and apocalyptic diatribes led Winston Churchill to allegedly describe Dulles as the "only bull who carried around his own China shop."

To cover his right flank, Dulles appointed hard-line anti-Communists to a variety of State Department posts and encouraged them to ferret out personnel of dubious loyalty. He fired one of the few senior "China hands" left in the depart-ment, John Carter Vincent. After sacking the veteran diplomat, Dulles stunned Vincent by asking whether he would agree to consult anonymously from time to time on China policy.

Although he was not personally close to Dulles (whose brother Allen simul-taneously served as director of the Central Intelligence Agency [CIA]), Eisenhower and his secretary of state worked together effectively. The president often utilized Dulles to play the public role of "bad cop" to Eisenhower's "good cop." Privately, Ike described Dulles as long winded and sanctimonious. The Secretary's tough language, Ike believed, kept the China Lobby mollified while deterring the PRC from taking reckless actions. Dulles derided the PRC as a godless, illegal regime that did "not conform to the practices of civilized nations" and was little more than a "creature of Moscow's Politburo." At one point he declared that "we owe it to ourselves, our allies, and the Chinese people to do all we can" to speed the regime's "passing."

Despite this ostracism and calls for regime change, both Eisenhower and Dulles considered Chiang a troublemaking fantasist who had to be kept on a leash. They understood that two Chinese governments existed and even supported low-level diplomatic contact with the PRC as a way of enmeshing the Communist regime in protracted, if inconsequential, talks. Despite Dulles's ritualized public praise of Chiang, privately, as one biographer noted, Dulles dismissed the Nationalist leader as an "arrogant, manipulative schemer more interested in self-aggrandizement than in the welfare of the Chinese people." Chiang, he feared, would happily drag the United States into war with China to boost his chance of recovering the mainland. The Generalissimo, he told an aide, had a "vested interest in World War III."

During 1953 and early 1954, the priorities of ending the war in Korea and managing the French retreat from Indochina took precedence over dealing with both China and Taiwan. Gradually, the administration's approach centered on containing China without becoming too entwined with Taiwan or fighting a new war in East Asia. Like their Democratic predecessors, Eisenhower and Dulles at various times considered deposing Chiang in favor of a more moderate Taiwan leader, turning the island over to a UN trusteeship, or even recognizing two separate Chinese governments. Ultimately, they developed a so-called wedge strategy designed to reduce China's threat by driving it apart from the Soviet Union. Rather than attempting to subdue China through direct military means, the administration implemented a program that combined elements of an economic embargo, political isolation, and covert military pressure to force the PRC out of the Soviet orbit.

The "wedge" could be "hard" or "soft." Dulles, and especially his deputy Walter Robertson and Joint Chiefs of Staff chairman Admiral Radford, doubted Mao would respond to diplomatic carrots. They urged tightening the embargo on China's trade with non-Communist nations (especially Great Britain and Japan) to force Beijing's complete reliance on the Soviets. Since the Soviet economy could not meet China's needs, they predicted, China would be forced to its knees— and its senses.

Eisenhower favored an alternative approach. He considered it "hopeless to imagine we could break China away from the Soviets and Communism short of some great cataclysm." A more relaxed trade policy, not rigidity, he insisted, would encourage China to change and could be used "as a weapon on our side." Ike worried that too strict an embargo would also create strains with Great Britain and Japan who looked to China as a market. If all trade "between the free world and Soviet bloc" was severed, he asked, how much would it cost the United States to subsidize "countries that depend on trade, such as Japan?" It was absurd to "simply slam the door in Japan's face" given that Japan, not China, was the key to American influence in East Asia.

At the end of 1953, Eisenhower told his cabinet that the only "sensible course of action" in regard to China trade was to "apply the criterion of the net gain. What do we get out of this policy in terms of what we put in." Only half joking, he claimed he would even sell jet fighter planes to the PRC rather than to Taiwan "if it could be shown to be to our net advantage." Speaking to congressional leaders in 1954, Eisenhower berated those who insisted on "no trade with Red China" yet opposed sending troops to Vietnam or taking in more Japanese exports. It was vital, he argued, to allow some trade with China while defending Vietnam and easing Japan's exports. Unless the United States did all three, "we would lose Japan" and the Pacific would become a "Communist lake."

The problem, Eisenhower told his aides, came from the pro-Taiwan China Lobby and "demagogues" like Senator Joseph McCarthy who incited public fear about any dealings with China. One particular lobbying group, the Committee of One Million, was organized during 1953–1954 (possibly with CIA support) with the aim of blocking China's admission to the UN. It circulated a petition that gathered a million signatures against UN membership for China and pressed many mainstream groups, such as the AFL-CIO and American Legion, to endorse its aims. The Committee increased its clout in Congress by threatening retaliation against any politician who questioned a hard-line approach toward China. Eisenhower generally reserved his criticism of the China Lobby for closed meetings with trusted aides. What the American people and Chinese leadership heard from Washington was the more extreme rhetoric of Dulles, Vice President Richard Nixon, Admiral Radford, and congressional hawks.

As a result of these divisions, American policy often combined the worst of the conflicting wedge strategies. Washington imposed rigid, but not absolute, limits on British and Japanese exports to China. Eisenhower publicly defended these restrictions while privately ridiculing them. In several meetings with British and Japanese leaders during the 1950s he virtually encouraged them to ignore the American imposed embargo. As critics of the policy noted, China often purchased forbidden Western products from its Soviet or Eastern European partners who were allowed to import a wide array of Western goods. Under mounting pressure from Great Britain and Japan, the United States finally relented in 1957 and abandoned the so-called China differential, allowing American allies to sell to China the same products they could sell to the Soviet bloc. Ironically, just as the United States relaxed its export controls in 1957–1958, Mao Zedong launched a radical economic development program called the Great Leap Forward that stressed self-reliance over foreign trade.

Stalin's death in 1953, followed by the Korean armistice, improved relations between China and the Soviet Union. Nikita Khrushchev, who eventually succeeded Stalin, accommodated Chinese needs and sensitivities more willingly than his suspicious predecessor. Khrushchev visited Beijing in 1954 and offered to return the naval base taken by Stalin in 1945 in the Manchurian port of Lushun (Port Arthur). He followed this gesture by granting China substantial economic and military assistance and sending several thousand technical advisers. These actions undercut the American hope of driving an early wedge between Moscow and Beijing.

Mao expressed mixed feelings when Khrushchev attacked Stalin's behavior and legacy in 1956. As Mao admitted, if he had followed Stalin's advice to the letter, the Communists might not have won the civil war and "I would have been dead." Nevertheless, Mao resented the new Soviet leader's failure to consult him in advance of this radical departure, suggesting it showed that Moscow still considered China a client state. He also faulted Khrushchev's iconoclasm for unleashing anti-Communist protests in Eastern Europe and for encouraging criticism of the Communist Party within China.

In 1957, Mao himself urged the Chinese to voice criticism of Communist Party policies. In launching the so-called Hundred Flowers campaign, he called on Chinese of various backgrounds to point out policy failures and other short-comings. The outpouring of grievances stunned Mao, who promptly reversed himself and launched an Anti-Rightist campaign that harshly punished around a half million regime critics.

Until 1958, the PRC relied heavily on Soviet assistance and a modest amount of trade with non-Communist nations. Especially after the Korean armistice, Chinese agricultural and industrial production showed significant gains. By 1958, however, Mao condemned Soviet-style planning and resolved to speed China's development by adopting his own economic model of self-reliance called the Great Leap Forward. The government forced peasants out of their homes into large agricultural communes and encouraged the proliferation of small, locally man-aged industrial enterprises. For a while, party propagandists boasted of surging harvests and rivers of steel pouring forth from backyard smelters. The actual re-sults proved disastrous. By the time Mao relented in 1960–1961, the Great Leap had caused widespread famine that killed an estimated 20 to 30 million people and played havoc with industrial production.

Soviet development assistance to the PRC had an analogue in U.S. aid to Taiwan during the 1950s. Despite their nominal support for Chiang's pledge to return to the mainland, Eisenhower and Dulles considered it likely the Nationalist government would remain entrenched solely on Taiwan. The regime's survival, they believed, depended as much on improving living standards on the island as in the shield provided by the Seventh Fleet. Chiang had previously ignored a decade or more of U.S.-promoted reforms, but he proved more flexible from his island redoubt. Perhaps he had learned from past errors or, as some observers recognized, the social structure on Taiwan differed significantly from that on the mainland. Native Taiwanese landlords, rather than the Nationalist supporters who swarmed to the island after 1949, owned most of the farmland. With the United States providing much of the money, Chiang approved government pur-chase of land and its redistribution to small farmers. This weakened the power of the local landlord class who often resented Chiang and the GMD while boosting regime support among formerly landless peasants. With cash or government bonds in hand, the former landlords often invested in factories, transforming the predominantly agricultural economy. At the same time, a variety of American agricultural, economic, civil service, health, and other advisers flocked to the small island. Although Taiwan remained a rigid, authoritarian state until the 1980s, its economy flourished and by the early 1960s it enjoyed a standard of living in Asia second only to Japan.

1950s CRISES WITH CHINA

After the Korean armistice, the United States and China nearly came to blows on three occasions: in Vietnam in mid-1954 and in the Taiwan Strait in 1954 and

1958. Each time the two countries approached what John Foster Dulles called "the brink," but pulled back. To some extent, both sides had learned a painful lesson in Korea and avoided making the same mistake. Although Mao labeled the United States a toothless "paper tiger" and called on the oppressed peoples of the world to fight imperialism, he made it clear that they would have to achieve their own liberation and that China was willing to accept "peaceful co-existence" with the main enemy—so long as Washington did not attack or threaten its borders.

Chinese and American interests collided in Vietnam in the spring of 1954. After four years of escalating economic and military aid to French forces fighting the Communist-led Viet Minh guerrillas of Ho Chi Minh, the insurgents had worn down colonial forces. As a condition to more aid, American military planners pressed the French to lure the Viet Minh into a pitched battle at Dien Bien Phu, a valley in northern Vietnam. There, the French and Americans hoped, the base's large number of troops, artillery, and aircraft would destroy the guerrillas. Instead, the French garrison was quickly surrounded, isolated, and put under siege. Chinese advisers and supplies, freed from Korea, assisted the Viet Minh. The loss of Dien Bien Phu in May 1954 destroyed French civilian and military morale and opened the path to Communist control of all Vietnam and, Americans feared, Chinese Communist domination of Southeast Asia.)

Months earlier, Dulles had warned that the Soviets and Chinese planned to seize Japan not through direct assault but "through what they are doing in Indochina. If they could get this peninsula . . . along with Siam, Burma, Malaya . . . they would have what was called the rice bowl of Asia." The Joint Chiefs of Staff also issued a warning that a Viet Minh victory would herald Communist control of all Southeast Asia. Japan, "the keystone of U.S. policy in the Far East," would then be forced by "economic and political pressure" to reach an "accommodation with the Communist bloc." With Japan neutered, "China would ultimately control the entire Western and Southwestern Pacific region and would threaten South Asia and the Middle East." In light of these concerns, the Eisenhower administration was prepared to intervene directly in Vietnam if Chinese combat troops joined the war.

Early in 1954, when he dispatched additional military advisers to Vietnam, Eisenhower declared "My God . . . we must not lose Asia." He spoke of Japan ultimately being brought down by a "row of falling dominoes" beginning in Vietnam. Defeat of France in Vietnam, he warned the British, would allow the Soviets and Chinese to "combine the manpower and natural resources of Asia with the industrial potential of Japan," upsetting the global balance of power.

Despite these concerns, Eisenhower ultimately rejected calls by some of his aides to commit U.S. troops, air power, or even atomic weapons to saving the French. Congressional leaders made clear their opposition to direct intervention. The British had no interest in backing Dulles's call for "United Action," which might require sending their own forces into battle. Even the beleaguered French were lukewarm about American intervention. Paris wanted help in saving the thousands of troops trapped in Dien Bien Phu, but spurned Washington's demand that it turn over management of the war to Americans.

At the same time as Dien Bien Phu fell in May 1954, an international conference to discuss Asian issues convened in Geneva. The Soviet Union, France, Great Britain, and China formally participated and the United States sent an "observer team," briefly led by Dulles. The Americans feared that in its rush to get out of Indochina, the government of French Prime Minister Pierre Mendes-France would cut a sweetheart deal with Ho Chi Minh. That, Dulles and Eisenhower worried, would make it difficult "to keep Japan in our orbit."

Dulles ostentatiously refused to shake hands with Chinese premier Zhou Enlai in Geneva. He even insisted that he not be seated close to any Communists. One diplomat recalled that he sat at the conference table, "mouth drawn down at the corners, his eyes on the ceiling, sucking his teeth." After a few days, Dulles left for home.

Despite gloomy predictions, the decisions made in Geneva proved far better than the Americans anticipated. The Soviets and Chinese hoped to ratchet down tensions with the west. In the wake of Korea, they had no wish to provoke American military intervention in Vietnam. Soviet and Chinese representatives leaned heavily on Ho Chi Minh to accept a compromise short of outright victory. This involved spinning off Laos and Cambodia as independent states and temporarily dividing Vietnam along the 17th parallel, far north of the demarcation the Viet Minh preferred. North of the "temporary" division, Ho's Democratic Republic of Vietnam could consolidate power. South of the division, the departing French would turn authority over to the so-called State of Vietnam, headed by the weak and unpopular playboy emperor, Bao Dai. In 1956, national unity elections would take place. Given the chaos in the south as the French withdrew, Ho and his followers were nearly certain to win national control. Both the French and the Viet Minh considered these so-called Geneva Accords an imperfect but acceptable deal. The United States did not sign the agreement but pledged not to "disturb it."

In fact, policy makers in Washington considered the temporary division a window of opportunity in which to consolidate anti-Communist strength in the south. Dulles stressed the importance of blocking the Communist north from extending its power "throughout Southeast Asia and the Southwest Pacific." To achieve this goal, the Eisenhower administration began replacing departing French army and civil administrators with American advisers. Advice and support soon flowed to Ngo Dinh Diem, whom Bao Dai appointed as head of government.

Diem (really his first name; his surname, Ngo, pronounced No, confused his American backers) came from an influential Vietnamese Catholic family and had ingratiated himself with influential Americans during a sojourn in the United States in the early 1950s. Although some U.S. officials in Saigon questioned his ability, key advisers, such as CIA station chief Edward Lansdale, strongly supported Diem's effort to build a viable regime. His religious faith and Western orientation, they believed, made Diem an ideal Cold War ally. Some even described him as a "new and improved" Chiang Kai-shek. To the consternation of skeptics, by 1956 Diem succeeded in crushing his main non-Communist rivals in the south. He moved quickly to depose and exile Bao Dai, canceled national unity elections, and created a Republic of Vietnam below the 17th parallel with himself as president.

The Eisenhower administration promptly recognized and pledged to support Diem's regime with its capital in Saigon. China and the Soviet Union appeared unmoved by Ho's protests of betrayal. Clearly, Vietnamese unification was not a priority for Moscow or Beijing. Nikita Khrushchev even proposed that *both* North and South Vietnam be admitted to the UN as sovereign states. The Eisenhower administration boasted that South Vietnam's emergence as what it called a prosperous democracy proved that the United States could successfully "build" a nation from the wreckage of colonialism. Without firing a shot, the United States had apparently blocked Chinese expansion and created an ally it portrayed as a beacon to other emerging nations in the so-called Third World.

During the period of South Vietnam's gestation, Dulles nurtured additional barriers around China. In September 1954, at a conference in Manila, he recruited Britain, France, New Zealand, Australia, Thailand, and the Philippines to join the United States in forming the Southeast Asia Treaty Organization (SEATO). Based loosely on the North Atlantic Treaty Organization alliance, SEATO—only two of whose members were actually located in Southeast Asia—did not commit any signatory to doing anything beyond consulting in case of an attack. It might give an aggressor pause but required no American military response. Within a few years, SEATO granted South Vietnam "observer status" and the United States declared that protecting the Republic of Vietnam was a treaty obligation.

The PRC hoped that its moderate behavior at the Geneva Conference, especially its pressure on Ho Chi Minh to compromise on the terms of the settlement, might encourage a dialogue with Washington. Instead, Dulles formulated the SEATO alliance and considered offering Taiwan additional security guarantees. In what proved a misguided move to deter the United States from granting Taiwan a new defense pact, Mao ordered artillery shelling of several small Nationalist-held islands off the coast of Fujian Province, the largest of which were Quemoy (Jinmen) and Matsu (Mazu). Chiang considered these coastal toeholds an important part of his claim to the Chinese mainland and had stationed about 50,000 troops on them. These garrisons threatened China's coastal shipping and sometimes launched raids against the mainland.

American diplomats and military planners questioned why Chiang stationed so many troops on the vulnerable offshore islands. In addition to provoking the PRC, they presented a danger to Taiwan itself. If, for example, Communist forces overran Quemoy and Matsu, or the Pescadores (Penghu) located closer to Taiwan, the loss of so many Nationalist soldiers might destabilize Taiwan and force the United States to come directly to its defense. It raised the question whether Chiang deliberately put his troops at risk to force American support. At the same time, Dulles and Eisenhower worried that if they disavowed Chiang's action or failed to defend the disputed islands, they would encourage a Chinese attack and be criticized by the China Lobby.

Mao probably had several reasons for shelling the islands. Forcing the withdrawal of Nationalist forces would reduce the threat they posed to coastal security and might weaken Chiang's grip on Taiwan. It would, he hoped, demonstrate the risk America would run by signing a defense pact with the Nationalist government while refusing to speak to Beijing. However, in Washington, administration hard-liners considered the shelling a preliminary move against Taiwan and urged the president to fully commit to the island's defense.

Eisenhower split the difference among his advisers. In December 1954 he authorized Dulles to sign a mutual defense treaty with Taiwan that shielded the Nationalist regime but did not extend a guarantee to the many offshore islands. The United States would defend these outposts only if an attack on them threatened Taiwan directly. In return for the pact, Chiang effectively gave Washington a veto over his operations against the mainland. At the administration's request, Congress enacted the so-called Formosa Resolution in January 1955 that effectively gave Eisenhower a blank check to protect the "security of Formosa, the Pescadores, and related positions and territories of that area." The president, who did not think China wanted a war with the United States, also issued some nuclear threats that he was certain would not need to be backed up. In fact, to reduce the likelihood of a future clash, Ike urged Chiang to voluntarily abandon some of the offshore islands in return for a stronger commitment to Taiwan itself.

As Eisenhower suspected, China had no intention of fighting the United States. In April 1955, while Zhou Enlai attended a conference of nonaligned Asian and African nations in Bandung, Indonesia, the Chinese premier and sometimes foreign minister announced that China would cease shelling Quemoy. He also proposed that the United States and the PRC begin ambassadorial talks on matters of mutual concern. Dulles, who insisted that U.S. resolve had forced China's policy reversal, agreed to discussions, first in Geneva, then in Warsaw.

These first direct contacts since 1949 achieved some small but important results. For example, since the Korean War China had detained several dozen American citizens, mostly students and missionaries. Citing security concerns, the United States had blocked the exit of several hundred Chinese students and scientists working at American universities. (They were cleared to go to Taiwan, but not the PRC.) The talks led to the repatriation of both groups. Unfortunately, the discussions deadlocked on such issues as UN representation and the status of Taiwan. China strongly hinted that if Washington and Beijing made progress on other issues, it would pledge to reunify Taiwan with the mainland primarily by peaceful means. Dulles insisted that China formally renounce the use of force, which it refused. He, in turn, vetoed China's proposal to permit mutual visits by journalists. After two years, the Chinese concluded that Dulles saw the discussions as a way to distract China in endless talks with no larger purpose. In 1957, they suspended the meetings.

Meanwhile, Chiang Kai-shek defied American advice and expanded troop deployments to Quemoy and other offshore islands. By 1958, more than 100,000 soldiers, twice the number stationed there in 1954, held forward positions. The Eisenhower administration criticized Chiang's actions but did nothing to stop him. In fact, the United States increased aid levels to Taiwan and stationed nuclear-capable Matador missiles on the island. Chiang's muscle flexing, seemingly abetted by the United States, persuaded Mao that his support for peaceful coexistence had yielded nothing and that the time had come to "probe the attitude of the Americans."

In preparation, Mao visited Moscow in November 1957, where he praised recent Soviet technological achievements, including the testing of long-range ballistic missiles and the launch of the first artificial space satellite, *Sputnik*. The "east wind was prevailing over the west wind," he declared, adding that the United States was merely a "paper tiger." Khrushchev approved Mao's request for Soviet aid in developing nuclear energy and weapons, so long as he promised not to provoke the United States.

Despite these agreements, Mao nurtured growing doubts about Soviet economic and foreign policies. Soviet advisers in China promoted centrally planned and managed development projects. They mocked Mao's call for the creation of vast agricultural communes and rural industry, hallmarks of the soon-to-be announced Great Leap Forward. Mao, in turn, accused Khrushchev of losing revolutionary zeal and trying too hard to cooperate with the United States. The time was right to challenge U.S. imperialism, he insisted. Mao also complained that the Soviets reneged on their promise to help China build nuclear weapons.

Suspicious of his Soviet ally, fed up with what he saw as provocations by the United States and Taiwan, and eager to initiate his radical Great Leap Forward, Mao provoked another crisis in the Taiwan Strait. He hoped this would reveal true Soviet intentions toward China and frustrate what he saw as American efforts to permanently separate Taiwan from China. A modulated crisis might also help to mobilize domestic support for the Great Leap.

With little or no notice to the Soviets, Mao initiated a massive artillery barrage against Quemoy beginning on August 23, 1958. Thousands of shells landed on the tiny island over the next three days, effectively cutting it off from resupply and blocking evacuation. When it seemed as if the garrison would surrender, American strategists contemplated "nuclear strikes deep into China" even at the cost of "millions of non-combat casualties." Over the next several weeks, Eisenhower deployed heavy naval reinforcement and 100 nuclear-capable aircraft to the area, but offered no public pledge to defend Quemoy. He still suspected that Chiang hoped to "drag us into attacking . . . the whole of China."

The president and his secretary of state once again played the roles of "good cop/bad cop" in their public messages. On September 4, Dulles announced that the attack on Quemoy threatened Taiwan and that under the defense treaty this required U.S. intervention. He made sure the press reported the deployment of nuclear-capable missiles and artillery to Taiwan. Eisenhower, however, struck a different chord, suggesting that the time was right for China to renounce the use of force against Taiwan and resume ambassadorial talks with the United States. On September 6, China agreed to hold talks in Warsaw starting on September 15. The shelling continued, but Chinese gunners took care to avoid hitting U.S. naval ships escorting Taiwan vessels supplying Quemoy. This effectively ended the effort to starve or bomb out the garrison.

In Warsaw, American negotiators proposed that both Chinese governments agree to demilitarize the offshore islands. Eisenhower again pressed Chiang to withdraw his troops, arguing that a voluntary pullout would reduce tensions without compromising Taiwan's security. Chiang balked at surrendering any territory. Mao also refused the deal. He feared that if the Nationalists actually abandoned the offshore islands and settled down exclusively on Taiwan, it would create a pretext for the United States and other nations to adopt a "two-China policy." This would mean treating Taiwan and the PRC as two legitimate but separate governments. Both Mao and Chiang rejected this, insisting each headed the one true government of *all* China.

To make certain the besieged Nationalists on Quemoy did not abandon the island, at one point a Communist military commander actually proposed that the PRC supply the besieged garrison. In October, Chinese officials suggested a face-saving deal. China would cease shelling Quemoy if the U.S. Navy ceased offering protection to Taiwan's supply ships. Washington agreed and Nationalist vessels delivered supplies. Soon the PRC announced it would shell the island only on odd-numbered days, a tactic Eisenhower compared to the plot of a Gilbert and Sullivan operetta. Soon the shelling ended completely and the crisis passed, as well as the idea of demilitarizing the islands.

At the end of 1958, Dulles visited Taiwan and in talks with Chiang again insisted that although the United States would defend the island, it would not support an invasion to retake the mainland. Pressed by the American, Chiang issued an ambiguous pledge that force might not be needed to "restore freedom to the mainland."

Meanwhile, the ambassadorial talks in Warsaw again stalemated. Washington demanded China renounce the use of force against Taiwan, whereas Beijing insisted that the United States withdraw its armed forces from Taiwan and nearby waters. Contacts soon lapsed and the two nations' positions remained frozen for another decade.

The confrontation in the Taiwan Straits claimed another casualty, as Sino–Soviet relations deteriorated. In September 1959 Khrushchev flew to Beijing directly after a surprisingly upbeat visit to the United States. Hopeful that he could reach a variety of deals with Eisenhower on issues such as banning nuclear testing and increasing trade, the Soviet leader called on Mao to "ease international relations" by showing new restraint toward Taiwan. The meeting descended into name calling as Khrushchev criticized China's threatened use of force to adjust

Near the end of his term in 1960, President Eisenhower visits Chiang Kai-shek and Soong Mei-ling on Taiwan. (Hank Walker/Getty Images)

its disputed border with India and labeled as "irresponsible" Mao's claim that China could survive a nuclear war with acceptable losses. Mao condemned Khrushchev as a "sellout" and went on to accuse Chinese who faulted the Great Leap for colluding with the Soviets. Soon, the Soviets began withdrawing most of their 1,400 economic and military advisers from China and aid from Moscow ceased.

Although American policy makers had for a decade hoped to drive a wedge between Moscow and Beijing, officials from Eisenhower down were uncertain what to make of the emerging split. Some dismissed it as superficial, whereas others claimed it was merely Communist disinformation. Not surprisingly, Chiang Kai-shek hammered this point in conversations with Vice President Richard Nixon and with Eisenhower when the president visited Taiwan in 1960. Many shared a view expressed by Dulles shortly before his death in 1959: the Chinese Communists, he opined, "seem to be much more violent and fanatical, more addicted to the use of force than the Russians are or have become." Even centrist career diplomats like Ambassador Chester Bowles agreed that "China is more likely to threaten our interests in the next twenty years than the Soviet Union." Neither Eisenhower nor most of his foreign policy advisers recognized that the rift between China and the Soviet Union ran deep and transcended ideological details. Most U.S. intelligence analysts ignored evidence that did not accord with their preconceptions of the threat posed by China. Military planners worried that acknowledging the collapse of a unified Communist bloc would make it harder to wrest from Congress a wide array of Cold War weapons appropriations. As a result, during his final two years in office, even as he worked to improve relations with the Soviet Union, Eisenhower made no effort to determine how China might respond to more flexible U.S. policies.

SELECTED ADDITIONAL READINGS

Robert Accinelli, *Crisis and Commitment: United States Policy toward Taiwan, 1950–1955* (Chapel Hill, N.C., 1996); Odd Arne Westad, ed. *Brothers in Arms: The Rise and Fall of the Sino–Soviet Alliance, 1945–1963* (Washington, D.C., 1999) and *Restless Empire: China and the World since 1750* (New York, 2012); Rosemary Foot, *The Practice of Power: U.S. Relations with China since 1949* (New York, 1995); Thomas Christensen, *Useful Adversaries: Grand Strategy, Domestic Mobilization, and Sino–American Conflict, 1947–1958* (Princeton, N.J., 1996); John W. Garver, *The Sino–American Alliance: Nationalist China and American Cold War Strategy in Asia* (Armonk, N.Y., 1997); Nancy Bernkoph Tucker, *The China Threat: Memories, Myths, and Realities in the 1950s* (New York, 2012) and *Taiwan, Hong Kong, and the United States, 1945–1992: Uncertain Friendships* (New York, 1994) and *China Confidential: American Diplomats and Sino–American Relations, 1945–1996* (New York, 2001); Gordon Chang, *Friends and Enemies: The United States, China, and the Soviet Union, 1948–1972* (Stanford, Ca., 1990); Qing Simei, *From Allies to Enemies: Visions of Modernity, Identity, and U.S.–China Diplomacy, 1945–1960* (Cambridge, Mass., 2007); Frank Dikotter, *Mao's Great Famine: The History of China's Most Devastating Catastrophe, 1958–62* (New York, 2010) and *The Tragedy of Liberation: A History of the Chinese Revolution, 1945–1957* (London, 2013); Richard Immerman, *Piety, Pragmatism, and Power in U.S. Foreign Policy* (Wilmington, Del., 1996); Stephen Kinzer, *The Brothers: John Foster Dulles, Allen Dulles, and Their Secret World War* (New York, 2013); Stanley D. Bachrack, *The Committee of One Million: China Lobby Politics, 1953–1971* (New York, 1976); John L. Gaddis, *Strategies of Containment* (New York, 1982); Michael Schaller, *Altered States: The U.S. and Japan since the Occupation* (New York, 1997); John L. Lewis and Xue Litai, *China Builds the Bomb* (Stanford, Ca., 1988); Qiang Zhai, *China and the Vietnam Wars, 1950–1975* (Chapel Hill, N.C., 2000) and *The Dragon, the Lion, and the Eagle: Chinese–British–American Relations, 1949–1958* (Kent, Oh., 1990); Chen Jian, *Mao's China and the Cold War* (Chapel Hill, N.C., 2001); Zhang Shu Guan, *Deterrence and Strategic Culture: Chinese–American Confrontations, 1949–1958* (Ithaca, N.Y., 1992); Robert Schulzinger, *A Time for War: The United States and Vietnam, 1941–1975* (New York, 1997); Frederick Logevall, *Embers of War: The Fall of an Empire and the Making of America's Vietnam* (New York, 2012).

CHAPTER 9

China, the New Frontier, and the Vietnam War, 1961–1969

In the 1960 presidential campaign, candidates Richard M. Nixon and John F. Kennedy vigorously debated who could do a better job resisting Communist threats and stimulating economic growth. Neither man had much to say about the three issues that dominated the following decade, civil rights, poverty, and Vietnam. On topics such as Cuba, where Fidel Castro had allied himself with the Soviet Union, and in the race to produce long-range missiles, Kennedy criticized the Eisenhower administration as inept.[1]

During these first-ever televised presidential debates, Kennedy put Nixon on the defensive by mocking him as a "trigger-happy Republican" whose reliance on "tired thinking" would sacrifice U.S. troops and perhaps start a nuclear war to protect the Nationalist-held islands along China's coast. "Quemoy and Matsu," he insisted, where "not essential to the defense of Formosa (Taiwan)." Nixon struck back, accusing Kennedy of willingness to "hand over part of the Free World" to Communist aggressors. He assured his audience he would never "hand over one square foot."

Kennedy responded that Eisenhower had several times urged Chiang to withdraw troops from these outposts to focus on defending Taiwan. Nixon, he suggested, was at odds with his own boss. The flustered vice president faulted Kennedy's "wooly thinking" but the senator had the facts on his side. In any case, the real issue, Kennedy explained throughout the campaign, was not the fate of these tiny offshore islands but the fact that Republicans had overcommitted the United States to the nuclear defense of marginal areas. As president, he would expand conventional military power to credibly resist Communist threats in the emerging Third World. What Kennedy did not propose was re-examining the China policy he inherited.

---

[1]Eisenhower had a low regard for both his likely successors. He considered Nixon unworthy and told friends he could scarcely believe that the same electorate that had sent him twice to the White House "could turn the government over to a man like Kennedy."

[After he took office, JFK seldom spoke publicly about China. When he did, it was usually to describe the threat it posed to peace.] Kennedy's reluctance to engage China in negotiations or to recognize the PRC is sometimes attributed to a meeting he had with Eisenhower on the eve of his inauguration in January 1961. According to accounts by administration insiders Clark Clifford and Dean Rusk, Ike threatened to mobilize the public against the new president if he extended diplomatic recognition to China. Since Eisenhower himself had frequently lamented China's isolation and called for a more flexible approach, it is unclear why he would make such a threat or why Kennedy would take it especially seriously.

Shortly before his death in November 1963, Kennedy told reporters that he was not wedded to a policy of unremitting hostility toward mainland China. If and when Beijing showed a willingness to coexist peacefully, Kennedy indicated he was open to modifying American policy. Theodore Sorensen, a close presidential adviser, later wrote that Kennedy "felt dissatisfied with his administration's failure to break new ground" on China and might have initiated new policies during his second term. Of course, many of Kennedy's defenders also assert that despite sending more than 15,000 American soldiers to Vietnam, he intended to avoid escalating the conflict once safely re-elected. Although no one can know for certain what he might have done had he lived, Kennedy's record on China was not one that suggested a dramatic change was likely. Kennedy perceived China, like Cuba, as a challenge to his view of world order.

Like many Democrats of his generation, Kennedy recalled vividly the charge that his party had lost China. [As a young congressman in 1949, he was one of the few Democrats who joined the attack on Truman and Acheson.] He lamented how an ally whose "freedom we once fought to preserve" had been "frittered away" by "our diplomats and president." In the mid-1950s Kennedy joined the lobbying group American Friends of Vietnam and enthusiastically supported Ngo Dinh Diem. He described Diem and South Vietnam as "the cornerstone of the Free World in Southeast Asia, the keystone in the arch, the finger in the dike." South Vietnam, he stressed, was "our offspring" and played a vital role in sealing off Southeast Asia from Chinese Communism. Before entering the White House, Kennedy praised South Vietnam as a showcase of democracy and proof of how the United States could cultivate friends in former colonial areas.

By the time Kennedy became president, several influential policy groups challenged the position of the Committee of One Million and broached the idea of recognizing "two Chinas" or "one China, one Taiwan." During 1959, studies conducted by the Senate Foreign Relations Committee and by the prestigious Rockefeller Brothers Fund suggested the time had come to openly discuss a two-China policy, accepting the legitimacy of the governments in both Beijing and Taipei. The respected Democratic liberal and two-time presidential candidate, Adlai Stevenson, published similar views in an article that appeared in *Foreign Affairs* in January 1960. Taiwan, he argued, warranted recognition as an independent state and should be accorded this status—once Chiang Kai-shek abandoned his claim to the mainland.

Despite a quiet consensus among foreign policy experts that the time had come to revisit and revise China policy, few politicians aspiring to national office openly questioned orthodox thinking. Even Eisenhower, who had nothing to fear from voters after 1956, refrained from doing anything likely to provoke the wrath of the China Lobby and other groups committed to keeping China an outcast and out of the UN.

Tensions between China and the Soviet Union increased in the months before Kennedy took office. Mao ridiculed Khrushchev's "timid" attitude toward the West. He complained at the lack of support China received for retaking Taiwan and Soviet reluctance to help China develop nuclear weapons. Why, Mao asked, did Moscow express support for India in its border dispute with China? Khrushchev, the Chinese leader complained, had undermined the Great Leap Forward and refused to treat the PRC (or Mao) as an equal. When Mao boasted of China's capacity to survive a nuclear war, the Soviet leader retorted that after such a war, the living would envy the dead. By mid-1960, Khrushchev had heard enough and decided to give Mao the opportunity to practice the self-reliance he boasted of by withdrawing from China all remaining Soviet advisers and cutting off aid. For all practical purposes, the Sino–Soviet alliance was finished.

Kennedy and his senior foreign policy advisers, such as Secretary of State Dean Rusk and Defense Secretary Robert McNamara, remained wary of China's motives and behavior. The Soviets represented a long-term challenge, they agreed, but China seemed a more immediate threat. Mao's call for world revolution and support (more rhetorical than material) for "wars of national liberation" threatened the Third World. They were deeply troubled by China's quest in the early 1960s to acquire nuclear weapons and shared Eisenhower's ambivalence about the Sino–Soviet split. The Communist rivals' "dispute over how to bury the West is no grounds for Western rejoicing," Kennedy remarked to aides. The new president believed that to meet the threat posed by China and other enemies, the United States must rapidly increase military spending and develop a "flexible response" capable of countering both nuclear threats and Chinese-supported insurgencies. Where some American strategists had once thought it might be possible to cooperate with China against the Soviet menace, they now speculated whether the United States and Soviet Union should combine their efforts to contain a reckless China.

The growing threat to Diem in South Vietnam by Communist Viet Cong guerrillas struck Kennedy as partly a test of wills with China. During his thousand days in office, JFK increased the number of American military personnel in Vietnam from 1,000 to 16,000 and spent more than $1 billion in aid to the Saigon regime. Even after Kennedy authorized support for a coup to remove the increasingly erratic Diem in November 1963, he repeated his belief in the domino theory. If South Vietnam went, Kennedy told an aide, "it would give the impression that the wave of the future in Southeast Asia was China and the Communists."

A few senior diplomats, some members of the National Security Council, and two highly qualified academics serving as ambassadors (John Kenneth Galbraith in India and Edwin O. Reischauer in Japan) questioned administration policy.

China's revolutionary rhetoric, they insisted, was more bark than bite. For all Mao's talk of battling imperialism, China provided only modest aid and encouragement to revolutionary movements. When Galbraith sent an impassioned cable arguing that the United States should at least allow China to join the UN, Secretary of State Rusk replied, "to the extent that your position has any merit it has been fully considered and rejected."[2]

Kennedy promised Chiang that the United States would exercise its veto if the UN voted to admit China to its ranks. He also tacitly approved additional covert raids from Taiwan on the Chinese mainland. The terrible famine that still raged in 1961–1962 as a result of Mao's Great Leap policies kindled hope in Chiang's mind that the Chinese people would soon rise up against the Communist regime and pave the way for an invasion. Kennedy declined requests to assist such an invasion but agreed to supply equipment for limited airdrops and amphibious raids.

By the summer of 1962 Nationalist harassment provoked Mao to transfer large numbers of troops to the south China coast opposite Taiwan. If warfare erupted, Kennedy and his aides realized, the United States would likely be drawn into the fighting. Even Secretary of State Rusk, who harbored a deep loathing for the PRC, hoped to avoid missteps that might escalate into a Korean-type confrontation. Rusk reactivated the long-dormant Warsaw ambassadorial channel in June 1962. There, American diplomats told their Chinese counterparts that Washington would not support a Nationalist invasion of the mainland. Although this prompted both sides to step back from the brink, the divide between the United States and PRC remained unbridged.

During Kennedy's final year in the White House, his administration's view of China grew even bleaker. Two events during October 1962—the Cuban missile crisis and the China–India border war—convinced Kennedy that the PRC threatened global security. Although Soviet premier Nikita Khrushchev had several motives for attempting to deploy medium-range nuclear armed missiles to Cuba, many American intelligence analysts believed that Mao's ridicule of Soviet efforts to cooperate with the United States prompted him to take a dangerous gamble in Cuba.[3] Evidence of Chinese pressure on the Soviet Union came mostly after the

---

[2]U.S. officials discounted Chinese efforts at international cooperation in the early 1960s as insincere or nefarious. In fact, the PRC simultaneously opposed some of the norms of international behavior while seeking to join the community of nations. Barred from most international organizations, Beijing searched for ways to demonstrate Chinese accomplishments, such as in sport. In 1962 China recruited a Japanese table tennis champion to coach China's team. Zhou Enlai explained how "ever since the opium wars we have suffered many humiliating experiences. We reasoned that sport is a way to wipe away the source of inferiority created by the humiliations." The PRC soon became a dominant force in table tennis.

[3]Castro and Khrushchev hoped the missiles would deter another U.S. invasion of the island. Despite claims that the United States lagged behind the Soviets in rockets—the so-called missile gap—the United States had many more long-range missiles in its arsenal. Placing some shorter-range weapons on Cuba that could reach American soil would redress this imbalance, Khrushchev hoped. It might also blunt Chinese criticism that the Soviet Union cowered before the United States.

fact, when Mao criticized Khrushchev's retreat in the face of the U.S. naval blockade of Cuba. Kennedy saw this as a sign that Mao scoffed at the risks of nuclear war.

On October 20, 1962, in the midst of the Cuban crisis, China launched a month-long attack along its Himalayan border with India. Although described by the Western press as a case of unprovoked aggression on peaceful India, the facts were less clear. Even Chiang Kai-shek agreed with Mao that the Indians relied on maps drawn by British colonialists to illegally occupy Chinese soil. Indian military action, as much as the Chinese, provoked the attack. However, nearly all Americans perceived India as a victim of Chinese warmongering. When Chinese troops halted their advance after occupying the disputed territory, the U.S. government suggested that only the threat of American intervention had blocked a Chinese sweep into India.

The Cuban and Indian crises prompted the Kennedy administration to push harder for a long-delayed nuclear test ban agreement with the Soviets. A deal that put a lid on tests, Kennedy hoped, would restrain China's effort to develop atomic weapons. As the president put it, "any negotiations that can hold back the Chinese Communists are most important . . . because they loom as our major antagonists of the late-1960s and beyond." Kennedy's aides speculated that Khrushchev stalled on agreeing to a test ban because he feared Chinese criticism. As one negotiator reported, "this challenge by the Chinese Communists of Kremlin leadership" of world Communism "is causing the greatest concern" to the Soviets. Worried that a nuclear armed China would be the "greatest menace on earth," Kennedy sent Averell Harriman to Moscow in the summer of 1963 to secure a deal. The "Chinese problem," JFK told Harriman, was a threat to everyone. Even "relatively small forces in the hands of the Chinese Communists could be very dangerous to us all." To block China's acquisition of nuclear weapons, Kennedy broached the idea to Khrushchev whether "to take Soviet action or to accept U.S. action aimed at" stopping this. The president appeared to suggest either joint or separate Soviet–American air or missile strikes to destroy Chinese nuclear development facilities.

Neither power opted to strike, however, and in October 1963 Moscow and Washington signed a limited test ban treaty. Undeterred, China continued its effort to develop nuclear weapons and in October 1964 detonated its first atomic device. (When China tested a much more powerful hydrogen bomb in 1967, Dean Rusk warned of "a billion Chinese armed with nuclear weapons.") At the time of his death in November 1963, Kennedy remained extremely wary of the PRC and considered the growing war in Vietnam a test of America's resolve and ability to curb China's expansion.

ALL THE WAY WITH LBJ

In October 1966, almost three years after Lyndon Johnson assumed the presidency, National Security Adviser Walt Rostow sent a reassuring message to his boss. The United States had achieved much of value in Latin America, Africa, and

Europe, Rostow wrote, but "it is clear that a good part of your Administration's place in history will consist of the reshaping of Asia and our relations with it." This assessment proved true, but not exactly in the way Rostow imagined. By 1968, after four years of increasingly bitter combat in Southeast Asia, America's domestic tranquility, international stature, and Asia policy were in tatters. The disaster in Vietnam not only tarnished Johnson's Great Society reforms, but also stymied any hope of a new departure in Sino–American relations.

With the Vietnam war still just "a cloud on the horizon no bigger than a man's hand," as one presidential adviser put it at the start of his presidency in November 1963, some of Johnson's staff thought it a good time to discuss a change in China policy. A month after the president's death, Assistant Secretary of State Roger Hilsman spoke publicly about the value of recognizing two Chinas: one on Taiwan and the other on the mainland. The China Lobby largely ignored the speech, as did nearly everyone else. In January 1964, when French President Charles de Gaulle recognized the PRC and severed ties to Taiwan, the Johnson administration condemned the move. China should be permitted to join the community of nations, Johnson and Dean Rusk agreed, only after it abandoned its "doctrine of violence" and support for "wars of national liberation."

In Washington, Vietnam became the test of Chinese intentions. "We will not permit," Johnson declared, the "independent nations of the East to be swallowed up by Communist conquest." As the series of weak post-Diem governments in Saigon lost control of rural Vietnam during 1964 and 1965, Johnson and his advisers interpreted the fighting as a proxy battle between Washington and Beijing. LBJ considered Ho Chi Minh and North Vietnam little more than stand-ins for Mao Zedong and China, the tail of the powerful Chinese dog.

Some midlevel policy analysts, such as NSC China expert James Thomson, challenged the conventional wisdom about Vietnam. After all, as of 1964 China had provided only advisers, light weapons, and supplies to North Vietnam. In a memo to top Johnson aide McGeorge Bundy, Thomson questioned whether "this tail (Vietnam) even belongs to that particular dog (China)." He warned against the tendency to "push too far the thesis of Peking's responsibility for the South Vietnam crisis."

In fact, although both the Soviet Union and China supported Vietnamese unification and provided economic and military aid to North Vietnam, a victory by Hanoi was not of primary importance to either Communist power. If the United States chose to exhaust itself fighting in Southeast Asia, both Moscow and Beijing were perfectly happy to oblige. At a reasonable cost to themselves in the form of assistance to Hanoi, they could sustain the conflict till the last Vietnamese. At the same time, neither China nor the Soviet Union wanted to be accused by other communist states of failing to support Vietnam in its fight against imperialism. North Vietnam benefitted by playing China and the Soviet Union against each other in its quest for aid.

President Johnson felt trapped between his commitment to the Great Society social reforms and a belief that the loss of Vietnam to Communism would erode the barrier to Chinese expansion and embolden his Republican critics. Reflecting later on his decision early in 1965 to "Americanize" the war by committing substantial air and ground forces, Johnson told biographer Doris Kearns that he risked being "crucified" whatever he did.

> If I left the woman I really loved, the Great Society, in order to get involved with that bitch of a war on the other side of the world, then I would lose everything at home. All my programs. All my hopes to feed the hungry and shelter the homeless. All my dreams to provide education and medical care to the browns and the blacks and the lame and the poor. But if I left that war and let the Communists take over South Vietnam then I would be seen as a coward, and my nation would be seen as an appeaser and we would both find it impossible to accomplish anything for anybody on the entire globe.

Johnson reasoned by analogy, comparing Vietnam to the Chinese civil war and the domestic backlash that befell the Truman administration after the Communist victory in 1949.

> Everything I knew about history told me that if I got out of Vietnam and let Ho Chi Minh run through the streets of Saigon then I'd be doing exactly what Chamberlain did in [the run up to] W.W. II. I'd be giving a big fat reward to aggression. And I knew that if we let Communist aggression succeed in taking over South Vietnam there would follow in this country an endless national debate—a mean and destructive debate—that would shatter my presidency, kill my administration, and damage our democracy. I knew that Harry Truman and Dean Acheson had lost effectiveness from the day the Communists took over China. I believed that the loss of China had played a large role in the rise of Joe McCarthy. And I knew that all those problems taken together were chicken shit compared with what might happen if we lost Vietnam.[4]

He feared that "Who Lost Vietnam?" would become the mantra of those determined to undo his presidency, much as the loss of China haunted Truman. Containing Republicans at home required containing China abroad.

Following his huge election sweep in November 1964, Johnson began escalating the American military presence in Vietnam, first with air power and then with combat troops. Bombing the north, he hoped, would crack the enemy's morale and block its ability to send soldiers and supplies south. Meanwhile, coordinated air and ground attacks would destroy guerrilla units in the south. With enough firepower, Johnson and his advisers believed, the United States could, in a few years, reach a crossover point where an enhanced Army of the Republic of Vietnam could take over most of the fighting. By early 1968, nearly half a million uniformed Americans served in and around Vietnam. U.S. aircraft dropped

---

[4]In 1965 North Vietnamese leaders also cited the "lesson" of appeasing Hitler at the Munich conference in 1938 where the British and French sacrificed democratic Czechoslovakia. Any failure to match U.S. escalation of the war in the south, they argued, would further embolden Johnson. "No More Munichs!," they declared, to justify expanding the fight against U.S. forces.

more tons of bombs over Vietnam, Laos, and Cambodia than had been used against Germany and Japan in World War II.

Johnson often envisioned the war as a contest of wills between Beijing and Washington. In April 1965 he declared that "over this war—and all Asia—is another reality: the deepening shadow of Communist China." The "rulers of Hanoi," he claimed, were "pushed on by Peking," making the "contest in Vietnam . . . part of a wider pattern of Chinese aggression." Later that year he claimed that China targeted not only Vietnam, "but all Asia." Unless American troops held South Vietnam, Vice President Hubert Humphrey told a senate friend in 1965, the Chinese would take "all Asia. Because they saw the PRC as North Vietnam's main enabler, Johnson and his advisers were determined to curb China's ambitions. Only after it observed international norms could the PRC enter the family of nations. As one Defense Department official put it, China must learn better table manners before being invited to dinner.

Given Chinese rhetoric, some of these fears were understandable, if much exaggerated. Between 1960 and 1965, China pursued a variety of peaceful foreign contacts, especially among the emerging nations of Africa. It also tried to cement an alliance with Indonesia, a nation with a large Chinese minority.[5] It continued to seek UN membership, despite American opposition. In the fall of 1965, as the U.S. buildup accelerated in Vietnam, Mao's designated heir, People's Liberation Army commander Lin Biao, published an article that convinced Americans of China's hostile intent. Writing under the title "Long Live the Victory of the People's War," Lin proclaimed China's support for revolutionary struggles throughout the Third World. Johnson and his aides compared it to Hitler's infamous blueprint for expansion, *Mein Kampf.* In fact, Lin stressed that although China supported the goal of world revolution, the resources, leadership, and bodies to carry it out would have to be found locally.

Mao and other Chinese leaders debated the threat posed by the American air, land, and sea forces near their southwestern border. In addition to increasing military aid to Hanoi, they deployed fighter planes near North Vietnam and along the south China coast, which several times engaged American aircraft that strayed into Chinese air space. In 1966, even as Johnson dramatically escalated the war in Vietnam, he issued a call for some sort of reconciliation with China. But his words were drowned out by U.S. military actions. Meanwhile, Mao turned his gaze inward, questioning the very essence of the China he helped create.

Since the terrible consequences of the Great Leap Forward, Mao had contemplated how to revitalize what he saw as China's lagging revolutionary spirit

---

[5] In September 1965 Indonesian Communists, allied to the mercurial President Sukarno, staged a botched coup. Muslim army generals reacted fiercely, destroying the Indonesian Communist Party, killing many of its ethnic Chinese supporters, and reducing Sukarno to a figurehead. U.S. officials supported the generals and turned a blind eye to the slaughter that ensued. With Mao's hope of a Chinese–Indonesian regional alliance shattered, the PRC pulled back from most of its foreign initiatives.

and stagnant economy. As Japan, Hong Kong, and Taiwan grew more prosperous, China lagged further behind. In addition to foreign enemies such as the United States and the Soviet Union, Mao faulted domestic foes entrenched in the Communist Party and government bureaucracy for holding on to old ways of thinking rather than pursuing a "permanent revolution." Criticizing the content of his own government's propaganda, in 1966 Mao remarked that "the best thing he had read in years" was a 16-page pamphlet titled "How to Play Table Tennis." To combat what he saw as an ossified bureaucracy and to enhance his own power, in 1966 Mao launched the Great Proletarian Cultural Revolution.[6]

Mao called on groups of so-called Red Guards, many of them teens or young adults, to shake up the Communist Party, government organizations, factory management, and rural communes. China recalled all but one of its ambassadors from abroad, expelled or imprisoned many foreign residents, and suspended most of its foreign assistance programs. Mobs torched the British legation in Beijing and threatened the Soviet embassy. As fighting erupted between rival Red Guard factions in China's cities and activists seized control of government agencies, central authority practically dissolved.

American officials viewed China's upheaval as confirmation that Washington could do little to placate such a reckless and hostile adversary. Mao's frequent denunciation of Soviet "social imperialism" persuaded policy analysts that the Sino–Soviet split was real and irreconcilable. At the same time, China's descent into chaos made it less able to affect events outside its borders.

Despite China's reduced ability to engage in meaningful foreign policy, the PRC maintained its material support for North Vietnam. Mao considered aid to Hanoi necessary to counter both American and Soviet influence in Vietnam. Between 1965 and 1968, China deployed a total of about 320,000 noncombat troops to North Vietnam. They served in antiaircraft units, engineering battalions, and other logistic capacities, freeing Vietnamese for combat. Through a variety of indirect channels, Beijing cautioned Washington that it would respond to nuclear attacks on North Vietnam, an American invasion of the North, or air attacks on China by sending combat forces to Vietnam. To protect key industries from attack by either (or both) the United States or the Soviet Union, in 1965 China began relocating factories to the interior west, calling the move a "third line of defense" against foreign attack.

Although President Johnson deeply distrusted China, he desperately hoped to avoid fighting the PRC. Discussing with the Joint Chiefs moves to escalate troop levels in 1965, LBJ asked whether sending several hundred thousand combat soldiers to South Vietnam "won't cause Russia and China to come in." The army's chief of staff minimized the risk. But recalling the events of 1950 when he served

---

[6]Mao's doctor reported that the leader's favorite movie in the run-up to the Cultural Revolution was the 1952 American western, *High Noon*, starring Gary Cooper. Mao apparently identified with the rugged sheriff who, when deserted by his own supporters, battled on his own to kill the outlaws trying to take over his town.

in the senate, the president shot back, "MacArthur didn't think they would come into Korea either."[7]

Over the next two years American diplomats in Warsaw informed their Chinese counterparts that the United States intended neither to occupy or destroy North Vietnam nor to attack China. Chinese officials indicated that if American forces observed these tactical limits, Beijing would not directly enter the war on behalf of the north. These mutual signals reduced the likelihood of a repetition of the events of 1950 in Korea.

Even as the war in Vietnam expanded, some influential Americans articulated misgivings about administration policy. For example, Senator J. William Fulbright, chairman of the Foreign Relations Committee, held hearings in 1964 that provided a forum for dissenting views on China policy. When Secretary of State Rusk insisted it was not possible to get on peacefully with China while it aided Hanoi and threatened force against Taiwan, Fulbright dismissed this view and endorsed a policy of "competitive co-existence" with the PRC. Furious at Fulbright for challenging administration policy, Johnson declared that "it is not we who must examine our view of China. It is the Chinese Communists who must re-examine their view of the world."

Two years later, with the war in Vietnam ever larger, Fulbright convened another round of Senate hearings on China policy. He provided a forum for several academic experts, such as A. Doak Barnett and John K. Fairbank, who spoke passionately about the importance of positively engaging China. Fulbright characterized their approach as "containment without isolation." In response to calls by academics, journalists, and others to reassess policy, the State Department announced it would permit limited scientific, cultural, and educational exchanges between private Chinese and Americans. In 1967 and 1968, it relaxed limits on the export of medicine to China and offered a few entry visas to Chinese journalists, none of whom accepted.

Throughout the 1960s, ordinary Americans learned little about China except for occasional reports about rampaging Red Guards whose violence sometimes appeared as terrifying as the Soviet nuclear arsenal. As in earlier decades, Hollywood contributed to this fear-mongering. Six new Fu Manchu films were released during the 1960s, several starring Christopher Lee, who portrayed the villain with distinct "Communist" overtones. In the 1962 film *Dr. No*, Sean Connery as James Bond foiled a plot by the devious Doctor (a "Chinese gent" in a "Mao-suit") to disrupt America's space program. Two movies starring leading actors portrayed Chinese Communists as even more ruthless than the Soviet enemy. In *The Manchurian Candidate* (1962), Frank Sinatra played an army intelligence officer who uncovered a plot hatched during the Korean War by Soviet

---

[7]Johnson had reason to be wary. During a White House briefing on bombing targets in North Vietnam, a general pointed to a position on a large map indicating where U.S. planes would attack. The president realized he had pointed to a location in China, not Vietnam.

and Chinese leaders to brainwash captured American soldiers and send them home as sleeper agents to assassinate a presidential candidate and assure the election of their stooge. *The Chairman* (1969) depicted China convulsed by the Cultural Revolution. Gregory Peck portrayed an American scientist sent to Beijing by the U.S. *and* Soviet governments to steal the formula for an enzyme that would allow food crops to grow in any climate. During a ping-pong game (!) with Mao, Peck learns the chairman intends to use the enzyme to blackmail hungry Third World nations. He foils the plot by spirting the formula out of China and across the Soviet border hidden in a copy of Mao's book of revolutionary quotations.

Hostile stereotypes and policy conflicts were too deeply embedded in both societies to allow a policy change any time soon. Meanwhile, the escalating war in Vietnam overshadowed all American initiatives in Asia. At the end of January 1968, after three years of intensive bombing and heavy ground fighting by U.S. forces, about 100,000 Viet Cong guerrillas launched the Tet Offensive, their biggest operation yet. Although militarily inconclusive, the countrywide attacks exposed the weakness of the South Vietnamese government and the failure of the United States to eradicate the insurgency despite its best effort. As hope of imminent victory evaporated, the American public lost faith in its leaders and patience with the war. At the end of March, a despondent President Johnson announced he would cap force levels in Vietnam, seek a negotiated settlement, and not stand for re-election. Without formally responding to these decisions, the PRC implicitly acknowledged the change by reducing its own military assistance to North Vietnam. With the American threat receding, Mao spoke more frequently of the threat to China posed by Soviet "social imperialism."

Over time, the American pullback from Vietnam, along with increased Sino–Soviet tensions, altered East Asian politics. But in 1968, little had changed on the ground. In May, China again suspended the periodic ambassadorial talks in Warsaw, declaring that as long as the United States continued to defend Taiwan, "there is nothing to talk about." Only after Washington dramatically changed course in Vietnam and Taiwan—and the Soviet challenge mounted— did the options arise for a reset of Sino–American relations.

SELECTED ADDITIONAL READINGS

Noam Kochavi, *A Conflict Perpetuated: China Policy during the Kennedy Years* (Westport, Conn., 2002); Robert Dallek, *An Unfinished Life: John F. Kennedy, 1917–1963* (Boston, 2003); Odd Arne Westad, ed., *Brothers in Arms: The Rise and Fall of the Sino–Soviet Alliance, 1945–1963* (Washington, D.C., 1963); Rosemary Foot, *The Practice of Power: U.S. Relations with China since 1949* (New York, 1995); Gordon Chang, *Friends and Enemies: The United States, China, and the Soviet Union, 1948–1972* (Stanford, Ca., 1990); Diane B. Kunz, ed., *Diplomacy of the Crucial Decade: American Foreign Policy during the 1960s* (New York, 1994); Michael Lumbers, *Piercing the Bamboo Curtain: Tentative Bridge-Building to China during the Johnson Years* (Manchester, 2008); Nancy B. Tucker and Warren Cohen, eds., *Lyndon Johnson Confronts the World: American Foreign Policy,*

1963–1968 (New York, 1994); Michael Schaller, *Altered States: The U.S. and Japan since the Occupation* (New York, 1997); Chen Jian, *Mao's China and the Cold War* (Chapel Hill, N.C., 2000); Qiang Zhai, *China and the Vietnam Wars, 1950–1975* (Chapel Hill, N.C, 2000); Kai Bird, *The Color of Truth: McGeorge Bundy and William Bundy, Brothers in Arms: A Biography* (New York, 1998); Allen Whiting, *The Chinese Calculus of Deterrence: India and Indochina* (Ann Arbor, Mi., 1975); Robert Schulzinger, *A Time for War: The United States and Vietnam, 1941–1975* (New York, 1997).

CHAPTER 10

Only Nixon Could Go to China

During 1968 and 1969, American policy in Asia hit rock bottom. The Tet Offensive and its aftermath (more Americans died in the 12 months following January 1968 than in any other year in Vietnam) shattered the Johnson administration's credibility. The stalemate fueled dissent among "hawks" and "doves" alike, with a majority of Americans expressing opposition to the war. What began as an effort to reassure friend and foe that the United States could create and defend Asian allies ended up shattering the Democratic Party and driving Lyndon Johnson into retirement. America's friends in Western Europe and Japan complained that Washington's obsession with Vietnam had squandered U.S. influence and weakened its alliances.

Japan, America's closest Asian ally, both profited from and resented the Vietnam War. The U.S. military procured many of its supplies in Japan, boosting that nation's economy while worsening America's chronic trade deficit.[1] Tokyo's refusal to send troops to Vietnam or to revalue the Yen against the dollar and curb exports angered both the Johnson and the Nixon administrations. At the same time, a robust anti–Vietnam War movement among the Japanese undermined the security treaty that granted the United States extensive base facilities on the home islands and Okinawa, without which the Vietnam War could not be fought.

Superficially, China seemed to benefit from the ongoing conflict in Southeast Asia. By supplying logistic support to North Vietnam (including more than 300,000 noncombat troops during the 1960s) China claimed some of the credit for humbling "U.S. imperialism" without risking a direct war. In 1968, Mao urged Ho Chi Minh to spurn Johnson's call for peace talks (advice Ho rejected) and push for a quick military victory. The PRC shrugged off an offer from the outgoing

---

[1]To a lesser but important degree, U.S. military spending also spurred economic growth in Taiwan, Thailand, South Korea, and the Philippines.

Johnson administration to resume diplomatic contact in Warsaw. The two sides, a PRC spokesman responded, had "nothing to talk about."

In reality, China faced dire internal and external threats by the late 1960s. Between 1966 and 1968, rival bands of Red Guards, each claiming to support Mao against "revisionists" and "capitalist roaders," fought each other in the streets of major cities. Many government offices ceased to function. Only intervention by the People's Liberation Army prevented utter chaos. Although badly bruised in Vietnam, the United States was not beaten. More than half a million armed Americans remained on China's border. The standoff in the Taiwan Strait continued, as did tensions with India. The emergence of an increasingly rich and assertive Japan rekindled fears among many Chinese stretching back to the 1930s.

But the greatest challenge came from the Soviet Union, which shared a 4,500-mile ill-defined border with the PRC. Sino–Soviet tension increased after Leonid Brezhnev replaced Khrushchev in 1964. By 1965, each side labeled the other a "traitor" to true Communism and deployed large numbers of troops to the border. Mao declared that "social imperialism" now rivaled "capitalist imperialism" as a threat to peace. When Soviet troops invaded Czechoslovakia in August 1968 to depose a liberal Communist regime that had rejected Moscow's leadership, Mao considered it a portent of what the Soviets had in mind for China.

To make matters worse, Mao and his inner circle began to worry about the implications of an actual American withdrawal from Vietnam. The new president, Richard M. Nixon, spoke of the need to reduce the role of ground forces in Asia. If, following the end of the Vietnam War, the United States really withdrew from Asia, how could China resist Soviet military power or even a resurgent Japan? Along with the relocation westward of key industries, Mao instructed urban residents to build tunnels and store grain in preparation for an air attack.

After several years of minor skirmishes along the Sino–Soviet border, the clash turned deadly on March 2, 1969. Both sides claimed ownership of tiny Zhenbao, or Damansky, Island in the middle of the Ussuri River that separated the two countries in the northeast. That day, when Chinese troops held up portraits of Mao to assert their claim, Soviet soldiers dropped their trousers and responded by displaying their bare buttocks. The Chinese opened fire, killing about 60 Soviet border guards. Mao may have encouraged this show of force to deter the Soviets from other actions or to mobilize nationalist sentiment at home. Dueling demonstrations in Beijing and Moscow denounced the other side's "criminal aggression." When Soviet premier Alexei Kosygin attempted to speak by telephone to Mao or Zhou, the Chinese operator called him a "scoundrel revisionist" and refused to connect him.

In mid-March a Soviet artillery barrage near the site of the first clash killed somewhere between dozens and a few hundred Chinese. Ratcheting up the violence, in August the Soviets launched an attack in Xinjiang, near China's nuclear test site, that killed several dozen Chinese troops. Both sides reinforced their border forces and prepared for large-scale fighting.

At home and abroad, Soviet civilian and military leaders spoke openly of the threat from the "yellow hordes." One Soviet spokesman labeled Maoism a "criminal racist theory." The defense minister declared that the time had come to deal with the "squint eyed bastards," perhaps through nuclear strikes. Soviet diplomats at the UN and in Washington spoke of a coming offensive to "kill those yellow sons-of-bitches." Soviet representatives probed American officials about how Washington would respond to a Soviet attack on Chinese nuclear facilities or cities with the aim of "eliminating" the threat and "discrediting the Mao clique."[2]

During the autumn of 1969 key officials were evacuated from Beijing and Mao moved to restore domestic order by ordering an end to all internal "factional struggles by violent means." But any credible resistance to the Soviet threat required that China reexamine its foreign relationships. In a discussion with his physician in August 1969, Mao observed, "We have the Soviet Union to the north and west, India to the south, and Japan to the east." If "all our enemies were to unite," he asked rhetorically, "what do you think we should do?" Then, referring to the United States, Mao answered his own question. "Didn't our ancestors counsel negotiating with faraway countries while fighting those that are near?" It made sense to deal with foreign "rightists" like President Richard Nixon because at least "they say what they really think."

Mao turned for advice to four senior military leaders (Chen Yi, Ye Jianying, Xu Xiangqian, and Nie Rongzhen), all of whom had been purged during the Cultural Revolution. Among these four "old marshals," Chen Yi played the leading role. Although they spent much of 1969 preparing reports, Mao already knew that Chen Yi considered the Soviet Union the greatest threat to China. More specifically, Chen suggested the time had come for the PRC to "play the America card" against the Soviets.

For all his revolutionary romanticism and sometimes delusional view of reality, Mao's instinct about dealing with Nixon proved uncannily accurate. Nearly two years later, in June 1971, the president mused to his closest aides about why Mao hoped to improve relations with the United States. Fundamental shifts in the world balance of power, Nixon explained, made it vital for the two enemies to cooperate. In words nearly identical to what Mao told his physician, Nixon asserted that China "faced by the Soviets on one side, a Soviet-backed India on another" and a resurgent Japan that could "develop [military power and nuclear weapons] fast because of its industrial base" sought protection from the United States. The Chinese Communists might continue to ritually demand that the "U.S. should get out of the Pacific" but, Nixon surmised, they really "don't want that."

---

[2]In 1962–1963, the Kennedy administration had asked how the Soviets would view a preemptive U.S. attack on China's nuclear facilities.

As the American withdrawal from Vietnam proceeded, the president speculated that Japan might either "go with the Soviets or re-arm," both bad alternatives from China's perspective. The rulers in Beijing, he predicted, would come to understand that a continued U.S. military presence in Japan, South Korea, and elsewhere in Southeast Asia was actually "China's [best] hope for Jap restraint" and Soviet containment.

When Nixon took office in January 1969, it seemed improbable that this veteran Cold Warrior would consider China an incipient ally. Throughout the 1950s and 1960s, Nixon had called for expanding the military commitment to Vietnam and blamed China for most of the region's problems. During a debate with Kennedy in 1960 he insisted that the Chinese Communists wanted much more than the offshore islands or even Taiwan. In fact, "they wanted the world." He later faulted Kennedy and Johnson for not doing enough to contain China.

However, in private conversations with American diplomats during 1965–1966 and in an article he published in *Foreign Affairs* in October 1967 ("Asia after Vietnam"), he broached new ideas. For the moment, he explained, the United States must strongly support anti-Communist regimes in Asia and neither trade with nor recognize the PRC. This would convince China it could not "satisfy its imperialistic ambitions." But in the long run, the United States "cannot afford to leave China forever outside the family of nations, there to nurture its fantasies, cherish its hates and threaten its neighbors. There is no place on this planet for a billion of its potentially most able people to live in angry isolation." Mao reportedly read a translation of the article and speculated that if Nixon became president he might change policy toward China.

In a joint editorial of January 20, 1969, China's major state-controlled newspapers, *Renmin ribao* (People's Daily) and *Hong Qi* (Red Flag), mocked the new president as the "jittery chieftain" of "U.S. imperialists," a "jackal" from the same lair as Johnson. His inaugural address proved that the imperialist camp was "beset with profound crises both at home and abroad." Yet, at Mao's command, the government newspapers took the unprecedented step of publishing Nixon's entire speech alongside their criticism. Among his associates, Mao reportedly praised Nixon's pledge to seek an "open world—open to ideas, open to the exchange of goods and people—a world in which no people, great or small, will live in angry isolation."

Shortly after Nixon became president, Zhou Enlai convinced Mao to resume the on-again, off-again Warsaw talks. However, just before the first scheduled meeting, a Chinese diplomat in the Netherlands defected to the United States. When Washington refused to return him, Chinese hard-liners, including Defense chief Lin Biao and Mao's wife, Jiang Qing, persuaded Mao to cancel the encounter.

In many of his public statements, Nixon seemed wedded to the rigid views and policies of his predecessors. When he announced plans in March 1969 to deploy a limited antimissile defense, he claimed it was aimed at blocking a Chinese attack. Neither the United States nor the Soviet Union, Nixon asserted, wanted to "stand naked against a potential Chinese Communist threat." Beijing claimed Nixon was actually colluding with the Soviets in an "evil" conspiracy to wage "nuclear blackmail" against China.

Nixon and his national security adviser, Henry Kissinger, hoped both to engage the Soviets diplomatically and to prevent them from consolidating their position as the single dominant Eurasian power. During most of 1969 the president dangled the prospect of increased trade and other incentives if Moscow persuaded North Vietnam to accept a peace agreement in which they postponed their drive to unify Vietnam. In return for Hanoi agreeing to what was sometimes called a "decent interval," the United States would stop bombing and gradually withdraw American troops. Moscow, it turned out, either could or would not get North Vietnam to accept this plan. About six months into his first term, Nixon decided to see whether China could deliver what the Soviets had not.

On July 21, 1969, Nixon took the first of several incremental steps signaling a new approach to the PRC (Henceforth, American scholars, scientists, and journalists would be permitted to travel to China on their U.S. passports). This represented the first meaningful relaxation on travel in 20 years. A few days later, while visiting several Pacific allies, the president spoke of a new defense posture soon labeled the "Nixon Doctrine." After the end of the Vietnam War, he explained, the United States would refrain from using its own troops to fight in Asia and would rely primarily on its allies. Although China continued to be a "threat to peace," the president acknowledged that internal difficulties caused by the chaotic Cultural Revolution made it "less effective in exporting revolution."

As Henry Kissinger later explained, he and Nixon believed reconciliation with China would reduce Indochina "to its proper scale—a small peninsula on a major continent." The high "drama" of opening ties to the PRC would help "erase for the American people the pain that would inevitably accompany our withdrawal from Southeast Asia." In other words, the excitement – and domestic political advantage—of "finding" China might mitigate the political backlash from eventually "losing" Vietnam.

Chinese strategic thinking followed a roughly similar arc. Between February and September 1969, the "Four Marshalls" reported to Mao about the potential value of cooperating with the United States to counterbalance threats from both the Soviet Union and Japan. By the end of 1969, they broached what Chen Yi called their "wild idea." Even if the Soviet Union did not launch a full-scale attack on China (recent negotiations had somewhat reduced tensions along the border), it remained a greater threat than the United States. American setbacks in Vietnam, they reasoned, had forced the United States to modify its hostility toward China. Accordingly, the PRC now had an opportunity to "utilize the contradiction between the United States and the Soviet Union in a strategic sense, and pursue a breakthrough in Sino–American relations" through high-level talks. In other words, China could play Washington against Moscow.

Mao probably saw an opening to the United States more as a tactical shift than an abandonment of his revolutionary ideals. The danger posed by the Soviet Union and the chaos of the Cultural Revolution required recalibrating, not

Nixon's National Security Adviser, Henry Kissinger, meets Chairman Mao Zedong in 1972.
(© Bettmann/Corbis)

abandoning, his vision. Neither Mao nor his radical allies envisioned cooperation with the United States as a bridge to anything like capitalism. Although Mao
endorsed the wild idea of a tactical alliance with the United States, he continued
to criticize moderates like the hapless Chen Yi as a "sham Marxist" and "anti-
party careerist," even while soliciting his advice.

In August 1969 Kissinger asked Pakistani President Yahya Khan to have his
ambassador in Beijing inform Zhou Enlai that Washington sought to open a
dialogue with China.

Nixon and Kissinger envisioned the opening to China partly as a way to play
off the Soviets and Chinese against each other. For example, in September, when
Soviet Foreign Minister Andrei Gromyko visited the UN, Nixon told Kissinger,
"I think while Gromyko is in the country would be a good time to have another
move to China made."

During the summer of 1969, a Chinese official in Hong Kong mentioned to
an American journalist that if Washington wanted to demonstrate its goodwill,
it should begin by "withdrawing its forces from the Taiwan Strait." In October,
the administration responded by declaring an end to regular U.S. naval patrols in
the strait, ostensibly for "budget reasons." It sent word via Pakistan that this was
intended to set the stage for bilateral contacts. In December, the U.S. ambassador

in Warsaw, Walter Stoessel, literally chased down a Chinese diplomat, Lei Yang, when they both attended a Yugoslav fashion show and passed him a message saying that Nixon wanted "serious, concrete talks" with Beijing. A week later, the Chinese released from captivity two Americans who had accidently sailed their private yacht into Chinese waters a year before. Three days later, Lei Yang invited Stoessel to visit him for the first of several informal conversations.

At these meetings in December 1969 and January 1970, Stoessel explained that Nixon was willing to send a "special representative" to Beijing or to receive a Chinese envoy in Washington. The United States, he added, hoped for a peaceful resolution to Taiwan's status and "opposed any offensive military action by Taiwan against the mainland." Linking improved relations to reaching a settlement in Vietnam, Stoessel added that the sooner the fighting ended, the more rapidly the United States could reduce its military facilities on Taiwan. In a subsequent round of "formal" ambassadorial talks in Warsaw during early 1970, the Chinese representative declared that if the U.S. government wanted to send a representative of "ministerial rank or a special envoy of the U.S. president" to Beijing to explore questions of "fundamental principle," the Chinese government "will be willing to receive him."

This apparent breakthrough proved difficult to translate into action. China's leadership remained uncertain about how to play the "American card" and was reluctant to engage in open-ended talks without a resolution of the Taiwan issue. Nixon and Kissinger were cautious about how quickly to move in a radically new direction. Several State Department officials speculated that China only wanted to pressure the United States to abandon Taiwan and that any deals with Beijing would alienate America's Asian allies. Stung by this criticism, Nixon and Kissinger cut the State Department out of future negotiations.[3] Complicating matters, the Soviets, who probably bugged the Warsaw conversations, passed word to Kissinger that Washington should "not use China as a military threat" against Moscow.

It took more than a year, between the spring of 1970 and the spring of 1971, before Washington and Beijing harmonized their policies. In both countries the absence of established mechanisms to contact the other complicated even rudimentary communication. Moreover, 20 years of official hostility had made China's few "America specialists," like America's remaining "China hands," wary of getting too far in front of their political masters. In May 1970, the U.S. invasion

---

[3]Nixon had casually mentioned to some congressional supporters of Taiwan, including Senator Karl Mundt and Representative Walter Judd, that he favored new approaches to dealing with the PRC. They appeared to take the news in stride, convincing Nixon that the old China Lobby had lost its political punch. Both the president and Kissinger repeatedly assured Taiwanese officials that they only sought to reduce tensions in East Asia, not to recognize the PRC or to abandon Taiwan. "I will never sell you down the river," Nixon told Jiang Jingguo, Chiang Kai-shek's son, in 1970. A year later, in April of 1971, Nixon told Kissinger that although it was a "shame" that near the "end of his life" Chiang Kai-shek would be shocked by the turn in U.S. policy, "we have to be cold about it."

of Cambodia prompted Mao to denounce American aggressors and their "running dogs" and to cancel a new round of Warsaw talks. Nixon, although deeply offended by Mao's language, continued to focus on China.[4]

During a late-night ramble among antiwar protesters near the Lincoln Memorial following the Cambodian invasion, the president told a startled group of students they should travel and "see the world." The "great mainland of China," he predicted, would soon be opened. Over the next few months Nixon told journalists he hoped to visit China, and during an autumn 1970 banquet for Romanian strong man and Chinese ally Nicolae Ceausescu he publicly referred to the People's Republic of China, the first time a president had spoken the PRC's name in public. In addition to these public signals, both Nixon and Kissinger passed a variety of messages to China via the Pakistani channel and through General Vernon Walters, a military attaché in Paris, stressing their desire to open direct talks.

Messages from China seemed receptive to direct talks, so long as they focused on ending the U.S. security commitment to Taiwan. Nixon and Kissinger tried to finesse this problem by stating that although discussion should not be limited to the question of Taiwan, the United States intended to reduce its military presence on the island as tensions in the region—meaning the Vietnam War—abated.

Neither Nixon nor Kissinger knew that an emerging power struggle in Beijing had complicated the foreign policy debate. Between the summer of 1970 and September 1971, Mao's defense minister and designated heir, Lin Biao, had questioned the new direction in Chinese foreign policy. Although the details of the conflict remain murky, Lin and his followers criticized the wisdom of taking a hard line toward the Soviet Union while reconciling with the United States. They seemed to favor either improving relations with Moscow or maintaining hostile relations with both great powers. Lin may also have worried that in any reshuffling of policy or personnel, he would be odd man out, just like Mao's previous designated heirs. Mao may have deferred meeting with a presidential envoy until he isolated Lin.

On October 1, 1970, Mao felt confident enough to send what he considered a strong signal to Washington and perhaps to his own people. He invited his first American chronicler, author of *Red Star Over China* in 1937, Edgar Snow, to stand beside him atop Tiananmen while he reviewed a national day parade.

Snow had visited China several times since the Communist victory in 1949 and written positive accounts. Dismissed by some Americans an apologist for the PRC, Snow lived in self-imposed exile in Switzerland. Remarkably, Mao and Zhou believed (incorrectly) Snow must work for the CIA to have been allowed to

---

[4]Despite the cancelation and Mao's harsh words, in July 1970 as a good will gesture China released Bishop James Walsh, an American cleric imprisoned in China as a spy since 1958.

Mao Zedong invites his "old friend," American journalist Edgar Snow, to join him on Tiananmen on China's national holiday, October 1, 1970. (Pictures from History/Bridgeman Images)

travel internationally and publish criticism of U.S. policy. This affiliation, they concluded, made him an ideal communication channel. To show his receptivity toward Americans, Mao instructed the Chinese press to publish pictures of Snow standing beside him. When officials in Washington took no notice of the joint appearance, Mao invited Snow to interview him. Chinese press coverage highlighted Mao's statement that he would be happy to welcome Nixon to China in an official or private capacity. Nixon should "just get on a plane and come."

Ironically, while Mao thought Snow might work for the CIA, Nixon and Kissinger dismissed the journalist as a "Communist propagandist" and ignored his interview with Mao. Snow spent several frustrating months attempting to sell the story and photographs of his meeting with Mao to an American magazine. Ultimately, *Life* magazine, whose recently deceased publisher, Henry Luce, worked so hard to demonize the Communists, printed the sympathetic feature. By then, the months-old interview attracted little official interest.

In April 1971, the Chinese made a dramatic gesture to signal their desire to talk. After an unscripted exchange of greetings and small gifts between Chinese and American players at a table tennis tournament in Nagoya, Japan, Mao instructed the Chinese team to invite the Americans to play an exhibition match in China. Chinese officials assumed, incorrectly, that the American team had official government status.[5] In fact, the American players had no official affiliation and barely enough money to pay for their hotel in Japan. The Chinese invitation had the whiff of an imperial summons: since U.S. players had requested an invitation "so many times," China agreed to receive them. When it appeared that some of the American players could not pay their way, China offered to "render them assistance." With the blessings of the Nixon administration (whose top officials admitted they knew almost nothing about the U.S. Table Tennis Association), the ping-pong players flew to Hong Kong, traveled by rail to Guangzhou, and then flew to Beijing.

The visit of the first American delegation since 1949 elicited genuine excitement in both countries. American journalists who accompanied the team gushed with enthusiasm over the "new" China. Friendly Chinese crowds, with little official prompting, cheered the young athletes and official news accounts praised the restoration of friendship among the two peoples. Nevertheless, at the 18,000-seat stadium in Beijing where the exhibition matches were played, one prominent banner welcomed the American team while another declared, "Down with the Yankee oppressors and their running dogs." Chinese players allowed the overmatched Americans to win a few games, but dominated the competition. Zhou Enlai received the American team at the Great Hall of the People, near Tiananmen, complimenting them for "opening a new page" in Chinese–American friendship and indicating China hoped to send a team to play in the United States. (A Chinese team toured the United States during April 1972.) Although the Americans did not meet Mao, in Shanghai Mao's wife, Jiang Qing, invited the team to view a performance of her revolutionary ballet, *The Red Detachment of Women.*[6]

The positive reactions to the visit in both countries encouraged Mao and Zhou to move ahead with the plan to receive an official American envoy. The upbeat press coverage of the visit in the U.S. press also boosted Nixon's spirits. He expressed glee that TV news broadcasts focused on the team's visit "rather than Vietnam, for a change." The president instructed his aides to play up the fact that the "Chinese thing is going just the way we want it." He seemed especially pleased that the "Ping Pong team is worrying them [the Soviets] right up the wall," and jokingly asked Kissinger whether he "had learned to play ping pong yet."

---

[5]Table tennis was extremely popular in China and often played by leaders such as Mao and Zhou. In 1937, Edgar Snow had reported on the fierce competition among rank-and-file Communist guerrillas as well as Party leaders. During the first half of the 1960s, top players were national heroes and, until the Cultural Revolution, dominated world tournaments. China's participation in the Nagoya games marked a turn away from the isolation of Cultural Revolution, when even ping-pong had fallen under suspicion. Mao waivered over whether to invite the American players to China, but ultimately backed the approach.

[6]A year later, when Henry Kissinger was more or less forced to sit through another performance of the opera, he described it as an "art form of stupefying boredom [in which] as far as I can make out, a girl fell in love with a tractor."

Nixon told reporters that he "expected to visit Mainland China sometime in some capacity."

The only sour note came from Vice President Spiro Agnew. Never privy to administration foreign policy, Agnew, in Washington, called in a group of American journalists for an extended "chat" during the table tennis team's April visit to China. He criticized positive reporting on China, asserting that if Americans were forced to live under the conditions in China, liberals would call it "oppression of the poor." "Ping Pong Diplomacy," he griped, was little more than a "propaganda beating" for the United States. In private, Nixon disparaged Agnew as too dense to understand "the big picture in this whole Chinese operation, which is, of course the Russian game. We're using the Chinese thaw to get the Russians shook."

Around the time of the table tennis team's visit, Nixon and Kissinger exchanged a flurry of messages with Zhou Enlai. In late April the Chinese suggested that although the United States must pull its forces out of Taiwan before the normalization of relations, the matter could be discussed by a special envoy. Agreement was not a precondition to talks. The White House considered this positive enough to send a formal note on May 10 saying that Nixon himself was willing to visit China if Kissinger went first to set out the terms of a visit. In advance of a visit, the United States would make no deals at China's expense with the Soviet Union. The president also insisted that no prominent Americans, and especially no Democratic politicians, be invited to China before Nixon.

This message reached Beijing on May 17. Zhou assured Mao that the U.S. stance revealed the erosion of American power and desire for China's help in getting out of Vietnam. In the formal language of Maoism, Zhou explained that Nixon's initiative revealed the pressure exercised by the "broad mass of the people" in the United States. But since there was no certainty about when an "armed revolution" would erupt and topple the capitalist system, it would be prudent to accept Nixon's offer. At a minimum, bilateral discussions might speed the return of Taiwan, make the Soviets more cautious in their dealings with China, and widen the divisions between Moscow and Washington. If the talks went nowhere, China had little to lose.

On June 2, 1971, the Pakistani ambassador in Washington handed Kissinger a Chinese response. The first order of business in any meeting, Zhou indicated, must be a discussion of ways to expedite the withdrawal of U.S. forces from Taiwan. But this could be part of a broader dialogue, not something that must be decided in advance. Nixon called this the "most important communication that has come to an American president since the end of World War II." Kissinger went further, saying it surpassed all foreign policy initiatives since the Civil War! Nixon felt so exuberant at what he called this "fundamental" shift in the world balance of power that he uncorked a bottle of expensive brandy and with Kissinger drank a toast to "generations to come" who would have a "better chance to live in peace because of what we have done."

THE KISSINGER VISIT TO CHINA

Shortly before Kissinger's secret visit to Beijing, the appearance of the so-called Pentagon Papers rattled the administration. The publication first in *The New York Times* and then other papers of this documentary account of U.S. involvement in Vietnam from the 1940s through 1967 exposed the deception and hypocrisy of four presidents, as well as how fear of China underlay the obsession with Vietnam. Although the account ended with the Johnson administration, it threatened to further undermine popular support for the war in Vietnam and, by extension, Nixon's efforts to secure from Hanoi what he called "peace with honor."

Kissinger flew to Beijing on July 9 while ostensibly recovering from a stomach illness during a visit to Pakistan. As Kissinger and two aides (John Holdridge and Winston Lord) were driven from the Beijing airport to a guest house, veteran diplomat Huang Hua asked for assurance that the envoy would not refuse to shake Zhou's hand as had Dulles in Geneva in 1954. (During this and Nixon's subsequent visit, the Chinese made several references to the old snub.) In fact, Kissinger was entranced by Zhou, describing him as "one of the two or three most impressive men I have ever met."

In his various accounts of these first contacts, Kissinger insisted that his success derived from the simple fact that the United States offered China the single most important thing it wanted: "strategic reassurance, some easing of their nightmare of hostile encirclement." Zhou, Kissinger explained, made a pro forma demand that the United States abandon Taiwan, pull out of South Vietnam, and restrain Japanese militarism. But he reportedly assured Kissinger these were minor irritants.

The actual record of the discussion reveals that Taiwan remained a major point of contention, not an afterthought. Nixon had told his envoy to seem reluctant to "abandon much of our support for Taiwan *until it was necessary to do so.*" Complaining to Kissinger about the past misdeeds of Harry Truman, Dwight D. Eisenhower, and John Foster Dulles, Zhou made it clear that Beijing's priority was getting the United States to cut defense ties with the island and to acknowledge the PRC's territorial claim. If Kissinger would not agree to this, perhaps Nixon ought not to come at all. Kissinger, who, like Nixon, wanted China's help in pressing North Vietnam to make a deal with Washington, answered that most U.S. forces would leave Taiwan once peace returned to Indochina and that Taiwan's status would evolve over time, probably in China's favor. Henceforth, Kissinger promised, Washington would not support a "two-China policy," a "one China, one Taiwan" policy, or an independent Taiwan. Nor would the United States back any attack on China by Taiwan. If China could wait until Nixon's re-election in 1972, Kissinger indicated, the president would cut formal links to Taiwan and recognize the PRC.

When Zhou briefed Mao on the talks, the chairman remarked that it took time for a monkey to evolve into a human being. The Americans were now at the ape stage, "with a tail, though a much shorter one, in back." Since Washington's evolution was in a positive direction, Mao decided, "we are not in a hurry on the Taiwan issue." Although courteous to Kissinger, Zhou, like Mao, was less flattering in his private appraisal. He told colleagues that Nixon, through Kissinger, had "eagerly" sought an invitation and, like a whore, had "dressed up elaborately" to "present herself at the door."

Nixon and Kissinger, of course, considered realigning the global balance of power far more important than sparring over the status of an offshore island. Neither man understood that for China's leaders Taiwan was both a real and a symbolic issue of national legitimacy. The facts that U.S. spy missions against China originated on the island and that U.S. air, naval, and land forces for decades had protected the island were bitter vestiges of China's weak past. After some nimble rewording of a joint statement, the two sides agreed to announce simultaneously on July 15 that, "Knowing of President Nixon's expressed desire to visit," China had issued an invitation for him to come before May 1972 to discuss normalization of relations and to exchange views on "questions of concern to the two sides."

When Nixon learned of Kissinger's achievement via a coded message from Beijing, he mused to chief of staff H. R. Haldeman that in politics, "everything turns around." The Chinese "made a deal with us" because of concern regarding the Soviets," their former ally. He (Nixon) had "fought the battle" on Taiwan since the 1950s and had always "taken the line that we stand by the South Koreans . . . by the South Vietnamese, etc." How "ironic" that a conservative like himself was the "one to move in the other direction."

An era of cooperation between the United States and China, he predicted, would "shatter old alignments." The "pressure on Japan" might even push it toward an "alliance with the Soviets." Moscow would surely try to move closer to "Japan and India." Washington would need to "reassure its Pacific allies that we are not changing our policy" or selling out friends "behind their back." But they, like the American public, must understand that although there was "validity ten years ago to play the free nations of Asia against China," the United States could now "play a more effective role with China than without."

Although Zhou Enlai rebuffed Kissinger's suggestion that China press Hanoi to accept Nixon's peace terms, shortly after the visit Zhou conferred with North Vietnamese leaders. Like Nixon, he argued that improved Sino–American relations would stabilize Asia and ultimately benefit Vietnam. The North Vietnamese disagreed, complaining that China had "thrown a life buoy to Nixon, who had almost been drowned." Although more than a year passed before the combatants reached a tentative peace agreement in Vietnam, it was clear that China now placed a higher priority on cooperation with Washington than on assuring victory for Hanoi.

Nixon announced the China opening in a televised speech on July 15. The American public and politicians in both parties, weary of Vietnam, responded enthusiastically. Some Democrats brooded privately that Nixon—who had lambasted Truman for "losing China"—would reap the benefits of rapprochement.

Publically, however, they praised him. Conservatives who were Taiwan supporters, such as Senator Barry Goldwater and California Governor Ronald Reagan, seemed stunned by the policy reversal but accepted Nixon's private assurances that the move was primarily designed to weaken the Soviets.

The president persuaded Reagan to travel as his personal emissary to Taiwan in a bid to reassure Chiang Kai-shek that despite the opening to the mainland, Washington would not abandon the island. Nixon also hoped Reagan would mollify criticism from what remained of the so-called China Lobby. When Reagan delivered Nixon's message to Chiang, he supplemented it with his own pledge of support. "We will weaken no cherished associations; we will break no promises. Our defense commitment remains in full force and we will continue to support the full participation of the Republic of China [Taiwan] in the international community."[7]

Nixon had convinced a skeptical Reagan to undertake this hand-holding mission to Taiwan by assuring him that the purpose behind the China opening was primarily a tactical move to tie down and further weaken the Soviet Union. After all, he told Reagan, if the Soviets had to worry about the security of their 4,500-mile border with China, their ability to cause mischief elsewhere would be limited. Reagan explained Nixon's reasoning in a private letter he wrote to a friend during the president's historic trip to China in February 1972. Conservatives, Reagan observed, should ignore the "forgive-and-forget" nice words Nixon lavished on Mao Zedong and other Communist leaders.

The true purpose of the trip was not to appease Chinese Communism, but this could not be publicly revealed because it would "blow the whole diplomatic game plan." Nixon, Reagan asserted, recognized that the "American public opinion will no longer tolerate wars of the Vietnam type because they no longer feel a threat—thanks to the liberal press—from Communism." Unfortunately, Reagan explained, ordinary Americans had lost sight of the fact that wars like that fought in Vietnam were "really in defense of freedom and our own country."

Nixon, he continued, recognized the "disaffection between China and Russia, visits China, butters up the warlords, and lets them be because they have nothing to fear from us." This pivot would force the Soviets to commit "140 divisions on the Chinese border," increasing tension between the Communist giants and providing the United States "a little time and elbow room." This strategy, Reagan reassured his friend as well as himself, "was a million miles removed from the soft appeasement of previous Democratic administrations."

The new policy stunned Japan nearly as much as Taiwan. As the U.S. trade deficit with Japan ballooned in the early 1970s, a member of Nixon's cabinet told journalists that "the Japanese are still fighting the war, only now instead of a

---

[7]Despite this reassurance, many "mainlanders" who fled to Taiwan in 1949 were certain the island's days as the Republic of China were numbered. As a student in Taiwan in 1971–1972, the author lived with a family originally from Beijing who anticipated that Communist troops would soon storm the island's beaches.

shooting war it is an economic war." Echoing language recently used against China, he added that "their immediate intention is to try to dominate the Pacific and then perhaps the world." The president himself muttered on another occasion that the Japanese were "all over Asia, like a bunch of lice." A key benefit of the opening to China, Nixon and his aides acknowledged, would be less U.S. dependence on Japan as a strategic ally and a freer hand in pressing Tokyo to redress economic grievances.

Nixon was personally furious at the failure of Japanese Prime Minister Sato Eisaku to enact a promised reduction in textile exports to the United States, an important part of Nixon's effort to court southern politicians whose states still were major textile producers. In an act of vengeance, he ordered that Sato—who had loyally supported Nixon's policies in Asia—be given only a few minutes advance notice of the July 15 announcement. This would, he gloated, "stick it to Japan."

China, of course, had its own bitter feelings about Japan's wartime behavior. It also feared that Tokyo might use its economic power to build a strong military or otherwise dominate Southeast Asia, especially after a U.S. pullback. Cooperation with Washington, China hoped, would contain *both* the current Soviet and the potential Japanese challenges. Stunned by the sudden reversal of American policy toward China, as well as by the president's action in August to devalue the dollar and impose special tariffs, Japanese leaders described themselves as victims of "Nixon Shocks." Their American allies, the Japanese believed, had decided to "play a kind of China card" against Japan as well as the Soviet Union.

During the seven months that elapsed between Kissinger's "secret visit" and Nixon's February 1972 trip to China, negotiators wrestled with the wording of the communique to be issued at the conclusions of the presidential visit. Disagreements continued over Taiwan's membership in the UN and how to handle the island's security treaty with the United States. During September 1971, China was jolted by an attempt by Lin Biao and his son to topple Mao. Fleeing in the wake of the abortive plot, Lin and his entourage died in a plane crash in Mongolia, near the Soviet border. Lin's fall bolstered Zhou's position as the chief "moderate" around Mao. A short but bloody war between India and Pakistan during November and December (resulting in the creation of Bangladesh in former Eastern Pakistan) shifted public focus away from Sino–American relations in both Beijing and Washington.

In October, while again in Beijing, Kissinger persuaded the Chinese to agree to a statement that "all Chinese" on either side of the Taiwan Strait agreed there is one China and that the United States accepted that position. (Substance aside, Nixon's chief of staff noted that for publicity value a photo of Nixon being greeted "by a million Chinese is worth a hundred times the effect of a communique.") That same month, the UN, over American objections, gave China's seats in both the General Assembly and the Security Council to the PRC. Despite Nixon's hope that Taiwan could retain some form of representation, it was expelled. An angry Ronald Reagan urged Nixon to "put the bums in their place" by quitting, defunding, or boycotting the UN.

NIXON IN CHINA

H. R. Haldeman, Nixon's chief of staff, managed his boss's trip to China to assure maximum prime-time TV and photo coverage. In advance of the 1972 presidential election, journalists joked that the "first primary" was being held in Beijing. Although Nixon privately disparaged American journalists as "clowns," he insisted that the Chinese grant visas to 900, mostly television and photo journalists, to accompany him. During the lengthy flight (with intermediate stops) that reached China on February 21, 1972, Kissinger suggested ways Nixon might "bond" with Mao. The president ought to "treat him as an emperor," but claim both were "men of the people" who had contempt for intellectuals.

In notes he wrote to himself while traveling, Nixon speculated that the Chinese leadership wanted to meet him partly to "build up their world credentials." They desired, of course, to get the United States out of Taiwan and "out of Asia." He hoped the summit would speed a settlement in Vietnam and "restrain" both "Chicom" and Soviet expansion. The Chinese "expect action" on Taiwan just as Americans expect action on getting out of Vietnam. Although both developments were "inevitable," neither could be achieved "immediately."

Mao received Nixon and Kissinger soon after their arrival in Beijing. Following an exchange of pleasantries, Zhou conferred more substantively with the Americans.

President Richard Nixon meets his old enemy, Chairman Mao Zedong, in Beijing, 1972.
(© Bettmann/Corbis)

Meanwhile, the Chinese press covered Nixon's audience with Mao almost as effusively as did American journalists. At every "photo op" stop, such as the Great Wall, Ming Tombs, or the panda den at the Beijing zoo, hand-picked Chinese were on hand to greet the foreign guests. The message to the masses was clear—an opening to the United States was a good thing. Nixon, who hated small talk and sightseeing, asked his hosts to either cut out or shorten visits to sites such as the Forbidden City or restaurants that served Peking duck. But to everyone's surprise, and Kissinger's disgust, he seemed to enjoy watching a performance of Jiang Qing's revolutionary opera, *Red Detachment of Women.*

Etiquette required that Nixon host a banquet in Beijing. The event—with all food flown in from the United States—was televised globally and viewed by nearly as many people as had watched the recent lunar landing. At each table, the caterers placed a package of American cigarettes with the presidential seal attached. To the surprise of the heavy-smoking Chinese guests, each pack also contained the health warning mandated by the U.S. Surgeon General.[8]

When Nixon sat down for substantive discussions with the Chinese premier, Zhou again mentioned Dulles's refusal to shake his hand at Geneva in 1954, prompting Nixon to jump up and pump Zhou's hand. As Nixon anticipated, the issues of Taiwan and Vietnam came up quickly. Zhou called for the immediate withdrawal of U.S. forces from Vietnam and an end to support of the Saigon regime. Nixon rejected any immediate move to cease aid to the Saigon government, but added that once Hanoi accepted U.S. peace terms, the Americans would remove most of their armed forces and facilities from Taiwan. The faster the war ended and ties with China improved, the quicker the American exit from both Vietnam and Taiwan. Nixon and Kissinger made clear the United States would not formally cut ties with Taiwan or recognize the PRC before the 1972 election. But after that, the president explained, he hoped to quickly withdraw all U.S. forces from Taiwan and normalize relations with China.

Zhou told Nixon that the PRC could wait "a few more years" to retake Taiwan, by peaceful means if possible. But he rejected any suggestion that China lean on North Vietnam. Disingenuously, Zhou denied that China had given much aid or support to North Vietnam.[9] Mao had criticized Hanoi's engaging in

---

[8]As late as 1983, the Chinese government, which had a tobacco monopoly, did little to discourage smoking. When Communist Party Chairman Hu Yaobang met with the author that year, he offered up a cigarette and asked whether I was one of the many Americans concerned with the health risks of smoking. To avoid an international incident, I accepted the cigarette . . . but didn't inhale.

[9]China had, of course, supplied substantial economic and military assistance, including as many as 300,000 support troops who built roads, maintained weapons, and staffed missile batteries. Nevertheless, many Vietnamese Communists questioned China's reliability. They recalled China's historical efforts to dominate Vietnam and, more recently, its pressure to divide the country in 1954. In the Sino–Soviet dispute, Vietnamese communists tended to favor the Soviets who posed no threat to their territory. Throughout the long war in Vietnam, U.S. intelligence analysts had largely overlooked this fact.

peace talks with Washington in 1968, but by 1972 the Chinese saw the advantage of ending the war quickly. Although Zhou told Nixon that the PRC would not "meddle" in Hanoi's affairs, the North Vietnamese feared that China might "sell them out," much like Nixon and Taiwan. North Vietnam criticized Nixon's opening to China as a "perfidious maneuver" to divide socialist countries.

Shortly after Nixon left China, North Vietnam launched a "Spring Offensive" in hope of overrunning the south now that most U.S. combat forces had left—and before China became even more friendly with the United States. When Nixon unleashed punishing air attacks throughout Vietnam, China protested but took no action on Hanoi's behalf. Mao privately urged the North Vietnamese to accept the U.S. demand that in any peace settlement a non-communist government retain control in most of the south. This compromise, he predicted, would hasten the departure of U.S. forces. After "rest and reorganization," Mao added, "you can fight again to reach final victory." To the Vietnamese, this counsel must have sounded eerily similar to what China said in the 1954 Geneva Accords "temporarily" dividing Vietnam.

During the February talks in Beijing, both Chinese and American participants agreed on the need to "restrain" Soviet expansion. Nixon promised that in his upcoming summit in Moscow, he would make no deals at China's expense and do nothing that would "free [Moscow's] hand" for making mischief in Asia. When Zhou criticized the existing U.S.–Japan security treaty, Nixon and Kissinger asked him to ponder the alternative—a Japan uncoupled from America. "Do we tell the second most prosperous nation to go it alone—or do we provide a shield?" Wasn't a "U.S.–Japan policy with a U.S. veto" less dangerous to China than a "Japan only policy?" Without U.S. bases in Japan, the Philippines, and South Korea, Nixon argued, the potential "wild horse of Japan could not be controlled." In effect, Nixon described the security treaty with Japan as a way to keep it bottled up.The U.S. security pact with Japan, the president told Zhou, "is in your interest, not against it."

In the final hours of the presidential visit, disagreement surfaced over the joint communique. Originally, the wording indicated that Washington's new relationship with China would not come at the expense of its existing commitments to Japan, the Philippines, South Korea, Australia, and New Zealand—but made no mention of Taiwan. State Department officials who had been kept in the dark now insisted that Taiwan be included. When the Chinese balked, Nixon agreed to drop all references to U.S. regional pacts. The Chinese also wanted the joint statement to include promises to promote trade and cultural exchanges. Kissinger, who felt these inclusions were meaningless, agreed, but predicted that Sino–American trade would be "infinitesimal." The final wording of the February 28, 1972, Shanghai communique affirmed U.S. support for a "peaceful settlement of the Taiwan question by the Chinese themselves" and promised to progressively reduce U.S. forces on the island "as tension in the area diminishes." It briefly referenced the "highest value" it placed on its "relations with Japan" and pledged to preserve and "develop [those] existing close bonds."

The Chinese responded by including a statement of their opposition to the U.S.–Japan security treaty, condemned the "revival and outward expansion of Japanese militarism," and endorsed efforts by the Japanese people to "build an independent, democratic, peaceful, and neutral Japan."

In the year following Nixon's visit, the China initiative helped him achieve three long-sought goals: an arms-control deal with the Soviets, a ceasefire in Vietnam, and re-election. In May 1972 Nixon traveled to the Soviet Union and signed several accords, including a Strategic Arms Limitation Treaty. Soviet leader Leonid Brezhnev's willingness to host Nixon even while the U.S. air force stepped up bombing of North Vietnam revealed Moscow's desire to maintain détente with the United States, especially in light of the recent opening to China.

The failure of the North Vietnamese spring 1972 offensive, along with clear indications that both Moscow and Beijing wanted the war to end, compelled Hanoi to accept a peace agreement partially on American terms. The draft settlement of October 1972 called for a departure from Vietnam of all U.S. armed forces within 90 days. The United States retained the right to continue to support the Saigon government, but North Vietnamese and Viet Cong troops were permitted to hold on to territory they occupied in South Vietnam and to resupply their military forces there. As a sweetener, U.S. negotiators promised to provide reconstruction aid to North Vietnam if the ceasefire held. In reality, the peace accord was a ceasefire in place followed by a speedy U.S. exit. Few observers took seriously Nixon's claim of achieving "peace with honor." South Vietnam's President Thieu was so reluctant to give his consent that Washington had to ultimately threaten a cutoff of aid to get his reluctant consent to the deal. It required another round of heavy U.S. bombing in December before a final pact was signed in January 1973.[10] The impending truce in Vietnam had, by then, buried the presidential bid of antiwar Democrat Senator George McGovern. Nixon won reelection in November with a record 61 percent of the popular vote.

In February 1973, following the Vietnam settlement, Kissinger returned to Beijing. "The flood gates were open," he informed Nixon, in describing the warm reception he received. In place of the near secret conditions of earlier visits, the envoy's photograph was displayed on the "top half of the *People's Daily*" and Chinese soldiers "saluted" Kissinger when he entered official receptions.

On earlier trips Kissinger explained that he had hyped the Soviet threat to spur Chinese cooperation. This time he found the Chinese "obsessed" by fears of encirclement. Concern with the Soviet Union "dominated our conversation . . . and . . . permeated" his talks with Chinese leaders, he reported. Mao and Zhou sounded to him bizzarely like former Secretary of State John Foster Dulles, who during the 1950s had demanded greater efforts to "counter the Russians everywhere"

---

[10]Nixon and Kissinger blamed Hanoi for reneging on the draft peace deal, forcing them to resume bombing. In fact, it was largely Thieu's reluctance to accept the terms that led them to restart the air war, as a means of reassuring Thieu of future U.S. support if the truce collapsed.

by forming anti-communist alliances. Now it was Mao who demanded that China and the United States must cooperate to "deal with a bastard."

Kissinger repeated Nixon's pledge to "move toward normalization of relations," although he now pushed the date back, from 1972 until after the 1974 U.S. midterm elections. The United States, he thought, might follow Japan's lead by ending its diplomatic presence on Taiwan but maintaining an informal liaison office staffed by "retired" diplomats. However, Japan, unlike the United States, had no security treaty with Taiwan. This complication, Kissinger acknowledged, might even delay the establishment of full relations until 1976. Despite Chinese anger at the sudden change in the diplomatic timetable for normalizing ties, the two sides agreed to open liaison offices in Beijing and Washington.

During this visit, Kissinger was struck by the "major turnabout" toward Japan since Tokyo's own 1972 opening to China. Before then, Zhou had criticized the American decision to rebuild Japan after 1945. Now the Chinese "clearly consider Japan as an incipient ally," which could balance threats from India and the Soviet Union. Zhou described the U.S.–Japan security treaty as an important "brake on Japanese expansionism and militarism" and cautioned Kissinger against imposing trade sanctions on Tokyo (demanded by some American manufacturers) that might drive it toward Moscow. This reversal in tone made Kissinger suspect that China had begun a bidding war with America to "compete for Tokyo's allegiance."

By the time he left Beijing, Kissinger reached a remarkable conclusion. "We are now in the extraordinary position," he informed Nixon, that among all nations, "with the possible exception of the United Kingdom, the PRC might well be closest to us in its global perceptions." No other world leaders possessed the "sweep and imagination of Mao and Zhou nor the capacity and will to achieve a long-range policy." In "plain words," the United States and the PRC had become "tacit allies."

Despite hopes in both capitals that Nixon would quickly move forward to formally recognize China, the expanding Watergate Scandal dominated Nixon's final 18 months in office. As the president lost much of his domestic support, he hesitated to alienate conservative Republicans who retained affection for Taiwan. Nixon's focus on China was also diverted by the October 1973 war between Israel and its Arab neighbors that resulted in an Arab oil embargo that drove up energy prices and undermined the American economy.

With the process of normalization stalled and U.S.–China trade still at extremely low levels, dislike of the Soviet Union remained the primary attraction between the United States and China. Washington supplied a growing quantity of military intelligence to the Chinese. When Kissinger spoke with Mao and Zhou in November 1973 and in 1974, they swapped tales of Soviet perfidy and discussed ways of frustrating alleged Soviet designs in South Asia and the Middle East.

Despite the stall in normalization, the mere fact of a Chinese–American dialogue stripped the Cold War of many of its ideological trappings. After 1972, the Cold War in Asia, at least, largely disappeared. Regional conflicts no longer seemed of global significance. For example, when the North Vietnamese finally swept over South Vietnam in a two-month offensive in the spring of 1975, followed quickly by the fall of U.S. – supported regimes in Cambodia and Laos, few Americans considered the outcome a major "victory" for Communism or the Soviet Union or even much of a threat to the rest of Southeast Asia. Rivalries among the United States, China, and the Soviet Union continued but these resembled more traditional struggles for influence and appeared less like ideological contests for the hearts and minds of the world's people.

The foundation built by Nixon and Kissinger proved quite durable between 1973 and 1989. At its core was a shared belief in both capitals in the value of cooperation against the Soviet Union. This "organizing principle" of Sino-American cooperation lasted in one form or another until the collapse of the Soviet Union in 1991. Issues such as trade, human rights, and economic reform took a back seat. Any misgivings that Americans felt about China's authoritarian system were trumped by the value of strategic cooperation and belief that contact with the outside world would gradually transform the PRC. Presidents from Gerald Ford through Bill Clinton believed that the shared interests of the two countries outweighed the vagaries of world politics, including the decline of Soviet power.

SELECTED ADDITIONAL READINGS

Richard Nixon, *RN: The Memoirs of Richard Nixon* (New York, 1978); Henry Kissinger, *The White House Years* (Boston, 1979), *Years of Upheaval* (Boston, 1983), and *On China* (New York, 2011); John Holdridge and Marshall Green, *War and Peace with China: First Hand Experiences in the Foreign Service of the United States* (Bethesda, Md., 1994); James Mann, *About Face: A History of America's Curious Relationship with China, from Nixon to Clinton* (New York, 1999); Patrick Tyler, *A Great Wall: Six American Presidents and China* (New York, 1999); William Burr, ed., *The Kissinger Transcripts: The Top Secret Talks with Beijing and Moscow* (New York, 1998); Chen Jian, *Mao's China and the Cold War* (Chapel Hill, N.C., 2001); Robert S. Ross, *Negotiating Cooperation: The United States and China, 1969–1989* (Stanford, Ca., 1995); Michael Schaller, *Altered States: The U.S. and Japan since the Occupation* (New York, 1997); Robert Dallek, *Nixon and Kissinger: Partners in Power* (New York, 2007); Evelyn Goh, *Constructing the U.S. Rapprochement with China* (New York, 2007); Chris Tudda, *A Cold War Turning Point: Nixon and China, 1969–1972* (Baton Rouge, La., 2012); Margaret MacMillan, *Nixon and Mao: The Week that Changed the World* (New York, 2007); Nancy B. Tucker, *Strait Talk: United States–Taiwan Relations and the Crisis with China* (Cambridge, Mass., 2009); Nicholas Griffin, *Ping Pong Diplomacy: The Secret History of the Game that Changed the World* (New York, 2014); Odd Arne Westad, *Restless Empire: China and the World since 1750* (New York, 2012).

CHAPTER 11

From Tacit Allies to Tiananmen

In August 1974, as the House of Representatives prepared to impeach President Richard Nixon, he resigned rather than face near certain conviction by the Senate. The collapse of Nixon's political support resulted almost entirely from revelations about his role in the Watergate break-in and cover-up. Although most Americans applauded the triumph of legal and constitutional process over dirty tricks, the whole episode baffled Chinese officials. Mao and Zhou suspected that a dark conspiracy—perhaps aimed at China—underlay Nixon's fall from power.

In fact, Nixon's China initiative proved his most popular and durable accomplishment. Soon after Vice President Gerald Ford assumed the presidency, he dispatched Henry Kissinger—now secretary of state as well as national security adviser—to Beijing. There he reaffirmed that U.S. policy toward China remained steadfast and enjoyed bipartisan support.

THE FORD PRESIDENCY AND CHINA

Domestic politics complicated the new president's desire to normalize relations with China. From almost the moment he entered the White House, Ford found himself challenged by the growing influence of conservative Republicans from the "sun belt" as well as from traditional liberal Democrats. His speedy decision to pardon Nixon for his Watergate-related crimes—made on compassionate but short-sighted grounds—outraged Democratic politicians as well as a majority of Americans. Republicans inspired by California Governor Ronald Reagan were nearly as angry when Ford appointed the GOP moderate, former New York governor Nelson Rockefeller, as vice president. The rapid collapse of the South Vietnamese army in April 1975 and renewed tensions with Moscow further diminished the stature of Ford and Kissinger. At home, a combination of slow economic growth, high inflation, and rising oil prices—dubbed stagflation—eroded the administration's credibility.

When Ford took office, a coalition of conservative Republicans and liberal Democrats began to criticize détente with the Soviet Union. Moscow, they claimed, used arms control agreements as a fig leaf to increase its nuclear arsenal. In the Middle East, Latin America, and Africa, these critics asserted, the Soviets continued to aid anti-American groups. Although many of those opposed to détente agreed that it made sense to utilize China as a counterweight to the Soviets, none shared the enthusiasm Nixon and Kissinger had expressed about the value of ties to Beijing. In fact, critics of détente defended U.S. ties to Taiwan even if this delayed normalization of relations with the PRC.

Pressured from many directions, ridiculed by journalists, mocked by television comedians who parodied his alleged clumsiness, and dismissed by many in Congress as a foreign policy lightweight, Ford attempted to placate critics and burnish his own credentials by downplaying Kissinger's role. As part of his effort to counter Reagan's bid for the 1976 GOP presidential nomination by bolstering his conservative support, Ford backtracked on promises made to China. Accordingly, he decided to once again postpone normalizing relations with China until after the upcoming presidential election in 1976.

When Ford traveled to Beijing in December 1975 bearing the bad news, Chinese leaders complained about the new delay in recognition which Nixon initially promised would occur after the 1972 election. As compensation, Ford authorized the sale to China of advanced jet engines and computers with military potential. By then, the leading foreign policy moderate in Beijing, Zhou Enlai, was terminally ill with cancer (he died the next month), and an infirm Mao could barely rise out of his chair to greet the president. Vice Premier Deng Xiaoping, a short, spirited, and pragmatic disciple of Zhou who favored economic modernization coupled with closer ties to the West and Japan, took charge of dealing with the United States. However, Deng's position remained tenuous. A coalition of radicals, led by Mao's wife, Jiang Qing, who favored preserving Maoist orthodoxy, challenged Deng's authority. Ford's failure to sever links with Taiwan or formally recognize the PRC undermined Deng's position.

In his final years, Mao abandoned many of the so-called Maoist policies adopted by the radicals and attempted to govern more from the center by balancing off competing factions. Early in 1976, shortly after Zhou's death, Mao downgraded Deng and transferred many of his powers to a new premier, Hua Guofeng. A plump and jolly political cipher with few powerful allies, Hua was courted by followers of both Deng and Jiang Qing. The lack of settled power in both Beijing and Washington left Sino–American relations in limbo.[1]

Mao's death on September 2, 1976, precipitated a power struggle. In October Hua cast his lot with the moderates and ordered the arrest of Jiang Qing and her three closest allies, Yao Wenyuan, Zhang Chunqiao, and Wang Hongwen, a group soon derided as "the gang of four." Over the next two years Deng worked his way back into power, gradually displacing Hua. Even when in charge, Deng

---

[1]A severe earthquake flattened the northeastern city of Tangshan in late July 1976, killing between a quarter and a half million people. The inept response by central authorities, especially the radicals around Mao who argued the tragedy should not overshadow their efforts to denounce Deng Xiaoping, discredited them.

retained a relatively low rank in the Communist Party hierarchy, preferring to rule through surrogates, such as the new party general secretary, Hu Yaobang, and Premier Zhao Ziyang. But from 1978 until slowed by old age in the early 1990s and death in 1997, no one doubted that Deng wielded ultimate authority.

JIMMY CARTER AND THE POLITICS OF NORMALIZATION

Ford's effort to walk away from détente helped secure his renomination in 1976 but failed to salvage his bid for election that November. When Democrat Jimmy Carter entered the White House in January 1977, he, too, intended to fulfill Nixon's pledge of normalizing relations with China. But, as before, domestic and international factors complicated movement forward.

Carter, along with his new liaison to China, former United Auto Worker's president Leonard Woodcock, agreed on the importance of a strong relationship with the PRC. But Carter faulted Nixon and Kissinger for conceding too much in what he called their "ass kissing" negotiations with the Chinese. Nevertheless, it proved difficult for the new administration to reverse earlier concessions or settle the Taiwan issue other than on China's terms.

Although Carter called for greater reliance on open diplomacy, he relied heavily on national security adviser Zbigniew Brzezinski, who modeled himself on Kissinger, especially by keeping the State Department in the dark. The Chinese were actually more comfortable dealing with special presidential emissaries like Brzezinski than with career diplomats. Kissinger's indirect influence over policy persisted through several protégés, including Winston Lord, John Holdridge, Brent Scowcroft, Lawrence Eagleburger, Alexander Haig, and Richard Solomon. All played significant roles in setting China policy under Carter and his two successors. Carter encouraged more open cultural and academic exchanges with China, but high-level policy continued to be directed by a handful of officials, many still driven by anti-Soviet motives.

In August 1977, Carter dispatched Secretary of State Cyrus Vance to Beijing. Vance indicated that Washington hoped to move quickly to recognize the PRC so long as the United States could retain some form of reduced but official diplomatic tie with Taiwan. Deng accused Carter of backtracking on promises by Nixon and Ford and of fudging on the so-called Japanese model. (When Tokyo recognized Beijing in 1972, Japan severed *all* formal ties with Taiwan, shifting responsibility for managing trade and travel to a private organization staffed by retired diplomats.) Carter's proposal to retain at least some formal ties with Taiwan sounded like a new version of a two-China policy.

In addition to this impediment, domestic politics constrained Carter's actions. He had negotiated a treaty to transfer to Panama control of the canal that crossed its territory. Conservatives, galvanized by Reagan, condemned it as a surrender of U.S. primacy in Latin America. As one Republican senator declared, "we stole it, fair and square." To secure the Republican votes he needed for a two-thirds supermajority in the Senate, Carter backpeddled on China, delaying action on recognition until after Senate ratification of the canal treaty.

While China waited, its leaders pursued a more active regional policy in East and Southeast Asia. In August 1978 China signed a friendship pact with Japan, promoting greater economic cooperation. During a visit to Tokyo, Deng met with Emperor Hirohito, formerly a chief villain in Chinese propaganda. These actions were partly designed to show Carter that China could build its own alliances in Asia if the United States delayed recognition.

A few months before the reconciliation with Japan, the Chinese government invited surviving members of the wartime Dixie Mission to a reunion in Yan'an. Toasts and speeches by Chinese and American participants recalled the spirit of wartime cooperation and the effort to forge an incipient alliance in 1944–1945. As one ranking Chinese official noted, the PRC had been waiting for recognition for nearly 30 years, but had no desire to "wait forever."

Shortly after Senate ratification of the canal treaty, Carter sent Brzezinski to Beijing. The president hoped that a recognition deal with the PRC would prod the Soviets to conclude a long-delayed Strategic Arms Limitation Treaty (SALT) II treaty. Brzezinski, however, cared less about SALT than did Carter and considered cooperation with China a better way to contain the Soviet Union.

Carter, Brzezinski informed the Chinese, was prepared to recognize the PRC and to sever both diplomatic and security ties with Taiwan. The United States would suspend arms sales to the island for a year, but reserved the right to resume sales of defensive weapons depending on conditions. Like the Japanese, the United States would entrust management of trade and tourism to a nongovernmental agency staffed by retired diplomats. Brzezinski proposed mid-December 1978 as a target date for an agreement, following the midterm congressional elections but before the Senate took up ratification of a SALT II treaty with the Soviet Union.

Except for reserving the right to resume defensive weapons sales to Taiwan, Carter had accepted China's terms. Final negotiations were handled by Leonard Woodcock in Beijing. As under Nixon, State Department area experts were bypassed. Although China refused to concede the U.S. right to continue arms sales to Taiwan, Deng gave his blessing to the agreement. Diplomatic recognition by the United States, he reasoned, would speed the flow of Western capital and technology to China and promote modernization. Also, Deng had decided to punish Vietnam for invading and occupying Cambodia and for cooperating with the Soviet Union. He wanted to secure a deal with Washington before doing so.[2]

---

[2]Carter hoped to open diplomatic ties with *both* China and communist Vietnam by the end of 1978. U.S. and Vietnamese negotiators had settled many of the disputes that arose after the Communist victory in 1975. However, Hanoi's decision to sign a friendship treaty with Moscow in November 1978, along with Vietnam's expulsion of several hundred thousand ethnic Chinese residents, angered Deng. The PRC condemned Vietnam's invasion of Cambodia and overthrow of the brutal Khmer Rouge regime as evidence it had become a Soviet pawn. Beijing's harsh verbal attack on Hanoi as a tool of Soviet expansion resembled the language used by John Foster Dulles in the 1950s to denounce China. To placate China, Brzezinski persuaded Carter to postpone recognition of Vietnam. Another 18 years elapsed before U.S.–Vietnam diplomatic ties were restored under President Bill Clinton.

On December 15, 1978, without prior notice to Congress, the American public, or the nation's allies, President Carter announced that effective January 1, 1979, the United States would sever formal ties with the Republic of China on Taiwan and recognize the PRC as the sole, legitimate government of China. After the required one-year notification period, Washington would cancel its defense pact with Taiwan that dated to the mid-1950s. Before then, Carter explained, the United States would suspend arms sales to Taiwan but would be free to resume them after one year. Expressing hope that this would promote a peaceful resolution to the question of Taiwan's future status, Carter announced that Deng Xiaoping would visit the United States.

By 1979, the vast majority of Americans favored the normalization of U.S.–China relations. However, Carter's lack of consultation with Congress and seeming indifference to the fate of Taiwan raised hackles. Senators Barry Goldwater of Arizona and Jesse Helms of North Carolina were especially critical, accusing Carter of cowardly acts and "stabbing Taiwan in the back" in return for empty Communist promises. Even many moderate politicians voiced concern over the administration's action. Congress, in a broadly bipartisan vote, responded by passing the Taiwan Relations Act of 1979. The law, which Carter signed with misgivings, asserted that Congress favored continuing the sale of defensive weapons to Taiwan and that any military action by the PRC against the island would be of "grave concern to the United States." As discussed later, despite fears on Capitol Hill and on Taiwan that the Republic of China's days

During Premier Deng Xiaoping's visit to the U.S. in 1979, he gets into the spirit of a Texas rodeo. (© Wally McNamee/Corbis)

were numbered, the island nation thrived, both economically and politically, over the next 35 years.[3]

On January 28, 1979, declaring that he had always hoped to "visit America before going to see Marx," Deng Xiaoping arrived in Washington. His week-long cross-country tour captured headlines and won the diminutive Deng public affection. At a barbecue and a rodeo in Texas he put on a 10-gallon cowboy hat, picked up a six-shooter, and mugged for photographers. At Disney's Magic Kingdom he danced with Mickey Mouse. *Time* magazine featured Deng on its cover as "Man of the Year" for 1978, the first Chinese leader so honored since Chiang Kai-shek.

In discussions with American officials, Deng agreed to permit the United States to establish electronic listening posts in Western China. These replaced the facilities recently lost in Iran that monitored the Soviet Union. Deng informed Carter that China intended to strike a limited military blow against Vietnam in response to its invasion of Cambodia and expulsion of ethnic Chinese. Carter urged "restraint" but took no action to deter China. Neither leader remarked on the obvious irony that barely six years after American combat troops quit a war in Vietnam partly designed to contain China, the Chinese were conferring with a U.S. president about their plan to invade and contain Vietnam.[4]

Carter hoped to develop educational and cultural exchanges with China in addition to trade. Within a decade, more than 80,000 Chinese graduate students and other professionals came to the United States for advanced training. A few thousand American students, as well as a growing number of tourists, traveled in the other direction. Two-way trade with China remained quite modest during the late 1970s, but Carter also laid the groundwork for its later expansion. In the summer of 1979 Congress approved the president's call granting China provisional most favored nation status. This permitted China to export products to the United States at low tariff rates. For more than a century, Americans had anticipated a trade boom with China. Provisional most favored nation status, along with China's push for modernization, set the stage for China's entry into the world economy over the next two decades. Annual two-way trade between China and the United States increased from practically zero in 1971 to almost $13 billion in 1988.

Under Deng's leadership, Chinese authorities began relaxing the many constraints Mao had imposed on daily life. The new leader spoke of "seeking truth from facts," not from ideological preconceptions. He promoted economic modernization, foreign investments, creation of small-scale private enterprise, and

---

[3]On his father's death in 1976, Chiang Ching-kuo (Jiang Jingguo) assumed power on Taiwan and ruled for 13 years. Although an autocrat who spent some of his formative years in the Soviet Union, the younger Chiang proved a capable administrator and established the framework for a modern economy and what later became a robust democracy.

[4]The war between China and Vietnam lasted just over two weeks during the last half of February 1979. China declared it intended "to teach Vietnam a lesson." After 17 days of fighting along the border and suffering 20,000 casualties, Chinese forces withdrew. Vietnam continued to occupy Cambodia for more than a decade. The chief "lesson" seemed to be that China's antiquated army fought poorly beyond its own borders.

the return of individual farm plots to peasants. Although Deng praised democracy as a principle, he had little tolerance for political dissent. Like his successors, he hoped to build a prosperous and powerful China, not a democratic one.

At the end of 1978, student activists and urban intellectuals in several Chinese cities created a "democracy wall" movement. They displayed posters on public walls to spark debate on a variety of social and political issues ignored by the official press. But in March 1979, when some of the posters questioned the Communist Party's monopoly on power, authorities suppressed the movement. Dozens of activists, including Wei Jingsheng, author of a poster called the "Fifth Modernization—Democracy," were hustled off to prison.

President Carter had made support for human rights a major diplomatic initiative. He criticized political repression in countries as varied as the Philippines and the Soviet Union. Yet, the administration downplayed Chinese mistreatment of the regime critics. Given the rapid deterioration of U.S.–Soviet relations, Washington avoided picking a fight with Beijing.

In December 1979, Soviet troops invaded Afghanistan in an effort to bolster a tottering Afghan Communist regime that had come to power a few years before. The Soviets feared a loss of credibility if their Afghan client collapsed and worried about the spread of fundamentalist Islam so close to its central Asian border. The Carter administration dismissed these motives and accused the Soviets of using force to move in the direction of the oil-rich Persian Gulf. (In fact, Afghanistan's largely impenetrable terrain made it a path to nowhere.) Washington retaliated by postponing Senate consideration of the SALT II arms control treaty, canceling grain sales, imposing a boycott on the 1980 Moscow Olympics, and threatening military retaliation against any Soviet foray into the Persian Gulf. Carter also sent Defense Secretary Harold Brown to China, where he told Deng that the United States would sell "non-lethal" defense equipment to China, including air defense radar, computers, communications equipment, and transport helicopters. Over the next decade, the two countries would collaborate closely in the effort to push the Soviets out of Afghanistan.

By 1980, American anger over Soviet actions in Afghanistan, Africa, and Central America outweighed its concern with China's human rights record. Carter had taken office hoping to broaden the cultural and economic dimensions of the relationship with China. But the deteriorating ties with the Soviet Union had, by 1980, pushed the Sino–American relationship back into an anti-Soviet posture, where it began in 1971. In addition to rising tensions with the Soviets, high energy prices, inflation, slow growth, and the prolonged detention of U.S. hostages in Iran paved the way for the election in November 1980 of Ronald Reagan, the most anti-Communist and pro-Taiwan president since World War II.

REAGAN AND THE EVIL EMPIRE(S)

Reagan had frequently criticized his three predecessors—Richard Nixon, Gerald Ford, and Jimmy Carter—for trying to improve the U.S. relationship with the PRC. Like many conservative Republicans, Reagan, while governor of California, questioned this policy and especially worried how it would affect America's Cold War ally, Taiwan—officially the Republic of China.

Soon after Nixon startled the nation by announcing, in July 1971, that he was opening contact with the PRC, he persuaded Reagan to travel as his emissary to Taiwan in a bid to reassure its longtime leader, Chiang Kai-shek, that Washington would not "sell Taiwan down the river." As noted in the previous chapter, Nixon persuaded Reagan that the opening to China was primarily an anti-Soviet tactic, not an accommodation of the PRC.

The administration's lackluster effort to defend Taiwan's UN seat shook Reagan's faith in Nixon's policies. After the UN vote to expel Taiwan, Governor Reagan urged Nixon to appear on television to denounce the UN, or even to quit the world body. The president ignored this advice, adding to Reagan's growing misgivings about Nixon's domestic and foreign policies.

Following Nixon's resignation in August 1974, Reagan warned President Ford that he might contest the 1976 Republican nomination unless Ford ceased efforts to improve ties with both the Soviet Union and China. In June 1975, for instance, the now former California governor ridiculed Ford for his continuing efforts to reach arms-control agreements with the Soviets and to establish full diplomatic relations with what Reagan still called "Red China." In 1976, when Reagan announced his intention to seek the presidential nomination, he told Ford that one reason for his challenge was his opposition to any deal that called for abandoning Taiwan while normalizing relations with China. Reagan's position, which found growing support within the Republican Party, persuaded Ford to abandon efforts to normalize diplomatic relations with the PRC before the 1976 election. Ford narrowly secured the GOP nomination in the face of Reagan's challenge but lost the November 1976 election to Democrat Jimmy Carter.

Over the next several years, Reagan sniped at President Carter as he inched toward formalizing ties with China. To enhance his own foreign policy credentials prior to the 1980 election, Reagan traveled to Asia during April 1978. In visits to Japan and Taiwan, he stressed these countries' strategic importance in resisting Communist threats. In a meeting with Taiwan's new strongman, Chiang Ching-kuo (son of Chiang Kai-shek), and in a public speech, Reagan remarked, "It is hard for me to believe than any sensible American who believes in individual liberty and self-determination would stand by and let his government abandon an ally whose only 'sins' are that it is small and loves freedom" (Taiwan, in fact, remained a one-party dictatorship until the 1990s.)

Ignoring Reagan's appeal, Carter established full diplomatic relations with China on January 1, 1979. However, the United States maintained vigorous commercial ties with Taiwan as well as diplomatic relations through informal channels. As noted before, Chinese and American negotiators included ambiguous wording in their agreement as to whether the United States could continue to sell weapons to Taiwan. American officials interpreted the language as permitting sales for the time being, whereas Chinese officials insisted that it precluded new arms sales. Nevertheless, Reagan condemned Carter's act of "betrayal" and made a quick campaign trip to Taiwan, where he again promised to support the long-standing ally. Strong congressional majorities shared some of Reagan's concerns and enacted the Taiwan Relations Act in a bid to maintain the island's defenses.

During his 1980 presidential campaign, Reagan portrayed Carter's recognition of the PRC and the abrogation of the defense treaty with the ROC as yet another misguided effort to appease America's enemies by abandoning its friends. He compared it to Carter's "giveaway" of the Panama Canal. In both cases, Reagan charged, Carter had bowed to radicals and surrendered a strategic asset. The Republican hopeful also condemned Carter for abandoning the Shah of Iran and Nicaraguan strongman Anastasio Somoza. These signs of weakness, he claimed, emboldened America's enemies and worried its friends. Reagan further accused Carter of failing to press Vietnam for information about American soldiers still missing from the war. In angry tones, Reagan pledged, "There's one message I want to deliver more than anything in the world as president—no more Taiwans, no more Vietnams, no more betrayal of friends and allies by the U.S. government." A Reagan administration, he promised, would restore formal ties to America's "ally," Taiwan. When asked whether he would recognize Taiwan as an independent nation if it asserted autonomy from China, Reagan answered, "yes, just like a lot of countries recognized the thirteen colonies when they became part of the United States." The New China News Agency warned that any such action "would wreck the very foundations of Sino–U.S. relations."

Fearful that Carter might use Reagan's remarks as evidence that the challenger was not to be trusted as president, Reagan's advisers worked behind the scenes to qualify his statement. In August 1980, vice presidential nominee George H. W. Bush, along with two of Reagan's advisers, Richard Allen and James Lilley, flew to Beijing to reassure Deng's deputies that if elected, Reagan would not actually restore links to Taiwan or reverse Carter's policy. But when his aides told Reagan what they had promised the Chinese, he refused to back them up. The staff spent several tense hours pleading with Reagan before he agreed to modify his stand. He did so only after convincing himself that the Taiwan Relations Act already conferred a form of informal American recognition and protection to the island.

Shortly after Reagan took office as president in January 1981, the China issue reemerged. Part of the problem stemmed from differences among key members of the new administration. On one side, Secretary of State Alexander Haig, a Nixon–Kissinger protégé, lobbied for closer ties with the PRC, especially as a way to pressure the Soviets. On the other side, national security adviser Richard Allen and Defense Secretary Caspar Weinberger voiced strong sympathy for upgrading relations with Taiwan.

This bickering became a major problem when Taiwan requested that the Reagan administration approve sales of an advanced American fighter jet, dubbed the FX. Beijing objected, insisting that the United States was supposed to be curtailing, not expanding, the quantity and quality of arms sold to its rival. Haig proposed solving the problem by selling advanced weapons to *both* China and Taiwan. He claimed that such a deal would preserve cooperation with China, enhance Taiwan's security, and yield big profits for U.S. arms exporters whose corporate leaders were also strong Reagan supporters.

The president authorized Haig to explore this idea quietly during a visit to China in June 1981. Instead, Haig boasted during a press conference that Washington was poised to sell China some of the most advanced weapons in the U.S. arsenal while selling Taiwan less advanced equipment. Reagan promptly contradicted Haig, declaring that he had not changed his views on Taiwan and intended to sell to it, not China, advanced weapons. China then threatened to downgrade its relations with Washington if advanced weapons were sold to Taiwan.

The United States and China exchanged angry accusations of bad faith during the remainder of 1981 and the first half of 1982. When the Reagan administration decided to sell Taiwan an older model military jet, the F-5e, China demanded that the United States set a date certain for ending *all* military sales to the island. In June 1982, Haig resigned as secretary of state after mounting disputes with Reagan over foreign policy. (He later found work as a highly paid arms merchant for United Technologies, peddling weapons to a variety of nations, including China *and* Taiwan.) Haig's departure opened a path to compromise. On August 17, 1982, the United States and China issued a joint communique in which the American government promised to gradually reduce and eventually terminate arms sales to Taiwan, but only as regional security conditions permitted. Chinese leaders were pleased to get the U.S. government on record accepting the principle of terminating arms sales to Taiwan, even if no specific date was set. Reagan believed he had kept faith with Taiwan, even while accepting that weapons sales might cease at some future date. In a memorandum he wrote for the record, the president stated that the level and type of arms sold to Taiwan should reflect the balance of power between the island and China. If China gained strength and appeared to threaten Taiwan, the United States could increase arms sales. If relations improved, the United States could exercise restraint. In effect, the 1982 arrangement reaffirmed the ambiguity contained in Carter's 1979 agreement that normalized U.S.–China ties, a deal Reagan had harshly condemned.

Reagan then and later seemed uncertain about how to reconcile his deeply felt anti-Communism with China's evolution away from Marxist models and its utility as an anti-Soviet ally. When briefed by a National Security Council staffer about the significance of Deng Xiaoping's push to introduce market forces into the Chinese economy and to cooperate with the United States, Reagan's only response was to make a racist joke: "You mean our position should be 'no ticky, no laundry'?"

Haig's replacement as secretary of state, George Shultz, also questioned the value of enhanced military ties with the PRC, but not because he was enamored of Taiwan. Shultz simply doubted China's near-term geostrategic and economic importance. The PRC, he acknowledged, could be a useful ally in stabilizing Asia and leveraging U.S. efforts to reduce Soviet power. But, he argued, it was not vital to these efforts. Simply put, Shultz felt that the PRC was neither a great military nor an economic power and that the United States had no need to make fundamental concessions to it. America's priority in Asia, Shultz declared in a 1983 speech, should remain centered on enhancing trade and security relations with its long-term ally, Japan.

During 1982–1983, Chinese leaders suggested that they needed to reconsider the value of close ties to the United States. Since 1971 the PRC had relied on its "tacit alliance" with the United States to counter Soviet power. But Chinese strategists worried about Reagan's massive arms buildup and challenge to Soviet influence in Asia, Africa, Latin America, and South Asia. Beijing feared that China might be swept into an unwanted conflict between the two superpowers. At the end of 1982, Communist Party head Hu Yaobang told a gathering of party elders that China should follow a more evenhanded foreign policy, distinct from those of both the United States and the Soviet Union.

Despite these indications of Chinese–American friction, both nations remained on relatively good terms. In China, Deng Xiaoping's modernization policy required increased—not reduced—access to European, Japanese, and American technology and capital. As it industrialized, China must also find export markets in the West and in Japan. In addition, Deng's chief deputies, Hu Yaobang and Premier Zhao Ziyang, were, if anything, even more personally enthusiastic than their boss about the value of Western ties.

Despite their inclination to avoid a direct confrontation with the Soviet Union, China's leaders shared the Reagan administration's determination to oppose Soviet intervention in Afghanistan which had a short border with the PRC. When Soviet forces entered that unhappy land in 1979 to prop up a tottering Communist regime, the Carter administration began supporting anti-Soviet Islamist guerrillas known as *mujahideen*. Reagan, like Carter, perceived Soviet intervention in Afghanistan chiefly as a thrust toward the oil-rich Persian Gulf. To enhance aid to the Afghan guerrillas, the Reagan administration required Chinese cooperation. With covert funding from the CIA, Chinese military planners supplied thousands of mules to transport Chinese weapons (such as AK-47 assault rifles) to the Afghan resistance. This proved to be the most successful covert military operation of the Reagan administration and eventually forced the Soviets into a humiliating retreat. It also had the unintended consequence of promoting the fortunes of Osama bin Laden and other Islamist terrorists, especially in Pakistan, who later turned their wrath against the United States. Some of these radicals also supported Muslim Uighur separatists in China's Xinjiang province.

Despite this cooperation, Reagan's unscripted but provocative remarks often drove China's leaders to distraction. Several times during 1982 and 1983, Reagan called Taiwan an American ally, implying that the United States considered it a sovereign nation. If he continued saying this, Beijing hinted it might cancel a "goodwill" visit that Reagan planned to make early in 1984 as part of his reelection campaign. Chinese officials warned American diplomats, visiting businessmen, and scholars that Reagan risked a rupture in relations unless he dropped these references.

Author Michael Schaller presents a copy of an earlier edition of this book to Chinese Communist party General Secretary Hu Yaobang, Beijing, 1983. Shortly after this meeting, Hu was removed from power by Deng, allegedly for pushing democratization too rapidly. (Author's Collection)

For example, in December 1983, Communist Party leader Hu Yaobang raised the subject in a conversation with this book's author, Michael Schaller, then a Fulbright exchange scholar in Beijing. Hu asked for assistance in sending a "personal" message to the White House outside normal diplomatic channels. "Tell Reagan," Hu explained, "that if he wants a successful trip to China he can use to boost his re-election, he should keep his big mouth shut." Similar warnings conveyed from a variety of sources persuaded Reagan to mute his public references to Taiwan.

In April 1984, Reagan traveled to the PRC, a Communist state he had bitterly criticized since he entered politics in the early 1960s. He made the usual tourist circuit, visiting the Great Wall, the giant pandas in the Beijing Zoo, and the recently unearthed, life-size clay warriors in the city of Xi'an. In his public remarks, the president criticized the Soviet Union and praised democracy but said nothing provocative about Taiwan. Nor did Reagan explain why a Communist Soviet Union was an implacable threat but a Communist China was a worthy partner. At least in his own mind, he appeared to resolve the contradiction by telling journalists after his departure that he had visited "so-called Communist China," not a truly "evil empire" like the Soviet Union.

During Reagan's second term as president, relations with China remained generally positive and low key. Both nations encouraged thousands of Chinese graduate students to flock to American universities for advanced technical

President Ronald Reagan, who found China to be a useful ally against the Soviet Union, enjoys himself amidst the "buried army" of ancient Chinese clay soldiers near the city of Xi'an, 1984. (© Jean-Louis Atlan/Sygma/Corbis)

training. As noted earlier, Chinese exports to American consumers grew from virtually nothing to sales of $13 billion in 1988. Washington and Beijing continued to cooperate in the shadow war against the Soviets in Afghanistan. In 1984 China and Great Britain reached an accord to return Hong Kong to Chinese control after the 1997 expiration of Britain's 99-year lease on the colony. Since British Prime Minister Margaret Thatcher was Reagan's closest foreign ally, this deal eliminated a potential source of U.S. friction with China.

Perhaps more than any other factor, economic and political reform in both China and Taiwan during the 1980s reduced tensions in the region and gave the Reagan administration some breathing room. China's increased emphasis on economic growth and its gradual turn toward a market economy took precedence over recovering Taiwan. Even absent a formal security treaty with the United States, Taiwan's economy surged during the 1980s. Amid growing prosperity, the ruling clique began to relax many of the harsh political restrictions imposed over the previous 30 years. As both China and Taiwan sold an increasing volume of consumer goods to Americans, the immediate importance of the dispute over continued U.S. arms sales to the island faded. For Reagan, so long as China posed no immediate threat to Taiwan and cooperated with the United States in Afghanistan, it barely intruded on his thoughts.

Within China, however, student discontent over continued limits on political freedom resulted in several large demonstrations during 1985–1986. American journalists and diplomats paid little attention to these events. In January 1987, Communist party chief Hu Yaobang, who sympathized with demands for political reform, became the chief victim of the protests when Deng purged him and installed Zhao Ziyang as party leader. Only later did these protests reveal themselves as the forerunners to much larger antiregime movement that erupted in May 1989 and culminated in violent military suppression of protestors at Tiananmen Square that June, shortly after Reagan left office.

The Reagan administration criticized one Chinese government initiative: its entry into the international arms market. Although the United States was by far the world's largest arms merchant, it disputed the right of other nations to sell certain weapons to those regions or nations it considered unstable or unfriendly. As its military technology improved during the 1980s, China began marketing several types of short- and medium-range missiles to countries such as Iran, Pakistan, and Saudi Arabia. The Reagan administration even threatened trade sanctions if China continued its missile exports. Beijing alternately denied selling these weapons and promised not to do so again. But because arms sales were so profitable and represented a path toward global influence, China, like the United States, continued to export weapons.

GEORGE H. W. BUSH AND THE TIANANMEN INCIDENT

Although China policy was a "nonissue" in the 1988 presidential election, George H. W. Bush would have been pleased if it had been. He enjoyed giving people the impression that his service as head of the U.S. liaison office in Beijing in 1974–1975 qualified him as a "China expert." In fact, Bush had no particular interest in or knowledge of China and was eager to return to Washington after his brief assignment in Beijing. As Reagan's vice president, he remained outside the inner circle of those shaping foreign policy. Bush did, however, value stability and the status quo. By this measure, Sino–American relations in 1988 were thriving. Trade continued to increase, the Soviets retreated from Afghanistan, and China's modernization program surged forward. As economic growth hit double digits (and continued at this pace for the next 25 years), China signed 20,000 international business partnerships valued at $26 billion. Initially, many foreign factories were constructed in special economic zones such as Shenzhen near Hong Kong. Ordinary Chinese often first encountered American products in the form of fast food. For example, the first Kentucky Fried Chicken franchise opened in Beijing in 1987. By 2010, Kentucky Fried Chicken had 2,500 stores in China, with nearly as many Starbucks and McDonalds.

Although many American business interests complained about high levels of Japanese and European exports to the United States in the late 1980s, many envisioned Chinese exports—initially of low quality—as a less threatening alternative. In any case, most assumed China would require decades of progress, as well as capital and advice from American experts, before it competed seriously with advanced economies.

President George H. W. Bush Visits Beijing shortly before the Tiananmen Incident. (Kyodo/ Landov)

Like many Americans, President George H. W. Bush viewed Chinese prosperity as a stabilizing force and believed that economic growth and freer markets would promote Chinese democratization. On taking office in January 1989, Bush anticipated continuing the China policies he inherited.

In February 1989, after attending the funeral in Tokyo of Japanese Emperor Hirohito, Bush made a quick goodwill visit to Beijing. There he hosted a banquet for Chinese political leaders and prominent intellectuals. Among those on the guest list drawn up by the U.S. embassy was Fang Lizhi, a prominent astrophysicist, university president, and advocate of democratic reform. Chinese authorities grumbled at the invitation but had seemingly agreed to a deal that allowed Fang to be seated at a rear table, far from Bush. However, when Fang and his wife arrived at the banquet, Chinese police barred their entry. As news of the incident spread, Bush's aides blamed Ambassador Winston Lord for embarrassing the president by inviting Fang; Lord, a Kissinger protégé, soon lost his job.

Although in itself a minor ripple, the episode revealed dangerous trends. Bush, it appeared, would do almost anything to accommodate Chinese leaders. For its part, the Chinese government revealed its extreme fear of even mild, non-violent dissent. Neither the president nor the American public recognized that a political upheaval would soon erupt in China and cast a pall over relations.

During 1985 and 1986, student resentment over the Communist Party's monopoly on power and worker displeasure with the rapidly shifting economic landscape had prompted small demonstrations. Discontent exploded after April 15, 1989, following the death and funeral of former Communist Party head Hu Yaobang, a hero to those favoring democratic reform. By May, rallies protesting official corruption and repression had taken place in about 80 cities. Disgruntled students and workers gradually centered their activity in Beijing's Tiananmen Square. The massive plaza fronting the Forbidden City, Mao's tomb, and many government buildings symbolized central authority.

Those coming to Tiananmen had varying goals. Many simply wanted Communist authorities to loosen their grip on public life and allow greater freedom of expression. Others insisted on the creation of a pluralist, Western-style democracy. Factory workers called attention to low pay and primitive working conditions. At least a few hoped to spark a revolt against Communist rule. First tens, then hundreds of thousands of students, workers, and civil servants camped out in the square. This spontaneous action stunned Communist officials and fascinated the outside world.

The presence of many foreign journalists and television crews, as well as tourists, in Beijing transformed the demonstration into a global media event. As the size of the demonstration grew, President Bush and many of his advisers focused on the impending visit to China of Mikhail Gorbachev, the reformist Soviet leader. They worried that Gorbachev's flexible approach to international affairs might rapidly improve Sino–Soviet relations and thereby complicate Washington's dealings with Beijing. This concern led the Bush administration to mute criticism of how China handled dissent. Instead, it offered Beijing reassurance of American friendship.

By the time Gorbachev arrived in Beijing on May 15, 1989, about a half million people had occupied Tiananmen Square. Their ranks soon swelled to a million. Students and others exuberant at this taste of freedom and by the attention from the world's media cited Mohandas Gandhi, Patrick Henry, and Martin Luther King as role models. They displayed posters declaring "Give Us Democracy or Give Us Death." American journalists portrayed the demonstration as a Chinese effort to assert the rights Americans took for granted.

Senior government officials, including Communist Party chief Zhao Ziyang and Premier Li Peng, visited Tiananmen several times to discuss compromise measures to end the protest. But the movement's loosely organized leadership had no unified agenda or authority to act on behalf of those demonstrating. The more radical elements among the students refused to consider anything short of fundamental political change. Communist hard-liners expressed outrage when in late May students erected a 33-foot-tall papier mâché effigy dubbed the Goddess of Democracy near Mao's giant portrait. Western media and pundits noted its resemblance to the Statue of Liberty and cited this as proof that most Chinese favored an American-style democracy.

What flattered Americans terrified Deng Xiaoping. He branded the demonstrators as counterrevolutionaries, perhaps under foreign control. Deng and other hard-liners even claimed to have detected a lingering plot hatched by Secretary of State John Foster Dulles in the 1950s to restore capitalism! When Zhao defended

Students and workers demonstrating at Tiananmen Square in late May of 1989, captured the attention and affection of Americans by displaying a mock-up of the Statue of Liberty, dubbed the "Goddess of Democracy," in front of Mao's somber portrait. A few days later, the demonstration was brutally suppressed. (© Peter Turnley/Corbis)

the student protestors' goals, if not their methods, Deng stripped him of authority and promoted the more pliable Jiang Zemin, an official from Shanghai, as new head of the party. Warning that a turn toward multiparty democracy would kindle chaos worse than the Cultural Revolution, Deng tasked Premier Li Peng to restore order. When local police and military units hesitated to disperse the crowd, special troops were brought in from outside the capital.

Late on the night of June 3, following a final ultimatum to clear Tiananmen, troops and tanks assaulted the 20,000 or so people remaining in the square. Somewhere between several hundred and a thousand civilians were killed, most of them as they fled into nearby streets. Scientist Fang Lizhi and his wife sought sanctuary in the American embassy. In the following weeks, several thousand students, workers, and others who participated in the protests were arrested. Several thousand others fled the country. Although nearly all deaths occurred outside the square itself, the international media labeled the event the "Tiananmen Massacre."

American reporters seeking President Bush's response to the tragic events in China had to catch up with the chief executive as he jogged on June 4 near his vacation home in Maine. "Not while I'm running," the winded Bush replied to shouted questions. This seemingly flippant response dogged Bush for the remainder of his presidency. Although he recognized the gravity of Chinese events, he hoped to avoid saying or doing anything that would antagonize China's leaders and reduce American influence. At the urging of the State and Defense Departments, he suspended arms sales to the PRC, a policy that lasted five years. The White House also suspended high-level official contacts with Chinese leaders and in July the United States joined with Japan and Western European nations in suspending economic assistance and loans to China.

Although repressive acts by the Chinese government during the 1950s and 1960s far exceeded the scope of the violence of June 1989, the American public, media, and Congress reacted with special outrage to this crackdown. What had changed was the heightened visibility of events at Tiananmen, the display of Western symbols such as the Goddess of Democracy, and the assumption that with economic liberalization China was becoming "more like us." When Deng ordered the military to disperse the defiant protestors and arrest their sympathizers, he shattered American beliefs that reform moved in a straight line in familiar directions. In effect, the public blamed not only China's leaders, but also Bush, for its disappointment. Shortly before the violence, around 70 percent of Americans told pollsters that they had a favorable view of China. In the wake of Tiananmen, the number plummeted to about one-third.

Senate Majority Leader George Mitchell, Democrat of Maine, along with a broad, bipartisan spectrum of senators and representatives, condemned Chinese actions and Bush's apparent inaction. Many of the 43,000 Chinese graduate students in the United States participated in rallies in support of their fallen comrades and appealed for permission to remain in the United States. Congress swiftly passed legislation granting Chinese students automatic visa extensions. Bush vetoed the bill, although he instructed immigration authorities to grant visa extensions on request. Critics saw his veto as one more concession to the "butchers of Beijing."

Both the "left" and the "right" of the American political spectrum condemned China. Conservative journalist and sometime presidential candidate Patrick Buchanan proclaimed that "Mr. Deng . . . has declared war on the Chinese people." Americans must "stand with the people as allies against Mr. Deng." A group of leading China scholars at Harvard University's Fairbank Center for East Asian Studies signed a petition saying much the same thing.

Despite his order barring contacts with Chinese leaders, within weeks of the Tiananmen incident Bush dispatched top aides to Beijing to confer secretly with Deng. On June 30 National Security Adviser Brent Scowcroft told Deng that the president recognized "the value of the PRC–U.S. relationship to the vital interest of both countries." He hoped to see the relationship maintained. Accordingly, Bush wanted Deng to know that how the Chinese government "decides to deal with those of its own citizens involved in recent events in China is, of course an internal affair." The views of the U.S. government and its people were "equally, an internal affair." Chinese leaders interpreted this as a clear signal that they need not take too seriously American criticism or sanctions.

During a second mission to Beijing in December 1989, where Scowcroft was authorized to discuss Fang Lizhi's departure from the embassy and the possible sale to China of American aircraft and satellites, word of his secret trips to China leaked to the press. Members of Congress, the media, and the public voiced outrage that within weeks of the June crackdown Bush had violated his own policy and extended a hand to Deng. In a widely reported opinion piece published in the *Washington Post* on December 19, 1989, former ambassador Winston Lord accused Bush of sending "misguided missions to China" via "fawning emissaries."

Bush, however, was not alone in dismissing Tiananmen as merely a speed bump on the path of closer Chinese–American cooperation. Within months of the violence, both Henry Kissinger and Richard Nixon had traveled to China and given the regime absolution. Kissinger, now a private consultant, spoke out forcefully on the need to resume contact with China. The United States, he asserted, "needs China as a possible counterweight to Soviet aspirations in Asia." Former President Nixon also weighed in, telling Bush to "ignore extremist voices" from the human rights community and "stay the prudent course" of close ties to Beijing. Only this, Nixon cautioned, would permit the United States to "maintain the balance among China, Japan and the Soviet Union."

The trouble with this geostrategic argument, critics noted, was that by 1989–1990 the Soviet Union under Gorbachev's leadership was rapidly transforming itself into a more democratic state and dramatically reducing its commitments to Communist regimes in Eastern Europe, as well as to Cuba and Vietnam. Moscow also cut many of its ties to revolutionary groups in the Third World. Faced with a diminished Soviet specter as a reason to cooperate with China, Kissinger floated the idea, which Bush endorsed at a news conference in January 1990, that cooperation between the United States and China was needed to counterbalance Japanese, rather than Soviet, power. Japanese officials were stunned by Bush defining them as an emerging threat.

Early in 1990 Deputy Secretary of State Lawrence Eagleburger (who had accompanied Scowcroft to Beijing in June 1989) testified before Congress that unless China remained closely tied to the United States, it might sell missiles, nuclear weapons technology, or other weapons of mass destruction to rogue states in Asia and the Middle East. This new warning suggested that even China's supporters inside the Bush administration possessed a cynical view of the PRC.

During 1990, the United States, along with the Europeans and Japanese, relaxed many of the trade and economic sanctions imposed on China in June 1989. In June 1990 Washington and Beijing struck a deal to permit Fang Lizhi to leave the American embassy and assume an academic post at the University of Arizona. The administration described this humane but limited measure as a "far sighted and significant step" justifying the end of most sanctions.

After the Communist leadership had restored stability within China, Deng did another pivot and turned on leftist critics of economic reform. In 1992, he pressed for more rapid privatization in key economic sectors. However, Deng cited the chaos and collapse that befell the Soviet Union in 1991 as an example of why China must resist political liberalization. In effect, party leaders struck a bargain with the Chinese people: in return for delivering a rising standard of living and greater personal freedom, the Communist Party would maintain its political monopoly.

Bush was especially eager to put tensions with China behind him because of the crisis in the Middle East following Iraq's August 1990 invasion of Kuwait. The president sought UN approval of a resolution justifying the use of force against Iraq by an American-led coalition. In behind-the-scenes negotiations, China agreed not to veto the resolution and Bush agreed to receive China's foreign minister at a White House meeting that took place in November 1990. As the Bush administration grew more confident that it faced no domestic political backlash from resuming closer ties with China, it blocked efforts in Congress to restrict China's trade with the United States.

The U.S.-led success in pushing Iraqi forces out of Kuwait in February 1991 bolstered Bush's popularity and overshadowed lingering criticism of his China policy. In November 1991 Secretary of State James Baker became the first Cabinet member to visit China since June 1989. In January 1992, the president felt confident enough during a visit to UN headquarters in New York to greet Premier Li Peng, previously condemned as the chief villain behind the Tiananmen crackdown. The Bush administration believed it had put the events of June 1989 behind it.

Despite his confidence that China policy would not impede his re-election campaign, Bush's past actions shadowed him. During 1992, the afterglow of the Persian Gulf victory faded. The liberation of Kuwait seemed overshadowed by Saddam Hussein's survival in power and the brutal revenge he inflicted on Iraqi Kurds and Shia who had answered U.S. calls to rise up against his regime. At home, the U.S. economy experienced a steep recession that diminished Bush's stature as a good steward of domestic affairs. In these new circumstances, the president faced a barrage of criticism from both ends of the political spectrum. For example, Patrick Buchanan, who challenged Bush's renomination, condemned him for not restoring diplomatic ties and security guarantees with Taiwan. Democratic nominee Bill Clinton attacked Bush for ignoring China's human rights violations and called for punishing China by removing its most favored nation trade status.

Since Reagan's 1982 compromise with Beijing on the issue of arms sales to Taiwan, the issue had receded. Chinese leaders occasionally grumbled that weapons sales to the island represented U.S. interference in China's internal affairs but they generally avoided making too much of the dispute. Then, in the midst of Bush's lackluster re-election campaign, he suddenly declared his intention to sell Taiwan advanced F-16 fighter planes that would give the island's air force an edge over China's military.

This decision reflected a combination of political, strategic, and economic concerns. In March 1992, China had purchased two dozen Russian Sukhoi Su-27 jet fighters. Unable to match these with American aircraft, Taiwan planned to purchase French Mirage fighter jets. In July, the General Dynamics company announced it would lay off nearly 6,000 workers from its Fort Worth plant because it could not sell F-16s to Taiwan. Leading Democrats, including Texas Governor Ann Richards and Senator Lloyd Bentsen, blamed Bush for the impending layoffs. "I don't know what deals have been made between George Bush and Communist China," Richards complained, but "when it means the loss of [almost 6,000] jobs in Fort Worth, Texas, it's time to wake up and smell the coffee." Stung by this criticism, Bush visited the General Dynamics facility in Fort Worth on September 2 and soon announced approval of the sale of 150 F-16s to Taiwan, valued at $6 billion.

The sudden reversal infuriated the Chinese. However, because Deng Xiaoping much preferred dealing with Bush compared to the unknown Bill Clinton, Beijing muted its public response to the deal. Unfortunately for Bush, neither the big arms sale nor China's low-key response energized his campaign. Conservatives continued to accuse him of doing too little to help Taiwan, while Clinton ridiculed the incumbent as China's lapdog. Although Clinton focused on Bush's economic mistakes, in his speech accepting the Democratic presidential nomination, Clinton highlighted Bush's alleged moral failure toward both Iraq and China. If elected, he promised to lead "an America that will not coddle tyrants from Baghdad to Beijing." As president, he added in campaign speeches, he would settle accounts with those responsible for the deaths at Tiananmen. When the election results were tabulated in November 1992, Clinton defeated Bush and many observers braced themselves for a downward spiral in Sino–American relations.

SELECTED ADDITIONAL READINGS

Richard Madsen, *China and the American Dream* (Berkeley, Ca., 1995); James Mann, *About Face: A History of America's Curious Relationship with China from Nixon to Clinton* (New York, 1999); Patrick Tyler, *A Great Wall: Six American Presidents and China* (New York, 1999); Robert S. Ross, *Negotiating Cooperation: The United States and China, 1969–1989* (Stanford, Ca., 1995); William Kirby et al., eds., *Normalization of U.S. China Relations* (Cambridge, Mass., 2007); David Shambaugh, *Beautiful Imperialist: China Perceives America, 1972–1980* (Princeton, N.J., 1991); James Graham Wilson, *The Triumph of Improvisation: Gorbachev's Adaptability, Reagan's Engagement, and the End of the Cold War* (Ithaca, N.Y., 2014); Robert G. Sutter, *The China Quandary: Domestic Determinants of U.S. China Policy, 1972–1980* (Boulder, Co., 1983), *U.S. Policy toward China: An Introduction to the Role of Interest Groups* (Lanham, Md., 1998), and *U.S.–Chinese Relations: Perilous Past, Pragmatic Present* (Lanham, Md., 2010); Alan G. Gorowitz, ed., *The Taiwan Relations Act: Twenty-Five Years After and a Look Ahead* (Atlanta, Ga., 1999); Nancy B. Tucker, *Strait Talk: United States–Taiwan Relations and the Crisis with China* (Cambridge, Mass., 2009); Jimmy Carter, *Keeping Faith: Memoirs of a President* (New York, 1982); Zbigniew Brzezinski, *Power and Principle: Memoirs of the National Security Adviser, 1977–1981* (New York, 1983); James A. Baker III, *The Politics of Diplomacy—Revolution, War and Peace* (New York, 1995); Harry Harding, *A Fragile Relationship: The U.S. and China since 1972* (Washington, D.C., 1992); Jeffrey A. Engel, ed., *The China Diary of George H. W. Bush: The Making of a Global President* (Princeton, N.J., 2008); Liang Zhang and Andrew J. Nathan et. al., eds., *The Tiananmen Papers: The Chinese Leadership's Decision to Use Force against Their Own People— In Their Own Words* (New York, 2001); Louisa Lim, *The People's Republic of Amnesia: Tiananmen Revisited* (New York, 2014); Jan Taylor, *The Generalissimo's Son: Chiang Ching-kuo and the Revolutions in China and Taiwan* (Cambridge, Mass., 2000).

CHAPTER 12

Beyond Tiananmen, 1992–2001

Global politics, trade, and security relationships changed with startling speed during the 1990s. The unraveling of the Soviet empire beginning in 1989 culminated in the dissolution of the Soviet Union in December 1991. The removal of the "Soviet threat" altered the dynamics of the Sino–American relationship, creating a complex mix of shared interests and rivalries. China's remarkably rapid economic growth provided it with new leverage over foreign nations as well as a shared interest in maintaining stability. Growing wealth laid a foundation for China's emergence as a regional power. The Communist Party retained its political monopoly but China's domestic and foreign policies were increasingly driven by a combination of nationalist and market forces. In ways few could have predicted, after 1991 "making money" together served as a glue that bound the United States and China together for the next two decades.

Bill Clinton's election as president in November 1992 surprised China's leaders, who preferred George H. W. Bush as a far more reliable partner. Like many state officials, Clinton, as governor of Arkansas, had visited Taiwan several times on trade missions, but had never been to the PRC. As a presidential candidate, Clinton minimized the importance of foreign policy and charged that Bush's focus on international affairs had led him to mismanage the economy. However, the Democratic challenger had also criticized Bush for "coddling" the "butchers of Beijing." If elected, he pledged to hold China accountable for its human rights record and make its future most favored nation (MFN) trade access to the American consumer market conditional on its improved behavior.[1] Clinton's views matched those expressed by a large majority of Americans who told opinion pollsters they resented China's treatment of its own citizens and questioned its intentions toward the United States.

---

[1]Under U.S. law in the 1980s and 1990s, China's MFN status, giving it favorable terms of trade, had to be renewed annually.

On taking office in January 1993, President Clinton announced that he would insist on "continued progress" on human rights before renewing China's MFN trade status. In effect, he reversed Nixon's dictum of 1972 that it did not matter how China treated its own people, only how its external behavior affected the United States. It was vital, Clinton asserted, that Americans "stick up for ourselves and for the things we believe in and how these people are treated in that country." With questionable economic logic, the new president claimed that China's 1992 trade surplus of $15 billion with the United States gave Washington great leverage over Beijing since it showed China's dependence on exports to this country.

Clinton's views were influenced by several of his top foreign policy advisers, including Secretary of State Warren Christopher, Assistant Secretary for East Asia Winston Lord, and National Security Adviser Anthony Lake. Christopher told senators at his confirmation hearing that the administration hoped to promote China's transition from "Communism to democracy" by "encouraging the forces of economic and political liberalization." Lord told senators that trade liberalization and human rights were linked and that "Americans cannot forget Tiananmen Square." Privately, Clinton's aides held out a carrot, telling the Chinese that the administration would reward an improved human rights record by encouraging greater trade and resisting efforts by congressional Republicans to restore ties with Taiwan. Unimpressed by this, China's foreign minister declared that the United States should not meddle in his country's internal affairs.

The president attempted to balance the views of those in Congress and his own administration, who favored making any renewal of MFN dependent on China's human rights record, with business interests, who feared that imposing conditions would hurt American exports. In May 1993 Clinton issued an executive order that extended MFN to China for one year. Beijing, he explained, had one year to "shape up" or risk losing preferred trade status.

Increasingly, economic considerations drove both Chinese and American diplomacy. China entered a period of accelerated growth during the 1990s. In 1992–1993, as one of his last public acts before receding into unofficial retirement, Deng Xiaoping initiated reforms that encouraged private enterprise, welcomed foreign investment, and emphasized production for export. As the PRC became the world's fastest-growing economy, American business executives beat a path to Beijing in hope of selling airplanes, computers, and satellites. As recently as 1989, two-way trade between China and the United States totaled only $13 billion. Over the next decade, China became one of America's top four trading partners (behind Mexico, Canada, and Japan), with two-way trade in 2000 reaching $116 billion. The fabled "China Market" seemed to have finally arrived, but in an unanticipated form: the United States that year sold China goods valued at about $16 billion while importing $100 billion in Chinese products.

Unprecedented numbers of Chinese and American tourists and students also crossed the Pacific. About 54,000 Chinese students enrolled annually at American universities during the 1990s, with the numbers growing to 235,000 by

2014. For the first time since the nineteenth century, large numbers of Asians, about 250,000 per year, largely Chinese, took advantage of the 1965 immigration law and moved to the United States. During the 1990s, the Asian-origin population of the United States doubled, from 2 percent to 4 percent. By the end of the decade, about 40 percent of all immigrants to the United States came from the PRC, Taiwan, and nearby parts of Asia. These new Americans ran the gamut from scientists and engineers to unskilled laborers. Hollywood "action films" attracted large audiences in China while martial arts films from China, Hong Kong, and Taiwan became staples in U.S. theaters. The kung fu master Jackie Chan displaced Charlie Chan as the most popular Chinese film hero.

In November 1993, during a conference in Seattle attended by leaders of several Asian-Pacific nations, Presidents Clinton and Jiang Zemin met briefly. Each espoused their contrasting positions on whether trade should be linked to human rights behavior. Following the encounter, Jiang visited local factories and several "typical" American families. Addressing an assembly of Boeing aircraft workers, the Chinese leader urged American business and labor groups to remove "all the negative factors and artificially imposed factors" that inhibited trade. During a visit to the home of a Boeing employee, he gave a stuffed panda toy to the children and consumed a plate of homemade chocolate chip cookies. To demonstrate that China could find alternate sources of foreign investment and technology, Chinese officials made a great public show over the next several months of purchasing high-technology items from European and Japanese suppliers.

Two of the president's top economic advisers, Treasury Secretary Lloyd Bentsen and Commerce Secretary Ron Brown, urged Clinton to sever the link between MFN extension and human rights. U.S. pressure, they argued, hurt American exporters without advancing Chinese democracy. At the same time, Secretary of State Christopher continued to push linkage. In the run-up to a trip to Beijing in March 1994, he asserted that "human rights will be at the top of my agenda." This prompted Prime Minister Li Peng to tell the visiting diplomat that "China will never accept the U.S. concept of human rights." Noting Christopher's past role investigating the 1992 race riots in Los Angeles following the acquittal of police officers who beat black motorist Rodney King, Li added, "you've got racism and human rights problems in the United States . . . so don't come over here and talk to us about human rights problems."

In May 1994 Clinton bowed to pressure from U.S. business interests and announced that China's MFN trade status would continue to be extended annually without regard to its human rights record. Without saying so, the administration acknowledged that although the Chinese government might sometimes behave ruthlessly toward its own people, the United States had to do business with it. Some members of Congress and many human rights organizations continued to criticize China's treatment of dissidents and ethnic and religious minorities, its use of prison labor, and its policy of forced abortions. But the determination of policy makers and business groups to "engage" China outweighed these concerns. During the remainder of the Clinton presidency through 2000, trade disputes arose over issues such as China's pirating of music, movies, and computer soft-ware. But human rights faded as a bargaining point. China had called Clinton's bluff over the threat to impose trade sanctions and the president had folded.

After lying dormant for some time, the Taiwan issue resurfaced in the mid-1990s as an acute problem. In 1994, Taiwan president Lee Tung-hui "popped up" in Honolulu when his aircraft made a refueling stop en route to Latin America. In deference to Beijing, the State Department refused Lee's request for an entry visa that would allow him to deplane and walk around during the service stop. (Ordinary travelers from Taiwan entered the United States without hindrance. Restrictions only applied to senior officials.) Lee's appearance was part of a cam-paign by lobbyists to raise his profile in advance of Taiwan's first free election and to mobilize support among Republicans and Clinton haters in Congress.

The Senate quickly passed by an overwhelming margin a resolution calling on the administration to grant Lee and other Taiwan officials entry visas. A few months later, in May 1995, both the House and the Senate approved by nearly unanimous votes a resolution to grant Lee a visa to attend a college reunion at his alma mater, Cornell University, in Ithaca, New York. These votes stemmed partly from Republican desire to embarrass Clinton and partly from effective lobbying by Taiwan. The votes also revealed a changing attitude among many Americans.

Since the United States cut formal ties in 1979, Taiwan had become much more prosperous and more democratic. The process began after Chiang Kai-shek's death in 1975 when his son and heir, Chiang Ching-kuo, relaxed the harsh rule imposed by his father and stressed economic modernization. By the time the younger Chiang died in 1988, Taiwan had become a modern industrial power and exporter. His successor, Taiwanese-born Lee Tung-hui, had earned a PhD in agricultural economics from Cornell and accelerated the process of political lib-eralization and economic development. Although only a fraction of the size of mainland China, Taiwan, in 1993, purchased $16 billion worth of American products, more than the PRC. (By the end of the decade, two-way trade between Taiwan and the United States totaled $54 billion.) As an emerging democracy and valued trading partner, Taiwan followed a path Americans had hoped to see the PRC emulate.

Congressional support for Taiwan, however, had tangled roots. As in past decades, the GMD party operated a well-funded lobbying operation in the United States. Republican politicians, sympathetic journalists, and state and local officials and community leaders were frequently invited on expense-paid VIP tours of the island. Retired members of congress often found employment with Taiwanese companies. Under official guidance, many Taiwanese companies made politically motivated investments and purchases in the United States. As noted earlier, while governor of Arkansas, Bill Clinton traveled four times to Taiwan on trade missions.

These efforts paid dividends in November 1994 when Republicans, under the leadership of Georgia Representative Newt Gingrich, captured control of the House for the first time since the 1950s. Elected Speaker in 1995, Gingrich became Taiwan's top booster. He called on Clinton to invite Lee Tung-hui to the United States as an official guest, demanded that the UN readmit Taiwan as a member nation, and lavished praise on the Taiwan government during a good-will visit to the island. It was in this new political atmosphere that Lee requested a visa to attend his Cornell reunion.

Anxious to avoid a dispute with China, the State Department suggested that the Taiwanese leader be allowed to visit only Honolulu, where he could play a round of golf. Such foolishness, Clinton realized, would play into the hands of Gingrich and his House majority who wanted to amend the Taiwan Relations Act of 1979 by restoring formal links to the island. In addition, Clinton felt a certain admiration for Taiwan's political evolution and resented China's effort to dictate who could and could not visit the United States. "Just as the Chinese demand to be respected in their way," he told aides, "they have to respect our way." They should be mindful of American traditions and history, as Americans should be mindful of China's. In approving Lee's visit to Cornell, the president described the congressional majorities who supported it as evidence of democracy at work. In his June 1995 speech at his alma mater, Lee called Taiwan a member of the "family of nations" that was "here to stay."[2]

As the State Department feared, the PRC reacted to Lee's visit by throwing a fit. Beijing recalled its ambassador from Washington for consultations, refused to accept the credentials of the newly appointed U.S. ambassador, and canceled on-going informal talks between the PRC and Taiwan. More ominously, during July China announced a series of air, sea, and ground military exercises in and around the Taiwan Strait. PRC vessels fired several nuclear-capable test missiles in the vicinity of Taiwan.

In an effort to mollify China, Clinton sent a personal message to President Jiang Zemin, assuring him that the United States stood by a one-China policy and opposed Taiwan's independence or readmission to the UN. This temporarily cooled tempers, although China continued to accuse the United States of med-dling in its internal affairs.

The complaint grew more serious in the fall of 1995. In the run-up to the Taiwan presidential election in March 1996, President Lee hinted that he might soon declare Taiwan's independence from the mainland. China threatened retaliation if he did so. Clinton reacted in February 1996 by sending the aircraft carrier USS *Nimitz* into the Taiwan Strait. When China massed soldiers across the strait from Taiwan and resumed firing test missiles toward the island, Clinton dispatched two additional aircraft carriers and naval support vessels to the region. An armed attack on Taiwan, the White House warned, would have "grave consequences" for China.

---

[2]Clinton may have had an additional motive for approving Lee's visit. Middlemen acting on Taiwan's behalf contributed generously to U.S. congressional campaigns. If Democrats seemed overly hostile, Taiwan's dollars might flow exclusively to Republicans. Allowing high-profile visits could prevent a GOP lock on this funding. As noted below, Republicans accused Democrats of taking money from China, even as they took money from Taiwan.

President Lee's victory in Taiwan's first genuinely free election altered the dynamic. Walking back his inflammatory campaign rhetoric, Lee made clear he had no intention of proclaiming independence from China any time soon. With that, both U.S. and Chinese forces pulled back. Chinese officials recognized their modest naval power compared to that of the U.S. fleet and resolved to quickly enhance their own maritime strength.

While tensions flared between Beijing and Washington, American officials placed renewed emphasis on the semidormant security alliance with Japan. Since Nixon's opening to China and the end of the Vietnam War, American military forces based in Japan and on Okinawa had few functions. During the 1980s, President Reagan tried, with modest success, to enlist Japan as a more active anti-Soviet partner. This effort faded with the end of the Cold War and the dissolution of the Soviet Union.

In April 1996, with an eye toward China, President Clinton visited Japan. He and Japanese Premier Ryutaro Hashimoto agreed to renew and revitalize the U.S.–Japan mutual security pact. The United States would assist Japan in developing an antimissile defense system, primarily to counter a North Korean threat but which might also neutralize China's small rocket arsenal.

Many Americans questioned why China made such a fuss about Taiwan's status. After all, the island had been separated from the mainland since 1949 and no longer posed a threat to the PRC. Not only did the United States, Japan, and Europe enjoy profitable ties with both regimes, but also the two rivals had become major economic partners. During the 1990s Taiwanese invested about $50 billion on the mainland. Joint business ventures prospered and many thousands of Chinese traveled and worked freely on either side of the Taiwan Strait. Why upset these arrangements?

The answer had as much to do with internal Chinese politics as with international relations. Since Mao's death, the Chinese Communist Party faced mounting challenges to its identity and legitimacy. Ordinary Chinese appreciated their growing sphere of personal freedom and material abundance. Standards of living rose for tens and then hundreds of millions of Chinese. But this begged the question of what, in this new age, the Communist Party actually stood for. Maoist dogma about permanent revolution and class struggle had been supplanted by Deng's proclamation that "getting rich is glorious." But how did this justify one-party rule?

As China's ruling elite decentralized the national economy, encouraged private enterprise, and returned land rights to peasants, it searched for ways to legitimize its control. With many Chinese complaining about official corruption and growing inequality, the Communist oligarchy celebrated its role as champion of Chinese nationalism and greatness. Defense of the nation and reclaiming China's historic dominant role in East Asia were said to justify authoritarian rule. Political pluralism, the party warned, would lead to factionalism and regionalism that might tear the nation apart. Moreover, only strong Communist rule could assure the return of lost territories such as Hong Kong, Macao, and Taiwan—and prevent foreign powers such as Japan or the United States from dominating Asia's future as they had its recent past. To this end, Communist officials encouraged a rebirth of nationalism that sometimes verged on "victimhood," stoking resentments against a supposedly U.S.-supported Taiwan independence movement.

Events in 1999 and again in 2001 revealed this tendency. In May 1999, during air attacks by the North Atlantic Treaty Organization against Serbia (which had committed war crimes while attempting to hold the breakaway Kosovo province), American aircraft accidentally bombed the Chinese embassy in Belgrade, killing three Chinese journalists. Although Washington accepted responsibility for the error and offered compensation, Beijing accused the United States of deliberate "criminal aggression," a charge widely accepted in China but nowhere else. Demonstrators, including many college students, burned a U.S. consular office in Chengdu and ransacked several McDonald franchises in Beijing while police stood aside. China's official paper, *Renmin ribao* (People's Daily), compared the United States and the North Atlantic Treaty Organization to the Western armies that invaded China in 1899. A poem published in another newspaper declared,

When we are wearing Pierre Cardin and Nike

When we are driving Cadillacs, Lincolns, and going to KFC and McDonalds

Do we have a clear conscience?
NO!!

Can we still find glory by using foreign products?
NO!!

Two years later, in April 2001, Chinese officials and ordinary citizens expressed outrage when an American reconnaissance plane on a routine mission in international air space off the south China coast collided with a Chinese air force plane tailing it. The Chinese plane and pilot were lost and the American aircraft made an emergency landing on Hainan Island. Although electronic data indicated that the Chinese plane caused the collision, Beijing condemned the United States and demanded an apology before releasing the 24-person crew. When, after 11 days, a compromise deal led to the crew's release, many Chinese criticized their government for not taking tougher action. Several times during the 1990s and beyond, demonstrators attacked Japanese-owned factories and diplomatic facilities in response to charges that Japan had not adequately atoned for its wartime injuries to China. Although these incidents were approved by the government, they also tapped into popular feelings.

China's heavy-handed actions in the mid-1990s prompted American politicians and the press to voice the most strident anti-Chinese rhetoric since the Nixon era. In the run-up to the 1996 U.S. presidential election, Republican nominee Senator Bob Dole attacked Clinton for a "soft" China policy, although the incumbent had stood by Taiwan. Dole demanded that the president provide increased military assistance to Taiwan and China's other neighbors.

Many of China's critics in and out of government tapped into a growing fascination with Tibet. An ethnically and religiously distinct region dominated by China since 1950, Tibetans practiced a form of Buddhism that looked to their religious leader, successive Dalai Lamas, as spiritual and political heads of state. Despite Chinese promises to respect the region's autonomy, Tibetans chafed under Communist rule. In 1959, aided by the CIA, Tibetans revolted. When the rebellion collapsed, the Dalai Lama fled into exile in India.

Over the next three decades, the Dalai Lama received the Nobel Prize for peace and proved a media-savvy advocate for the cause of Tibetan autonomy. He conducted seminars for wealthy Westerners in expensive resorts and even appeared in U.S. television commercials. His popular appeal, as well as foreign anger over China's continued heavy-handed rule, nurtured sympathy among Americans for Tibet's plight. Several popular Hollywood films produced during the 1990s, including *Seven Years in Tibet*, *Little Buddha*, and *Kundun*, presented Tibet in—quite literally—glowing colors that evoked images of Shangri-la, the heaven-on-earth depicted in the 1937 movie *Lost Horizon*. These films brought the Tibet question before a large public and prompted congressional Republicans to pass resolutions condemning China's occupation.

Until Dole and his GOP colleagues launched these attacks, Chinese officials had not shown much enthusiasm for Clinton's re-election. But Republican rhetoric made the incumbent more appealing to Beijing. To avoid making trouble for Clinton, China resolved several small irritants between the two countries and picked up on an American suggestion of an exchange of presidential visits after the 1996 election. Although Clinton's victory in November eased China's concerns, allegations soon surfaced in Washington that Beijing had bought influence among Democrats by making illegal campaign contributions. This, along with the Whitewater real estate and Monica Lewinski sex scandals, dogged Clinton throughout his second term.[3]

Clinton and Vice President Al Gore had aggressively raised campaign funds. They tapped many donors among the growing, affluent Asian American community. The generally lax laws governing donations stipulated that only U.S. citizens or legal residents could make contributions. In the aftermath of the 1996 election, evidence surfaced that some foreign nationals and Chinese-owned businesses had given funds to the Democratic Party and individual candidates. When this came to light, the Democratic National Committee returned the questionable money. This failed to mollify Republicans, who retained control of both houses of congress despite Clinton's re-election. For most of the next four years, Representative Dan Burton and Senator Fred Thompson conducted drawn-out, intensely partisan probes of Democratic fundraising determined to prove that China had "poured illegal money" into Democratic campaigns designed to "subvert our electoral process." Clinton, they claimed, had skated to victory in 1996 on bundles of Chinese cash.

---

[3]Neither Whitewater—a real estate investment by the Clintons in Arkansas in the 1980s on which they *lost* money—nor the Lewinski affair had anything to do with the president's official duties or job performance. However, like the far more serious Watergate scandal of the 1970s, these uniquely American kerfuffles puzzled Chinese leaders.

Congressional hearings focused on a few obscure Chinese American individuals who bundled contributions from small donors in return for VIP treatment, including White House tours and photo opportunities with the president. These murky relationships revealed more about the muddled nature of campaign funding law than about any organized Chinese effort to manipulate American politics. Congressional sleuths failed to show any collusion between the president and Chinese officials. In fact, many of the Chinese Americans, Chinese nationals, and Chinese-owned businesses linked to questionable contributions were actually associated with Taiwan or Chinese communities in Southeast Asia, not with the PRC. For example, Republicans ridiculed Al Gore for accepting donations from Buddhist monks during a brief visit in 1996 to their temple in Los Angeles. Gore had not known that local Chinese American business groups had used the monks as a cover for their contribution to his campaign. More telling was the fact that the religious sect in question was based in Taiwan, not China. When further inquiries revealed that Republicans had received donations from sources linked to Taiwan, the investigation ceased. In any case, the dubious "Chinese money," whatever its source or destination, comprised chump change—far less than 1 percent of the total of more than $2 billion spent by the Democratic and Republican parties in 1996.

Persistent, partisan attacks put Clinton's domestic and foreign policy agendas on the defensive. Nearly all diplomats, academic experts on China, and business groups agreed that the best way to encourage China to respect international trade norms, observe copyright laws, and treat its labor force fairly was to grant Beijing "permanent, normal trade relations" rather than annual MFN status and to speed its entry into the World Trade Organization (WTO). But Clinton hesitated to take action that might be labeled "pro-Chinese."

Criticism of Clinton's approach to China was exemplified by the March 24, 1997, cover of the conservative journal, *National Review*. Dubbing the president the "Manchurian Candidate" (a reference to the 1962 film depicting a sleeper agent and assassin programmed by Chinese Communists), the cover portrayed Bill and Hillary Clinton and Al Gore in "yellow face." It depicted the president as a buck-toothed, squinty-eyed house boy wearing a straw hat serving tea. The similarly buck-toothed and squinting First Lady wore a Red Guard outfit and waved a copy of Mao's "Little Red Book." The hapless vice president wore Buddhist robes and carried a monk's begging bowl stuffed with cash. The *National Review* article repeated the patently false mantra that China had bought the 1996 election and "owned" the president.

In February 1997, after three years out of public view, Deng Xiaoping died at the age of 92. In power almost as long as Mao, Deng left nearly as dramatic an imprint on the PRC as its founder. President Jiang Zemin, a Deng protégé, filled his mentor's place. On June 30, 1997, in a ceremony designed to erase the ignominious defeat in the first Opium War, Jiang presided over the return of Hong Kong to China. Portuguese Macao followed in 1999, after 442 years as a colony. This left only Taiwan separated from the motherland.

President Bill Clinton, with Chinese President Jiang Zemin, reviews Chinese troops near Tiananmen Square, June 1998. (© Wally McNamee/Corbis)

As agreed to the year before, Jiang visited Washington in October 1997. He and Clinton spoke politely but left unresolved most issues dividing their countries. Clinton refused to cease arms sales to Taiwan and chided Jiang by telling him that China stood on the "wrong side of history" by refusing to expand political freedom for its people. In return for American agreement to sell China some civilian nuclear technology, Jiang promised to stop assisting Iran's nuclear development program.

After the Chinese leader's departure, the State Department issued a statement repeating American opposition to Taiwan independence or any sort of two-China policy. China responded by releasing from prison democracy rights crusader Wei Jingsheng, who had spent nearly 18 years in jail. Sent into exile in the United States, Wei received an invitation to the White House and took a job at Columbia University.[4]

In June 1998, amid the furor of the Lewinski sex scandal, a politically wounded President Clinton traveled to China. There he spoke forcefully about the reasons many Americans questioned Chinese government behavior. In an unprecedented, live, televised press conference held with President Jiang in Beijing, Clinton spoke directly about the 1989 violence at Tiananmen. Both he and the American people, Clinton asserted, "believe that the use of force and the tragic loss of life was wrong." Jiang defended his government's action, declaring

---

[4]Wei proved a more inspiring symbol of democracy while in China than in exile. He did not easily adjust to life in the United States and alienated many of his American supporters.

that "had the Chinese government not taken the resolute measures, we could not have enjoyed the stability that we are enjoying today."

During this and subsequent public exchanges in Shanghai, the two presidents engaged in a spirited discussion about the nature of democracy, the treatment of dissidents in both countries, and American concern about conditions in Tibet. This was the most wide-ranging political debate between a Chinese and an American leader aired publicly in China since 1949. In a speech Clinton delivered in Shanghai, he showed his appreciation for the opportunity by endorsing China's "Three No" policy. The United States would not support an independent Taiwan, would not recognize two Chinas, and would oppose UN membership for Taiwan. For the moment, this reassured Beijing that Washington would not challenge its self-image as the sole, legitimate government of all China and all Chinese.

The Taiwan issue emerged again in mid-1999. Facing an election the following year, Lee Tung-hui resumed speaking of Taiwan as a sovereign nation that China must deal with on a "state-to-state" basis. This appeal to Taiwanese who favored some form of independence infuriated the PRC. Lee's rhetoric, however, alienated as many voters as it attracted and in March 2000 Chen Shui-bian won the presidential election. Chen, candidate of the pro-independence Democratic Progressive Party, was the first Taiwan leader from outside the GMD. Although both Beijing and Washington braced for a crisis, Chen surprised everyone by downplaying talk of independence.

In the midst of the Taiwan election, California Republican Representative Christopher Cox released a 700-page portion of a larger, classified report (commissioned by Speaker Gingrich who had earlier promoted the bogus investigation of Chinese political donations) that accused China of engaging in a massive espionage scheme while the Clinton administration turned a blind eye. Cox claimed that the report of May 1999 proved that China had spent the last several years secretly collecting computer codes and design information from the nuclear weapons laboratory in Los Alamos, New Mexico, and from other sites. This, he alleged, had enabled China to miniaturize atomic warheads that could be placed on missiles. As a result, China now posed a "credible direct threat against the United States."[5]

The report claimed that Chinese espionage began in the 1940s abetted by a Chinese-born scientist, Qian Xuesen, a veteran of the wartime program to build an atomic bomb and then a cofounder of the Jet Propulsion Laboratory at Cal Tech. In 1950, after his effort to obtain U.S. citizenship and his security clearance were rejected because of his alleged Communist sympathies (which he denied), Qian attempted to return to China. Instead, he was held under virtual house

---

[5]As of 2000, China had a large but defense-oriented army, a tiny navy, an obsolete air force, two to three dozen nuclear-tipped missiles capable of reaching the United States, and several hundred short-range rockets that could reach Taiwan. The United States, after substantially cutting its arsenal following the Soviet collapse, still possessed more than 8,000 nuclear weapons that could reach targets anywhere on the planet.

arrest until 1955. After his exchange for several American pilots downed during the Korean War, he returned to China and helped develop its ballistic missile and nuclear weapons program. The Cox report implied that Qian, like every Chinese exchange student, visiting scholar, or even ordinary Chinese American, might be a potential spy. Initially, these allegations were accepted at face value. Even the normally sober *New York Times* praised the Cox committee for "invaluable service with its unsparing investigation."

China, like the United States, certainly gathered military, technical, and economic secrets from abroad. The Cox report justifiably criticized the lax security at many American weapons labs and defense facilities that had allowed the Chinese and others to scoop up information. But impartial experts concluded that China's intelligence gathering exploited a combination of open sources, accidental disclosures, and pumping scientists at international conferences for useful data. Outright theft of secret information certainly occurred, but was neither the main problem nor a uniquely Chinese phenomenon. Ironically, many of the most strident critics of China based their conclusion on a handbook published openly in the PRC that suggested ways in which Chinese scientists could gather information from foreign books, articles, conference papers, and the Internet. Espionage had its place, the manual acknowledged, but massive amounts of data could be gleaned from open sources.

Despite its dubious evidence and conclusions, the Cox report gained some credibility in December 1999 when the Federal Bureau of Investigation arrested Wen Ho Lee, a Taiwan-born nuclear weapons designer who worked at the Los Alamos laboratory. Lee was suspected of downloading large amounts of secret data from his secure computer and passing the copied information to China. Federal officials told journalists that Lee had stolen the "crown jewels" of America's nuclear weapons program and that his betrayal threatened to tip the global balance of power in China's favor.

Denied bail and held for nine months in solitary confinement, Lee was threatened with possible execution unless he confessed. Ultimately, government sleuths were unable to prove that Wen Ho Lee had given any of the purloined data to anyone or that he even had access to the specific warhead diagrams that China had acquired. Investigators later admitted they focused on Lee and ignored other leads because of a mindset that targeted ethnic Chinese as potential spies.

Embarrassed by the failure to make a case, the Justice Department offered Lee a plea bargain. The scientist pled guilty to a single charge of improper handling of restricted data that, he insisted, was for his own use. The federal judge overseeing the case criticized the Federal Bureau of Investigation and the Energy Department for misconduct and misrepresenting facts. After the plea deal, investigators acknowledged that Lee may have intended to trade the nuclear data for a job with institutions in Australia, Switzerland, or Taiwan, rather than China. In 2006, the government and five media organizations agreed to pay Lee $1.6 million for leaking his name and damaging information before any charges had been filed.

In July 2000, as the Lee case unraveled, Cox released a follow-up report detailing a North Korean threat. Not only was North Korea a monstrous tyranny, Cox charged, but also it had become "one of the greatest threats to American and allied interests anywhere around the globe." Cox insinuated that the Clinton administration, in thrall to North Korea's patron, China, ignored this nuclear threat.[6]

Amid these Congressional spasms, the Clinton administration endeavored to remain engaged with China. China's economic growth and emergence as a major trading partner had enmeshed the United States and the PRC in ways almost unimaginable just a decade earlier. In 1999, the two countries agreed on terms for China to eventually join the multilateral WTO, which supervised trade relations among major exporters and importers. (China formally entered the WTO in 2001.) In 2000, Clinton recommended and Congress approved granting China permanent, normal trade relations status. In place of annually granting China conditional tariff preference, China would permanently receive the same low tariff treatment as America's other major trading partners. In turn, China agreed to open its domestic market to more foreign products and capital. Foreign firms gained increased access to Chinese financial, telecommunications, and legal sectors. Beijing also agreed to cut subsidies to state factories and to eliminate many quotas on agricultural imports.

The millions of Chinese and foreign visitors who entered the Forbidden City through Tiananmen each year, passing under a giant portrait of Mao as they walked on gray cobblestones past vermilion pavilions toward the Palace of Heavenly Purity, encountered a new monument to globalization in October 2000: Starbucks opened a coffee shop in the shadow of the residences of former Ming and Qing emperors. In June 2001, the Beijing municipal government sponsored a concert in the Forbidden City as part of their ultimately successful effort to attract the 2008 Summer Olympics. Nearly 30,000 affluent Chinese paid as much as $2,000 to sip a Starbuck's latte or vintage wine while listening to the "Three Tenors" perform Italian arias in a courtyard near the spot where Boxers and Red Guards had once attacked foreign devils and bourgeois revisionists.

Nevertheless, Sino–American relations remained unsettled at the start of the twenty-first century. Although China policy was hardly discussed by the major candidates during the presidential election of 2000, soon after he took office in 2001 President George W. Bush and his aides began describing the PRC as a "strategic competitor," a rival if not an enemy of the United States. The incoming

---

[6]Despite Cox's warning, the threat of war on the always volatile Korean peninsula actually decreased in 2000, at least for a while. Rival Korean presidents Kim Jong-il in the North and Kim Dae-jung in the South exchanged visits and pledged to improve relations. Both of Cox's inflammatory reports coincided with Republican efforts to revive the expensive but faltering antiballistic missile program begun under Reagan. Despite Republican pressure, Clinton resisted deploying the costly and unreliable system. To the considerable annoyance of the Clinton administration, China had sold missile technology to Pakistan and Iran during the 1990s, but this seemed not to overly concern Cox and his fellow Republicans.

president and his top aides spoke openly about defending Taiwan at any cost. A majority of Americans and their congressional representatives continued to condemn China as a human rights violator. In July 2001 China signed a new treaty of "friendship and cooperation" with its former enemy, Russia. The two erstwhile allies pledged cooperation against efforts by any outside power (i.e., the United States) to impose a unilateral security framework on Asia. A Russian official described this pact as an "act of friendship against America." As one astute policy observer noted, economic and political globalization had moved China and the United States continually closer without necessarily making them more cooperative. In the words of a Chinese proverb, they shared the same bed but had different dreams.

SELECTED ADDITIONAL READINGS

Richard Madsen, *China and the American Dream* (Berkeley, Ca., 1995); James Mann, *About Face: A History of America's Curious Relationship with China from Nixon to Clinton* (New York, 1999); Patrick Tyler, *A Great Wall: Six American Presidents and China* (New York, 1999); Robert G. Sutter, *U.S. Policy toward China: An Introduction to the Role of Interest Groups* (Lanham, Md., 1998) and *U.S.–Chinese Relations: Perilous Past, Pragmatic Present* (Lanham, Md., 2010); Odd Arne Westad, *Restless Empire: China and the World since 1750* (New York, 2012); Alan G. Gorowitz, ed., *The Taiwan Relations Act: Twenty-Five Years After and a Look Ahead* (Atlanta, Ga., 1999); Nancy B. Tucker, *Strait Talk: United States–Taiwan Relations and the Crisis with China* (Cambridge, Mass., 2009); Louisa Lim, *The People's Republic of Amnesia: Tiananmen Revisited* (New York, 2014); Jay Taylor, *The Generalissimo's Son: Chiang Ching-kuo and the Revolutions in China and Taiwan* (Cambridge, Mass., 2000); David M. Lampton, *Same Bed, Different Dreams: Managing U.S.–China Relations, 1989–2000* (Berkeley, Ca., 2001); Robert Ross, ed., *After the Cold War: Domestic Factors and U.S. China Relations* (New York, 1998); John W. Garver, *Face Off: China, the United States, and Taiwan's Democratization* (Seattle, Wa., 1997); Ezra F. Vogel, ed., *Living with China: U.S.–China Relations in the 21st Century* (New York, 1997); Richard Bernstein and Ross H. Munro, *Coming Conflict with China* (New York, 1998); Bruce Cumings, *Parallax Visions: Making Sense of American–East Asian Relations at the End of the Century* (Raleigh–Durham, N.C., 1999); James L. Watson, *Golden Arches East: McDonalds in East Asia* (Stanford, Ca., 1997); *Report of the Select Committee on U.S. National Security and Military/Commercial Concerns with the People's Republic of China [Cox Report]* (Washington, D.C., 1999).

CHAPTER 13

China Ascending, 2001–2015

Since 1967, when presidential candidate Richard Nixon wrote that the United States "cannot afford to leave China forever outside the family of nations," nurturing fantasies and threatening its neighbors, he and his successors have engaged China in the global economic and political system. All Nixon's successors agreed with him that it made no sense "on this small planet for a billion of its potentially most able people to live in angry isolation." In January 2011, President Barack Obama repeated this mantra in remarks welcoming Chinese President Hu Jintao to the White House. The United States, he declared, "welcomes China's rise as a strong, prosperous and successful member of the community of nations." For four decades American leaders, along with those in Western Europe and Japan, have worked to wean China away from Maoist dreams of world revolution and policies of domestic repression. To foster change, the United States opened its markets, provided loans, transferred technology, educated hundreds of thousands of Chinese students, and promoted China's membership in international organizations such as the UN (1971), the International Monetary Fund and the World Bank (1980), and the WTO (2001).

By the second decade of the twenty-first century China, by most measures, had moved from the margins to the center of the international system. Its wealth and power have increased beyond anyone's expectations. It possesses global influence even if it does not yet exercise global power. The PRC now boasts the world's second biggest economy and has become America's second largest trading partner as well as its largest foreign creditor. Economic historian Niall Ferguson coined a term for this new relationship: "Chimerica."

CHINA AND AMERICAN POLITICS BEFORE AND AFTER 9/11

Although Republican presidential candidate George W. Bush chided Bill Clinton and Al Gore for "coddling" Beijing, China policy was not a major issue in the

2000 election.[1] Friction over Taiwan, human rights, and trade had diminished by the end of the Clinton presidency. Nevertheless, once the Supreme Court affirmed his disputed election, Bush indicated that as president he would pursue a more strident policy toward the PRC. During the first nine months of the new administration, relations between Washington and Beijing soured and seemed on a downward spiral.

During the 2000 election campaign, George W. Bush described China as a "strategic competitor." If the PRC threatened Taiwan, he asserted, the United States would do "whatever it takes" to defend the island. Most of the president's top foreign policy advisers had come to maturity during the Cold War and continued to focus their attention on Russia and the Middle East, rather than on East Asia. Their views of China often seemed stuck in a time warp, thinking of the PRC as either a counter to Soviet power or a Communist threat by itself.

Tensions with China flared in April 2001 when a U.S. reconnaissance (i.e., spy) aircraft flying 70 miles off the south China coast collided with a Chinese jet that had been shadowing it. The Chinese plane crashed, killing the pilot, and the damaged American plane with its crew of 24 made an emergency landing on China's Hainan Island. Although tracking data showed the Chinese plane to be at fault, Beijing accused the Americans of causing the collision and refused to release the crew until the United States apologized. Following an 11-day standoff, China accepted an "expression of regret" by the Bush administration for the incident. After the crew left Hainan, Chinese experts scrutinized the American plane's electronic gear before eventually returning it. Many Chinese publicly complained that their government had treated the Americans too lightly. How, they asked, would the United States respond to a Chinese spy plane patrolling off the coast of Florida or California?

In the United States, the episode soured both public and congressional opinion. Shortly after the collision, Congress voted 406 to 6 to condemn China for violating the human rights of political dissidents and religious minorities. The State Department cautioned Americans who had criticized China's policies toward Taiwan or Tibet against visiting the PRC. In July, China partly responded to these criticisms by signing a treaty of "friendship and cooperation" with Russia. The two recent antagonists pledged to boost trade and resist efforts by any outside power (i.e., the United States) to impose a unilateral security framework on Asia. A Russian official described this pact as an "act of friendship against America." Chinese leaders felt even more confident during the summer of 2001 when the International Olympics Committee selected Beijing to host the 2008 games. Also at the end of 2001, the PRC formally joined the WTO, signifying its membership among the world's largest economies.

---

[1] In spite of hype by Congressional Republicans and their allies in the media, the public showed little interest in ongoing but unfounded allegations that Democrats had benefitted from illegal Chinese campaign funds.

The terrorist attacks of September 11, 2001, quickly overshadowed the recent spats between Washington and Beijing. Within days of the tragic events, Chinese President Jiang Zemin called Bush to express sympathy and pledged to cooperate in "combatting all sorts of terrorist violence." As the Bush administration launched its "global war on terror," Beijing assisted U.S. efforts to halt money laundering by terrorists, shared intelligence with Washington, and supported the American military campaign to remove the Taliban regime in Afghanistan. In return, the United States tacitly approved China's harsh policy of suppressing radical Muslim Uighur separatists in Xinjiang province. Chinese leaders were content to see the United States devote most of its attention to the Middle East and terrorism, leaving China a much freer hand in Asia.

George W. Bush commemorated Nixon's 1972 opening to China by traveling there himself in February 2002. He and President Jiang Zemin pledged cooperation against terrorists and ignored most other questions.

Wearing traditional clothing, President George W. Bush and Chinese President Jiang Zemin greet each other. (© Reuters/Corbis)

Vice President Hu Jintao, Jiang's heir-apparent, reciprocated and met with Bush that spring in the Oval Office. Bush had signaled his upbeat feelings about China by inviting Jiang to visit his ranch in Texas, an honor reserved for special occasions.

The American-led invasion of Iraq in March 2003 – based partly on bogus intelligence indicating the regime had produced or soon would weapons of mass destruction -unsettled the Chinese, who enjoyed a lucrative trade relationship with Saddam Hussein's regime. However, the PRC did not attempt to block Bush's effort to organize a "coalition of the willing" to invade Iraq. Bush reciprocated by dropping U.S. backing for a UN resolution condemning China's human rights record. When Hu Jintao became China's president on the eve of Iraq war in 2003, Secretary of State Colin Powell described bilateral relations as "the best they have been since President Nixon's first visit."

But, as in the past, developments in Taiwan again rocked U.S.–China relations. During 2002 and 2003, Taiwan president Chen Shui-bian (as part of his re-election strategy) taunted China by suggesting that the island might soon declare itself an independent country. When Chen ignored a private message from Bush to tone down his rhetoric, the American president publicly chided Chen. During a White House visit by Chinese Premier Wen Jiabao, Bushdeclared U.S. opposition to any move by Taiwan to assert independence.

Nevertheless, after Chen won re-election in 2004, he repeated his threat to declare independence, angering both Washington and Beijing. The Bush administration, like its predecessors, relied on a policy of "strategic ambiguity" to maintain peace in the region. Washington believed that if both Taiwan and the PRC were unsure how far the United States would go to defend the island, Taiwan would not risk declaring independence from China, nor would China risk attacking Taiwan.[2] Chen's provocations and the resultingChinese military buildup across the strait continued until the spring of 2008 when residents of Taiwan elected a new president, Ma Ying-jeou, who pledged to improve relations with the mainland.

Trade disputes, American complaints of Chinese human rights violations, Beijing's trade with Iran despite American sanctions, and Chinese disapproval of Bush's penchant for "regime change" in Iraq and elsewhere also complicated bilateral relations. However, China's determination to expand trade with the United States, as well as American efforts to encourage China to become a "responsible stakeholder" in world affairs, as one official put it, mitigated these tensions. In November 2005, Bush and Defense Secretary Donald Rumsfeld visited China and reassured their hosts that America valued China's friendship and trade. After a return visit to Washington by PRC President Hu Jintao in April 2006, U.S. and Chinese military forces initiated cooperative training exercises and the two governments agreed on the need to restrain North Korea's nuclear

---

[2]Bush and Congress had approved substantial new arms sales to Taiwan. However, the Taiwan legislature, controlled by Chen's opponents, refused to appropriate funds to buy most of the weapons, thus tempering Beijing's anger with Washington.

weapons program. In December 2006, Bush again called the bilateral relationship "the best ever." In the summer of 2008, ignoring critics of China's human rights record, Bush attended the Beijing Olympics. Like the huge global audience watching on television, he marveled at how well China handled the spectacle. By year's end, the Bush administration had dropped China from its list of "worst" human rights violators.

CHINA AND THE OBAMA ADMINISTRATION

Since the opening to China in the 1970s, new presidents often took office promising to take a tougher line on Chinese trade practices and human rights violations. Yet, every one expanded America's economic and diplomatic relationship with China. Surprisingly, Barack Obama, the first president born in the Pacific region (Hawaii) and partly raised as a child in Southeast Asia (Indonesia), proved the exception. During the 2008 campaign he refrained from criticizing Bush's China policy.However, after he took office relations between the two nations soured.

As a senator, Obama joined most Democrats in criticizing China's manipulation of its currency and blamed Beijing for unfairly contributing to the U.S. trade deficit. But during his presidential campaign, Obama stressed his desire to cooperate with China on solving a range of economic and security issues. Although Obama questioned whether Bush should have attended the Beijing Olympics in light of Chinese behavior in Tibet and elsewhere, he downplayed China's human rights record as a campaign theme.

The 2008 Beijing Olympics, occurring just as an economic crisis began to engulf the United States and Western Europe, seemed evidence of China's ascendance and the West's relative decline. As part of his effort to promote recovery, President Obama hoped to engage China on a range of economic, security, and environmental issues. These included cooperation on climate change, nuclear nonproliferation, and dealing with "rogue" states such as North Korea and Iran. Obama met with Chinese president Hu Jintao in April 2009 at an economic conference in London and both pledged to cooperate in stabilizing the world economy. Obama also moved to enhance the strategic and economic dialogues—high-level meetings between key U.S. and Chinese officials—that began late in the Bush administration.

When Obama traveled to China for an official visit in November 2009, U.S. press coverage was surprisingly critical. Reflecting the economic despair caused by the worst downturn since the Great Depression of the 1930s, many American—and some Chinese—journalists depicted Obama as a supplicant, seeking alms. The meeting achieved little of substance. To make matters worse, at an international climate change conference in Copenhagen late in 2009, China scuttled American efforts to reach a comprehensive deal to reduce emissions. The plan, Beijing charged, unfairly penalized economies such as China, which relied heavily on coal.

During 2010, Obama and his foreign policy advisers saw China as uncooperative on a range of issues that concerned the United States. China, in turn, interpreted several U.S. actions as hostile. These included Obama's approval in

Two wary leaders, Barack Obama and Hu Jintao, size each other up as their nations become competitors. (© Lan Hongguang/Xinhua Press/Corbis)

January of a $6.4 billion arms sale to Taiwan and his February meeting with the exiled Dalai Lama. In March, when North Korea sank a South Korean warship, China refused to join a U.S.-led condemnation of the unprovoked attack.

Beginning in 2010, China more forcefully asserted territorial claims to several uninhabited islets and shoals in the South and East China seas, areas also claimed by Vietnam, Taiwan, Indonesia, the Philippines, Japan, and South Korea. In 2012 and 2014, Chinese naval vessels challenged Japanese, Filipino, and Vietnamese ships near these islets. The surrounding waters were believed to have valuable oil and mineral resources. They also lay astride shipping lanes vital to China's maritime trade. At home, this type of muscle flexing also appealed to domestic nationalist sentiment and bolstered the Communist Party's determination to cast itself as the nation's source of prosperity, pride, and strength. These displays revealed Beijing's determination to act as regional hegemon while compelling its neighbors to ponder the value of their ties with the United States.[3]

President Obama responded to these events by undertaking a so-called Pivot to Asia. Speaking before the Australian parliament in November 2011, Obama declared that the United States intended to play a "larger and long-term role" in

---

[3]The United States supported the claims of Japan, the Philippines and Vietnam to these islets, buturged all parties to negotiate territorial disputes.

shaping the Asia-Pacific region. It hoped to do so in partnership with "our allies and friends." Administration officials described the new approach as a "rebalancing" of American priorities. Elements of the pivot included more strident criticism of Chinese trade practices, including theft of intellectual property, currency manipulation, and export subsidies. To counter alleged "dumping," the Obama administration imposed special tariffs on Chinese automobile tires and then solar panels.[4]

Early in 2012 the United States also deployed several thousand Marines to Australia, the first increase in regional troop levels since the end of the Vietnam War. Their purpose, U.S. officials explained, was to serve as "first responders" to humanitarian and natural disasters, not as a combat force. But the Chinese press accused Washington of trying scare other Asians about China's intentions. PRC military spending had grown considerably since 2000, but the size and quality of its armed forces remained far less potent than those of the United States.

NEW ECONOMIC REALITIES

Starting in the early 1980s, China's economic growth startled the world. Many of the oppressive structures of Maoism—both political and economic—faded, even if the nation did not democratize. With its economic interests spanning the globe, China gradually became something of a status quo power. Since the early 1990s, most of China's traditional rivals either stumbled or turned their attention elsewhere. The Soviet Union collapsed in 1991, succeeded by a post-Communist Russia that struggled economically and politically. India's foreign policy focused on threats from Pakistan. Japan experienced more than a decade of economic drift and remained uncertain whether to limit or expand military cooperation with the United States. After 2001, the United States focused on combatting Islamist terrorism while fighting wars in Iraq and Afghanistan. With its global economic reach and military potential, China emerged as the only nation that might plausibly challenge U.S. military predominance in Asia. By the second decade of the twenty-first century, some Americans wondered if their previous support for China's rise confirmed the adage, "Be careful what you wish for."

Between 2001 and 2012, as the United States fought costly wars in Afghanistan and Iraq and spent hundreds of billions of dollars to defend itself against real and imagined terror threats, China's economic growth surged. The Great Recession that hobbled Western economies and financial institutions during 2008–2010 barely registered in China. China became America's largest foreign creditor, holding as much as $1.6 trillion in U.S. government debt bought with export profits. Washington used the borrowed money to pay for the unfunded wars and tax cuts enacted by Bush and the Republican Congress after 2001. While the American economy seemed to lurch from crisis to crisis, Chinese officials took to lecturing American bankers and politicians about how to manage their affairs.

---

[4]Dumping referred to one country selling goods abroad below the actual cost of production, partly due to government subsidies.

Beijing worried, of course, that a U.S. default could threaten the trillion dollars or more in U.S. Treasury bonds and other dollar assets held by China as well as the ability of American consumers to buy Chinese exports. As one Chinese economist put it, "our teachers now have some problems."[5] Some Chinese officials grumbled that U.S. consumers relied on "cheap Chinese labor" to allow them to live beyond their means.

From the founding of the PRC in 1949 until the mid-1970s, Mao promoted a rigid, Soviet-style economy. The system relied on central planning, government control over agriculture and industry, the abolition of most private property, and the use of ideological campaigns and terror, rather than material incentives, to mobilize production. Until 1959, China benefitted from trade and aid with the Soviet bloc, but after 1960 had limited economic contact with the outside world. During the quarter century after 1949, China achieved basic industrialization, but it lacked modern technology, barely produced enough food to feed itself, and sacrificed millions of lives in misguided domestic crusades such as the Great Leap Forward. As living standards in Japan, South Korea, and Taiwan surged, China lagged far behind.

Following his rise to power in the late 1970s, Deng Xiaoping steadily reversed Mao's policies. Initially, he proposed using modest material incentives to boost agricultural and industrial production in state-owned facilities. Peasants gradually gained the right to lease private plots and later took ownership of agricultural land. Deng also sanctioned the creation of a few "special economic zones" to attract foreign investment and produce goods for export. When these proved successful, he approved additional export production zones in several coastal provinces. In 1992, in one of his final public acts, Deng traveled to several of the most economically dynamic areas in south China and called for the entire country to adopt similar models of growth through global economic engagement. Soon, nearly all of China opened for foreign investment and export production.

China's economic growth and transformation since the 1990s resembled nothing in world history. In less than two decades it achieved results that took other industrialized economies such as Great Britain, Germany, the United States, and Japan at least a half century. For example, in 1984, during President Reagan's visit to China, the *Wall Street Journal* mocked those who predicted China would become a major trading nation. While the United States sold China weapons and advanced electronics, the *Journal* editorialized, China gave the United States "panda bears." As late as 1990, the American business press lamented that already the "balloon is out of the China bubble."

But although some pundits predicted the failure of another China market dream, actual trade exploded. For example, in the mid-1990s, China's national economy was about the size of Italy's. In 2012, after 20 years of double-digit

---

[5]When reports surfaced in 2008 of China exporting to the United States a variety of tainted products, economist Paul Krugman wryly observed, "they send us toxic food and toys and we send them toxic securities in return."

growth, it was the second biggest in the world. One economist called coastal China "one big export platform" and by 2009 China surpassed Germany as the world's largest exporter of manufactured goods. Most of these exports went to developed countries in Western Europe and to Japan and the United States. To sustain growth, China imported massive amounts of energy and raw materials, mostly from less developed countries, especially from Africa and the Persian Gulf. It displaced the United States as the world's largest oil importer.

One common measurement of national income, per capita gross domestic product (GDP), grew from about $200 per year in 1978 to nearly $7,000 in 2013. (In comparison, U.S. per capita GDP rose only a bit more than 10 percent in these years, to about $53,000 in 2013.) Some of China's GDP rise reflected its large population, and on a per capita basis many of the country's 1.4 billion people remained poor. Nevertheless, tens of millions of Chinese rose out of poverty during the late twentieth and early twenty-first centuries. By 2014, a majority of the world's millionaires and billionaires lived in China. As China industrialized, it also urbanized at a frantic pace. In 2012, for the first time in its history, more Chinese—about 700 million—lived in cities than in the countryside.

In 1972, the first year in which China and the United States resumed trade, the United States imported Chinese goods valued at $32 million. China imported American products worth $63.5 million. At the start of the twenty-first century, China exported to the United States goods worth $100 billion while American exports to China reached $16 billion. By 2013, Chinese goods sold to Americans had a value of just over $440 billion. U.S. exports topped $122 billion, producing a deficit of $319 billion in China's favor. China was the United States' third largest export market (behind Canada and Mexico) and the largest supplier of goods imported to the United States. Until the onset of the Great Recession in 2008, China used most of its trade surplus to purchase U.S. Treasury securities. Since then, it has devoted more of its foreign currency reserves—valued at about $4 trillion in 2014—to buying foreign resources, stocks, and commodities. Seventy percent of China's reserves were in dollar-denominated assets. This degree of economic enmeshment—so-called Chimerica—had few if any historical precedents.

Several factors accounted for this astounding growth over the past 30 years. China entered the world economy at a time when trading barriers were falling globally. As an exporter, China benefitted from a large, disciplined work force, low labor costs, the embrace of market ideas by government bureaucrats and entrepreneurs, the proliferation of low-cost ocean shipping using cargo containers, and the willingness of the American government and consumers to buy much of what China produced.[6]

---

[6]The use of standardized cargo containers that moved easily among trucks, ships, and trains lowered the cost of transoceanic shipping by up to 90 percent compared to costs before 1970. This made it profitable for China and other countries to produce and export globally inexpensive consumer goods, such as garments, toys, or small electrical appliances. In 2013, Walmart alone stocked products, mostly from China, that came to the United States in 370,000 8 × 40 foot cargo containers.

Some politicians, business, and labor groups blamed Chinese competition for the "hollowing out" of the U.S. industrial sector. In fact, most of the products China exported to American consumers before 2010 (toys, garments, inexpensive electronic devices) were items that U.S. factories had ceased producing decades before. Production of these goods had already moved to Japan, South Korea, Taiwan, and Southeast Asia. Part of China's gain in U.S. market share came at the expense of these suppliers. Most American sales to China consisted of high-end technological goods, upscale consumer brands, and agricultural products. More recently, Chinese exports include high value-added manufactured goods ranging from automobiles to computers and home appliances.

The U.S. government and business groups have long complained that China manipulated the value of its currency, the *Ren min bi* (RMB), to gain market share. By keeping the RMB undervalued in relation to the dollar, for example, Chinese goods could be sold more cheaply. Washington periodically pressed Beijing to revalue the RMB. Although China has gradually done so, the net effect on the trade balance with the United States has been small.

Washington also criticized China for unfairly subsidizing some manufacturers, allowing them to "dump" goods on the world market at below the cost of production. U.S. trade officials cited automobile tires and solar panels as examples. To level the playing field, the Obama administration slapped tariffs on these imports. This helped revive domestic production of solar panels. But even accounting for currency manipulation and subsidies, Chinese producers simply manufactured items Americans wanted at lower cost. In calculating their "bottom line," manufacturers around the world had to beat the so-called China Price if they hoped to find consumers.

CHINESE POWER AND AMERICAN SECURITY

China's military power increased substantially over the past 25 years. Into the 1990s, China's defense posture relied on what Mao had called a "peoples' war" strategy. The large but unwieldy People's Liberation Army (which included land, sea, and air forces) and peasant militias were configured to fight technologically superior invaders (such as the United States, Soviet Union, or Japan) by trading space for time. In the 1970s, China also developed a small nuclear deterrent of a few dozen intercontinental ballistic missiles.

In 1989, Deng Xiaoping urged his colleagues to behaved "modestly" and keep a low profile in foreign policy while promoting economic growth. It was best, he explained, to "hide our light and nurture our strength." As the economy prospered, military modernization would follow and China could gradually reclaim its traditional role as a dominant power in Asia. Between the late 1980s and 2012, China reduced the size of the People's Liberation Army by half, to about 2.25 million troops. It improved the training of military officers and put special emphasis on upgrading the quality of its naval, air, and nuclear forces. During the 1990s and the early years of the twenty-first century, China purchased many naval vessels and aircraft from Russia. Since 2007, it has produced its own advanced weapons. China deployed thousands of short-range missiles along its southern coast, available for use in a confrontation over Taiwan. It expanded its arsenal of nuclear-tipped missiles capable of hitting the United States to about 65 land-based intercontinental ballistic missiles and three dozen submarine-based missiles. As of 2014, China's military budget was the second largest in the world, but still far behind that of the United States.[7]

Even with new weapons, ships, and aircraft, China's security posture remains defensive. Its priorities include avoiding the loss of territory, reclaiming Taiwan, preventing domination of East Asia by one or a combination of outside powers, and maintaining international conditions that permit it to import energy and other raw materials and to export manufactured goods. China tries to influence its 22 large and small neighbors without seeming to dominate them, lest they seek protection from an outside power. Unlike the United States, China maintains no foreign bases or military alliances. A small number of its troops serve in UN peacekeeping operations. Although it aspires to create a "blue water navy," China currently has limited ability to project military power beyond its periphery or nearby maritime areas, including Taiwan. The PRC, as China watcher David Shambaugh has noted, has become a global *actor* but not yet a global *power*.

Some American politicians and pundits have warned that a hostile China might attempt to intimidate or harm the United States by "weaponizing" its hoard of dollars and Treasury bonds. Selling off these assets at bargain prices, the argument runs, could destroy the credit market and sink the American economy. In fact, any attempt to do so would hurt China as much or more than the United States. Here, another adage applies: "You owe the bank a thousand dollars and default, you're in trouble; you owe the bank a million dollars and default, the bank's in trouble."

Despite various tensions, Chinese and American leaders have maintained open lines of communication. Chinese President Hu Jintao paid a goodwill visit to Washington early in 2011. In February 2012, the PRC vice president and Hu's designated successor, Xi Jinping (who ascended to the top post in 2013), also visited the United States. These meetings routinely concluded with the release of joint statements stressing bilateral cooperation and common interests shared by both nations.

Following the Soviet collapse in 1991, China improved its relations and economic ties with Vietnam, India, and South Korea. Its main interest in Russia and the central Asian republics has been in sources of raw materials and energy for

---

[7]The United States, even after substantial reductions in the 1990s, possesses about 5,000 nuclear warheads on land and submarine-based missiles and on long-range bombers. The United States also maintains a global and Asian network of military alliances, bases, and other security arrangements, some dating from the 1950s, with Japan, South Korea, Thailand, the Philippines, Taiwan, Australia, New Zealand, and several central Asian republics. Not surprisingly, many Chinese consider these alliances and bases aimed at them.

domestic industry.[8] Despite extensive trade relations, Beijing remains wary of Japan. Since the late nineteenth century, China and Japan have each feared the other's plans to usurp the role of leader of East Asia. Recent Chinese efforts to control the uninhabited but disputed Diaoyu (in Chinese) or Senkaku (in Japanese) islets in the East China Sea are part of this ongoing contest. Leaders of both countries have mobilized nationalist sentiment in support of their claim. China may have hoped to fracture the U.S.–Japan alliance by making threats. If so, the tactic backfired, since Japan has moved to beef up its own military power, solidified its security ties to the United States, and initiated plans to adopt constitutional change to permit creation of a larger and more flexible defense force. Similarly, Chinese pressure in 2014 on Vietnam over maritime rights in the South China Sea prompted Hanoi to discuss with U.S. military officials the possibility of the U.S. Navy returning to some of the bases it occupied during the Vietnam War. Washington, once set on using anti-Communist South Vietnam to contain China, now ponders cooperating with Communist Vietnam to achieve a similar result.

BACKLASH

Just as Japan's economic surge in the 1970s and 1980s evoked fears of a "new Pearl Harbor," China ascendance since the 1990s revived a new "yellow peril" literature.[9] Although some authors, such as Richard Bernstein and Ross Munro (*The Coming Conflict with China*, 1997), Steven Mosher (*Hegemon: China's Plan to Dominate Asia and the World*, 2000), and Martin Jacques, *When China Rules the World* (2009) grounded their alarmist interpretations on facts, other titles—and lurid book jackets—resembled tales of Fu Manchu. This genre, produced by authors with little actual knowledge of China, included *Red Dragon Rising* (1999), *The China Threat* (2000), *The Coming China Wars: Where They Will Be Fought and How They Can Be Won* (2007), and *In the Jaws of the Dragon: America's Fate in the Coming Era of Chinese Hegemony* (2008). These books combined factual errors, misinformation, and outright distortions to arouse readers' anxieties. Some lurid novels, such as Clive Cussler's *Flood Tide* (1997), revived fears of invasion by masses of illegal Chinese immigrants. Popular writer Tom Clancy demonized both China and Russia in the novel *The Bear and the Dragon* (2001) and depicted Chinese as arch villains in several video games based on his writings.

Chinese officials often express their own fear of American-sponsored subversion. During the 1980s and 1990s, Communist officials sometimes described Western books and values as sources of "spiritual pollution," designed to subvert

---

[8] In 2001, China and Russia signed a treaty of "Good Neighborliness and Friendly Cooperation." Between 2004 and 2008 they completed the peaceful demarcation of their lengthy and long-disputed border.

[9] For example, in 1985 respected journalist Theodore White wrote in the *New York Times* that Japan's trade offensive aimed to subdue the "whole world" by reversing the outcome of "who finally won the war fifty years before."

China. Since 2000, several Chinese authors have written popular books that claim to reveal Western plots to degrade and humiliate the PRC. As recently as 2012, President Hu Jintao warned the Chinese they must carefully defend their "cultural security." Hostile forces, he explained, had intensified "the strategic plot of westernizing and dividing China, and ideological and cultural fields are the focal areas of their long-term infiltration." In an effort to stem the tide, the government ordered Chinese television to limit the airing of imported game, reality, and talent shows. Who knew that *Dancing with the Stars* could threaten national security? In 2014 and 2015, several high officials warned that using Western textbooks might distort the thinking of Chinese college students.

Many Americans, in and out of government, express surprise and dismay that China has adopted a market economy but not democracy. The PRC has remained a one-party, authoritarian state, restricting political freedom, barring independent labor unions, and strictly controlling the Internet. However, the government allows its citizens far more personal liberty than they enjoyed before the 1980s. It encourages Chinese to travel and study abroad and has promoted the rise of "Western" consumer lifestyles. Continued Communist Party monopoly rule relies partly on sustaining economic growth, and that depends in large part on good relations with the United States, Western Europe, and Japan, as well as access to oil and raw materials.

Unlike the situation in the late nineteenth and early twentieth centuries, amid the Western fears of the yellow peril or the Chinese Boxer's antiforeign attacks, contemporary China and the United States are far more thoroughly enmeshed than at any previous time. As noted above, they are among each other's largest trading partners, with China the world's largest exporter and the United States the largest importer. The United States invests heavily in China, and China is the largest foreign creditor of the United States. Cooperation with the United States, Western Europe, and Japan remains a foundation of China's prosperity. China, in turn, has helped keep the U.S. economy afloat, whereas American naval power polices the sea lanes on which China's global trade depends.

Each day, around 10,000 people—tourists, commercial travelers, and students—travel between the two countries. Between 1978 and 2003, nearly 700,000 Chinese studied abroad, mostly in the United States. Initially, only about 25 percent returned home. That changed dramatically in the early twenty-first century as business and other professional opportunities increased. As of 2014, around 235,000 Chinese (more than from any other country), mostly graduate students, enrolled in American institutions of higher learning, and some 20,000 Americans study annually in China. Many U.S. colleges and universities have opened branch campuses in China. Programs in business management, science, and technology are especially popular. Nearly all of China's 100 million high school or college students study some English, and about a quarter million Americans study Chinese. The Chinese government sponsors more than 300 so-called Confucius Institutes worldwide, including 75 in the United States, promoting study of Chinese culture. Between 2000 and 2010, American couples adopted 65,000 Chinese orphans, most of them girls. Many well-to-do Chinese families send their children to American high schools and summer camps to improve their chances of admission to elite U.S. colleges. NBA players are sports heroes in China, whereas Americans are in awe of Chinese martial artists. Although none of these factors alone determines official policy or makes conflict impossible, together they make it far less likely.

Since 2001 American officials have called on China to play a more active and responsible role in world affairs, even while questioning its expansion of military power in ways seen as undercutting U.S. security interests in the Persian Gulf, Latin America, and Africa. During the Clinton and Obama administrations, Washington criticized China for blocking expansion of a liberal world political and economic order by cooperating with rogue regimes such as North Korea, Iran, and Sudan. They also accused the PRC of blocking efforts to reduce greenhouse gasses contributing to climate change. In 2014, however, China and the United States reached a draft agreement to reduce both nations' carbon footprints. Chinese leaders complain that the United States selfishly pushes its own political values on others and that the Obama administration, like its Cold War predecessors, is trying to contain China. In fact, China and the United States are not and need not become adversaries. They are competitors with many parallel, rather than colliding, interests.

For example, in 2015 China's president, Xi Jintong, called for creation of a China-led Asian development bank that would serve as the regional counterpart to the U.S.—created World Bank and International Monetary Fund that spurred global development aid since 1945. In spite of Washington's wariness that China would use its new economic muscle to exercise political pressure on aid recipients, most of American allies rushed to join the project.

Rhetoric aside, since 2001 China has not been a disruptive force in the world economy or done anything to upset the global balance of military power. Beijing has focused on modifying the existing world order, not on overthrowing it. Should any of China's larger neighbors, such as Russia, India, Pakistan, and Japan, grow too weak or too strong, it might create conditions for Chinese intervention. A precipitous U.S. economic or military decline might also produce a power vacuum China might feel compelled to fill. The key to stable Sino–American relations, as with U.S. foreign policy generally, is for the United States to maintain domestic prosperity and defend global stability. Under those circumstances, both nations can thrive.

As described earlier, between 1971 and 1991, shared wariness of the Soviet Union drew the United States and China together after twenty years of estrangement. During the twenty years after the collapse of the Soviet empire, as China's economy and its overseas trade expanded rapidly, "making money" served as a foundation of stable bi-lateral relations. Now, well into the second decade of the twenty-first century, China and the United States must discover and cultivate a broader range of common interests that assure their cooperation in a world where they are the two most powerful military and economic powers.

SELECTED ADDITIONAL READINGS

Rosemary Foot and Andrew Weller, *China, the United States and Global Order* (New York, 2010); David Shambaugh, *China Goes Global: The Partial Power* (New York, 2013), and ed., *Tangled Titans: The United States and China* (Latham, Md., 2013); Robert G. Sutter, *U.S.–Chinese Relations: Perilous Past, Pragmatic Present* (Latham, Md., 2010); Odd Arne Westad, *Restless Empire: China and the World since 1750* (New York, 2010); Louisa Lim, *The People's Republic of Amnesia: Tiananmen Revisited* (New York, 2014); Andrew J. Nathan and Andrew Scobell, *China's Search for Security* (New York, 2012); Susan L. Shirk, *China: Fragile Superpower* (New York, 2008); Chi Wang, *George W. Bush and China: Problems, Policies, and Partnerships* (Lanham, Md., 2008); Jeffrey A. Bader, *Obama and China's Rise* (Washington, D.C., 2013); Aaron L. Friedberg, *A Contest for Supremacy: China, America, and the Struggle for Mastery in Asia* (New York, 2012); Evan Osnos, *Age of Ambition: Chasing Fortune, Truth, and Faith, in the New China* (New York, 2014); Howard French, *China's Second Continent: How a Million Migrants are Building a New Empire in Africa* (New York, 2015).

Index